Electra and the Empty Urn

The University of North Carolina Press | Chapel Hill and London

Electra and the Empty Urn

Metatheater

and Role Playing

in Sophocles

Mark Ringer

© 1998 The University of North Carolina Press
All rights reserved

Designed by April Leidig-Higgins
Set in Electra and Kadmos Greek
by Keystone Typesetting, Inc.
Manufactured in the United States of America

Library of Congress Cataloging-in-Publication Data
Ringer, Mark. Electra and the empty urn : metatheater and role playing in Sophocles / by Mark
Ringer.   p. cm. Includes bibliographical references
and index.
ISBN 0-8078-2391-0 (cloth: alk. paper)
ISBN 0-8078-4697-X (pbk.: alk. paper)
1. Sophocles—Criticism and interpretation.
2. Greek drama (Tragedy)—History and criticism.
3. Electra (Greek mythology) in literature.
4. Mythology, Greek, in literature. 5. Sophocles—
Knowledge—Theater. 6. Role playing in literature.
7. Sophocles. Electra. 8. Drama—Technique.
I. Title.   97-24548
PA4417.R56   1998   CIP

02 01 00 99 98 5 4 3 2 1

For my wife, Barbara,

my father, Gordon,

and most of all,

for the memory of my mother,

Professor Virginia Hartt Ringer,

ἥν ἂν Σοφοκλῆς ἐπήνεσεν.

Contents

Preface

The world evoked in the seven Sophoclean tragedies is a dangerously theatrical place where seeming and being are often disastrously different things. The present study is an examination of the metatheatrical aspects of Sophocles' art. Throughout his long career Sophocles was interested in exploring the aesthetic boundaries of the theater. Metatheater means theater about theater, drama that pushes at the limits of the theater and its conventions. Metatheater is drama that exhibits a high degree of self-consciousness. To examine Sophocles' plays from this vantage point, the texts have been approached from theatrical as well as philological perspectives. The Sophoclean tragedies are, first and foremost, blueprints for performance within the Theater of Dionysus, and only secondarily great literature. This study, like earlier books on Sophocles, calls attention to the playwright's language, but with focus placed on dialogue that hints at performative self-awareness, giving special attention to the *roles* played by Sophocles' characters. These seven plays are peopled by a wide range of dramatic personages who assume roles within their roles—posturing, posing, and often deceiving their fellow characters, and sometimes even themselves. This issue of internal role playing is a defining feature of metatheatricality, since all drama entails actors pretending to be fictional characters on stage. When a character within a play sets out to deceive other characters or the theater audience through disguise or deceptive behavior, the audience is made aware of the performative nature of the play which hosts such doubly mimetic activity.

Along with internal role playing, this study also examines literal role playing in Sophoclean drama. It is an established fact that, except for the performers constituting the chorus, all roles in the fifth-century tragic theater were shared among no more than three actors. This convention contains implications for any study of tragedy as a performative art; yet, in spite of its fundamental importance, the three-actor rule is an aspect of Greek drama that is largely ignored by theater historians and practitioners as well as classicists. This issue of the literal role playing within Sophocles' theater must be addressed if we are to get any sense of the effect of the plays in performance. Casting configurations reflect the playwright's technical ingenuity and often reveal rich and essential layers of performative irony. Consequently, role playing, in both its metaphoric and literal dimensions, forms a vital facet of Sophoclean metatheater.

Metatheater is a neologism created during the 1960s and has strongly affected criticism of twentieth-century as well as Shakespearean drama. The first chapter gives a short introductory sketch of metatheatrical criticism, charting its movement from modern drama back to ancient tragedy and the roughly synchronous emergence of performance criticism of Greek and Latin theater. The second chapter offers a brief examination of Gorgias' aesthetic ideas and the quasi-theatrical atmosphere of Greek politics, suggesting that the society for which Sophocles presented plays would have been particularly attuned to the paradoxes inherent in the metatheatrical experience. Subsequent chapters examine the seven extant tragedies. The ordering of the tragedies is roughly chronological and reflects the introduction and development of metatheatrical themes throughout the Sophoclean corpus. The sequence builds toward the two most overtly metatheatrical tragedies, *Philoctetes* and *Electra*, which are taken out of chronological sequence.

The third chapter explores *Ajax*, which opens with a prologue constituting a marvelous paradigm of tragic drama. *Ajax* also presents the theater audience with Sophocles' first examples of such metatheatrical phenomena as a character becoming an audience-within-the-play, and role-playing-within-the-role. Chapter 4 deals with *Trachiniae* and examines how many of the themes and metatheatrical effects Sophocles used in *Ajax* are presented in a more subtle and troubling guise. The fifth chapter looks at Sophocles' three most famous plays, *Antigone*, *Oedipus Tyrannus*, and *Oedipus at Colonus*, as explorations of the theme of seeming and being—issues inextricably bound to the theater experience. The sixth chapter discusses *Philoctetes*, a tragedy permeated by a series of enacted deceptions, which seem to destabilize any interpretation of the play. The seventh and longest chapter is an extended examination of *Electra*, the epitome of Sophoclean metatheater, and a tragedy wherein the boundaries between fiction and reality are dissolved in one of the more self-conscious plays in the history of the drama. The Lloyd-Jones and Wilson text of Sophocles has been used throughout this book. The translations of Sophocles are my own.

I wish to thank many people who have helped me with this book. I am indebted to Sian Hunter White of the University of North Carolina Press for her perceptive comments and buoyant good spirits. Barbara Fowler, Richard Hornby, Barbara Hanrahan, Robert G. Egan, W. D. King, Francis Dunn, Simon Williams, and Marilyn Sundin have all offered constructive criticism and encouragement throughout the various stages of this project. I am particularly indebted to Steven Lattimore for many years of learning and friendship. Deborah Bosch has given invaluable technical assistance throughout all stages of this project. Lillian Bosch has afforded unflagging moral support and encouragement. I have received financial assistance during various stages of this work from Denison University and the Department of Dramatic Art at the University of California, Santa Barbara. I owe a great debt of gratitude to Carl Mueller and Bert O. States, in whose seminars I began thinking about Sophocles and his relationship to his art. I also wish to thank Professors Wendy Raschke, Michael Haslam, and Thomas Habinek, who taught me the Greek language. Finally I wish to acknowledge my family and friends, whose love and support I value above all other things.

Electra and the Empty Urn

1 | Introduction

Polus and the Urn

Sometime in the fourth century B.C., an Athenian named Polus became established as a leading tragedian in a generation of actors who
carried the histrionic art to new heights of public acclamation. The
glamour that the Hellenistic theater gave acting led to an increased
interest in actors and their personal idiosyncrasies. Many centuries
after his death, Polus' fame was still sufficient to earn him a place in
Aulus Gellius' *Attic Nights*, a second-century A.D. miscellany. Gellius'
story about Polus may be apocryphal. The story's value rests in what is
suggested about one of Polus' greatest roles, the Sophoclean Electra. It
speaks to the public perception of the tragedy in antiquity, and the

play's troubling mixture of emotional truth and theatrical artifice. The brief story occurs in the sixth book of Gellius' compendium:

> There was in the land of Greece an actor of wide reputation, who excelled all others in his clear delivery and graceful action. They say that his name was Polus, and he often acted the tragedies of famous poets with intelligence and dignity. This Polus lost by death a son whom he dearly loved. After he felt that he had indulged his grief sufficiently, he returned to the practice of his profession.
>
> At that time he was to act the *Electra* of Sophocles at Athens, and it was his part to carry an urn which was supposed to contain the ashes of Orestes. The plot of the play requires that Electra, who is represented as carrying her brother's remains, should lament and bewail the fate that she believed had overtaken him. Accordingly, Polus, clad in the mourning garb of Electra, took from the tomb the ashes and urn of his son, embraced them as if they were those of Orestes, and filled the whole place, not with the appearance and imitation of sorrow, but with genuine grief and unfeigned lamentation. Therefore, while it seemed that a play was being acted, it was in fact real grief that was being enacted.[1]

Here is perhaps the most fascinating description of an actor and his creative process to survive from the classical world. What does the story suggest to us about the ancient perception of Polus and his chosen role? Gellius is at pains to emphasize Polus' technical control and craft. "Clear delivery and graceful action" and "intelligence and dignity" do not describe an undisciplined opportunist. It is interesting to note that, after his son's death, Polus waited a "sufficient" time, presumably to recover from the trauma before resuming his career. The story calls to mind the practice of modern method acting technique, an approach developed by Constantine Stanislavski and Lee Strasberg. Polus' ghastly prop must rank among the most extraordinary uses of a "personal object" in the history of acting. A "personal object" in method acting is an emotionally evocative personal item used by an actor, usually during the rehearsal process, to stimulate the actor's identification with his or her role. Polus' waiting a "sufficient" time also has reverberations in the teachings of Stanislavski and Strasberg. Students studying the method are trained to use "affective memory" or "emotional recall." This process entails an actor recalling a personal moment in real life that stimulates an analogous emotional response to the situation required by the playwright. Instruction includes a warning, however, to refrain from using traumatic memories that are too recent to allow the actor to maintain aesthetic distance and emotional hygiene. The mention of Polus' hiatus from performing suggests a similar calculation on his part. Presumably, without the distance of time, his use of the ashes would have seemed the morbid and deranged act of a grieving parent. Instead, Gellius claims that the prop was a potent tool for drawing inspiration from a disciplined actor.

This story is fascinating in its portrayal of an actor's deliberate blending of real life and the fictive world of drama. The remark that "Polus, clad in the mourning garb of Electra, took from the tomb the ashes and urn of his son" deepens this confusion. Is Gellius conflating the retrieval of the ashes with Polus' later performance? Did Polus carry on some sort of rehearsal in the cemetery? At the very least, Gellius has made the situation highly ambiguous. What remains clear is that the actor's use of the ashes represents an extraordinary interpenetration of life and art.

In Gellius' anecdote, Polus emerges not as a morbid neurotic but as a consummate artist, aware of his own emotional life and prepared to exploit it cold-bloodedly in the service of his art. The Polus story may remind a theater historian of remarks made by the great French actor Talma (1763–1826), who wrote, "I scarcely know how to confess that, in my own person, in any circumstance of my life in which I experienced deep sorrow, the passion of the theatre was so strong in me that, although oppressed with real sorrow, and disregarding the tears I shed, I made, in spite of myself, a rapid and fugitive observation on the alteration of my voice, and on a certain spasmodic vibration which it contracted as I wept; and, I say it, not without some shame, I even thought of making use of this on the stage, and, indeed, this experiment on myself has often been of service to me."[2] Clearly an analogous acting process was described by Gellius.

Polus was able to fill "the whole place, not with the appearance and imitation of sorrow, but with genuine grief and unfeigned lamentation." The place (the theater or cemetery?) is filled not with imitation but real emotions. Gellius' last lines enunciate all the ambiguous tensions between reality and imitation. "Therefore, while it seemed that a play was being acted, it was in fact real grief that was enacted." Polus' enacted grief is real, and very powerfully projected to his audience. Despite this real grief, "it seemed that a play was being acted."

This confusion between art and reality is all the more fascinating because of the play and scene wherein Polus chose to use his very real prop. Polus' fourth-century audience was moved by a convoluted series of paradoxes generated by a famous actor's interpretation of one of the more paradoxical scenes in Greek tragedy. An examination of these paradoxes and their interrelationships may serve as a convenient point of entry into the cold, hard-edged self-consciousness of Sophocles' text. Polus' audience beheld a man pretending to be a woman wearing a tragic mask. Those in the audience who knew of Polus' bereavement may have realized the strange harmony between the tragic mask's frozen exterior and the actor's recent loss.

Sophocles' first audiences in the fifth century would have appreciated a rather different phenomenon. Within the artifice of the play, Electra, mistakenly believing that her brother Orestes has died, grieves over an urn that she has been told contains his ashes. By keening over this false and empty urn, Electra creates a situation of tremendous irony. Sophocles gave his audience a man pretending to be a woman grieving over an empty urn. Electra's sorrow, within the artifice of Sophocles' play, is real, but the audience is privileged to know that her emotional state lacks a real cause. Polus' audience experienced the gratuitous paradox of an actor channeling his real grief over an urn actually containing his loved one's ashes. The urn in Sophocles' play serves Orestes and his friends in accomplishing his revenge. The fact that the urn is empty, that it contains no ashes, that it is not what it appears to be, is fundamental to the entire play. The urn is a prop in both the fictive world of the play and the real world of the audience. By this seeming exploitation of the play, Polus has forced an examination of the various possibilities for meaning that fill Sophocles' empty urn and, by extension, the world of the play. The urn serves as a metaphor not only for the theatrical experience but for the very idea of metaphor itself. It represents a *vessel* capable of *transferring* meaning and significance from one conceptual plane to another.

The Polus' anecdote affords a tiny window on ancient appreciation of Sophoclean metatheater. The audience knows Electra's sorrow has no "real" cause; Orestes is alive and actually standing by her side. Polus was aware that the more real his mourning appeared, the greater would be the effectiveness of the entire performance. The more harrowing Electra's grief, the more cruel and unsettling the experience becomes for the audience. This empty urn is but one of the self-conscious theatrical elements in Sophocles' play. A reading of the *Electra* text, paying close attention to self-referential theatricality, or metatheater, reveals one of the most significant but usually ignored aspects of Sophoclean dramaturgy. Theater, playwriting, and performance are fundamental issues informing the *Electra*. The play has been chastised for its cold and calculating manipulation of the Orestes myth. This alleged coldness and calculation are the residual emotional effects of a play that turns in upon itself, constantly reminding the audience of its theatricality and focusing attention upon the process of acting and storytelling within the Theater of Dionysus.

Just as the Polus anecdote serves as an entry point for the exploration of *Electra*, *Electra* serves as a point of departure for an examination of the rest of Sophocles' tragedies. Sophocles was, throughout his career, a profoundly self-conscious playwright. This self-referential theatricality, or metatheatricality, is a vital aspect of all seven surviving tragedies. In varying degrees, they are all tragedies about tragedy, calling attention to their place within a performative tradition. *Ajax, Trachiniae, Antigone, Oedipus Tyrannus, Philoctetes*, and *Oedipus at Colonus* are metatheatrical works that point toward the *Electra* as a focal point of theatrical self-reflexivity. In this respect, *Electra*'s position within Sophocles' work resembles the status of *Hamlet* within the Shakespearean canon. While both *Electra* and *Hamlet* represent the high point of their respective creators' obsession with theatrical self-reference, all of Sophocles' and Shakespeare's remaining plays are highly metatheatrical. Their plays comment upon the process of theatrical art—that exchange which takes place within the theater between playwright, actors, and audience—and question theatrical tradition and expectation, pushing at the boundaries that separate either a play from its audience or one play from another. From a metatheatrical examination of all seven Sophoclean tragedies, a different vision of this playwright as artist and craftsman begins to emerge. The plays are revealed in a more troubling and ambivalent light. In this metatheatrical reading of Sophocles, questions involving duality, irony, and Sophocles' characteristic layering of perception among his characters must be reexamined.

According to the ancient *Vita*, Sophocles was the first tragedian to forsake acting in his own plays, allegedly due to a weak voice (*Vita* 4).[3] Lesky accepts the idea of Sophocles' withdrawal from acting but cautions that the ancient explanation concerning his weak voice "strongly resembles anecdotal aetiology" and is most likely apocryphal.[4] Sophocles' separation of tragic writing from tragic acting may well have created the myth of his defects as a performing artist. This myth materializes in one of several accounts of the poet's death, in which his demise is blamed on his failure to take a proper breath before reciting a long, uninterrupted section of the parodos from *Antigone* (*Vita* 14). While almost certainly a fabrication, the story of Sophocles' suffocation hints that the ancient imagination was intrigued by the prospect of a poet who was not a performer of his own work. Ancient commentators sought justification for this unusual separation in the poet's alleged shortcomings as a performer.

Aristotle names Sophocles as the inventor of skenographia.[5] The poet is also credited with inventing the tritagonist and composing a treatise on the tragic chorus. He is reported to have written plays with specific actors in mind and to have founded a *thiasos* dedicated to the Muses (*Vita* 6). These biographic details point to a lively involvement in the study and shaping of theatrical theory and technique, even though he declined to partake directly in the actual performance within the orchestra circle. Sophocles must have been aware of his unique status as a tragedian who did not perform but rather molded performances from the outside in. If not the first, he was among the first poets who experienced the comparatively modern separation of dramatic text from performance. Such an experience must have had profound impact on the practice of his art.

In an essay detailing the effect of literacy on ancient poetry, Charles Segal observes: "The literate poet becomes even more aware than the archaic bard that his words are the component parts of an artistic product, a crafted object. His work is no longer a memorial to other's deeds, as in Homeric epic or even the archaic encomium, but a distinctive entity of his own, the guarantor of his own, not his patron's fame."[6] This separation of text from performance must have sensitized the playwright to his paradoxical position as both "creator" and "outsider" in his finished art work—the performance within the Theater of Dionysus. It must have increased the aesthetic self-consciousness that permeates his surviving dramas.

Plutarch records that Sophocles reflected on his development as a dramatist as a tripartite process.[7] At first his style "played with the grandiosity of Aeschylus" (τὸν Αἰσχύλου διαπεπαιχὼς ὄγκον), and "then with the painful ingenuity of his own invention" (εἶτα τὸ πικρὸν καὶ κατάτεχνον τῆς αὐτοῦ κατασκευῆς). Finally, he "changed the character of the diction to what is most expressive of character and best" (τὸ τῆς λέξεως μεταβάλλειν εἶδος, ὅπερ ἠθικώτατον ἐστί καὶ βέλτιστον). The anecdote reveals a theater craftsman acutely aware of his own development as an artist. Sophocles describes Aeschylus' influence on his earlier work, his progression through "painful" (πικρόν) self-consciousness to arrive at a maturity that finds him renovating his language, becoming a master of both dramatic form and content.[8]

Sophocles lived and worked in a community involved in the literary and performing arts to an extent unrivaled by any modern society. He and his fellow playwrights could rely upon their audiences' extraordinary responsiveness to the finest nuance of tragic poetry and dramaturgical device. It is vital to understand Sophocles' awareness of his art and how this awareness is communicated, both in the study and in the theater.

Metatheater and the Greeks

ὁ κόσμος σκηνή, ὁ βίος
πάροδος· ἦλθες, εἶδες, ἀπῆλθες.

"The world is a *skene*, life
A *parodos*: you enter, take a look, then leave."
—Democritus 68 fr. 115 D-K

This book represents one of the first extended applications of metatheatrical criticism to a fifth-century tragic dramatist. It attempts to draw and expand upon both classical philology and the already sizable body of metatheatrical criticism of other dramatic genres. In addition to a definition of some terminology, a brief outline of the metatheatrical library and its influence on the present study is in order. "Metatheater" or "metadrama" means drama within drama as well as drama about drama. Perhaps the classic example of metatheater is the trope of the play within the play. Shakespeare's use of it in *Hamlet* and several other plays readily springs to mind, along with more modern instances, such as in Brecht's *Caucasian Chalk Circle*.

Metatheater, however, extends far beyond the boundaries of the literal "play-within-the-play." It encompasses all forms of theatrical self-referentiality. These may include role playing, various forms of self-conscious reference to dramatic convention and other plays, and the many ways in which a playwright may toy with the perceived boundaries of his or her craft. Other elements of metatheatrical phenomena include ritual or ceremonial enactments within the play and the rupturing of dramatic illusion. Metatheater calls attention to the semiotic systems of dramatic performance. It reminds the audience of the duality of the theater experience, the phenomenological fluctuation between illusion and the audience's appreciation of the mechanics and conventions of illusion. The significant dramatists of all ages frequently compel their audiences to "see double," to appreciate the airy bubble of their mimetic skills while maintaining awareness of the craft underlying their presentations. These dramatists encourage their audiences to perceive theater both as a reflection of the surrounding culture and as a self-conscious contribution to the traditions of playwriting and theatrical performance.[9]

Drama delights in mimetic mutation. An audience's experience becomes doubly exciting when characters within a play assume roles in addition to their main assignments. I call this kind of metatheatrical occurrence role-playing-within-the-role, wherein a character becomes an "internal actor," a doubly theatrical figure enacting a deceptive role as part of the "actual" role. Characters who play roles within their roles can be interpreted as commenting upon the phenomenon of *all* role playing within the theater. Another significant metatheatrical phenomenon comprises playwright/directors-within-the-play. This kind of metatheatrical figure is a character who manipulates and "scripts" the behavior of fellow characters, creating a play-within-the-play. The notions of "internal actor" and "internal playwright" are admittedly similar; often they are the same character but they are so frequently separate figures within the Sophoclean tragedies that it is necessary to make a distinction between the two. I combine the notion of playwright with director, tasks usually distinct in the modern theater, since the Greek tragic dramatists generally combined these duties. Sophocles, the *poietes* (poet, literally "maker"), functioned as the *didaskalos* in the Theater of Dionysus. *Didaskalos* (literally, "teacher") was the official name for the playwright/director at the tragic competition (*agon*). Play direction and playwriting were intimately connected in Sophocles' theater.

Another feature of metatheatricality is the presence of characters who serve as "internal audiences" or audiences-within-the-play. This occurs when characters are positioned within the tragedy so as to encourage the theater audience to view the play's actions through their eyes. The character of Odysseus serves as such an audience-within-the-play during the opening moments of *Ajax*. Odysseus conditions the theater audience's response to the rest of the play. Later plays such as *Trachiniae* and *Oedipus Tyrannus* will display a similar device within the figures of Deianeira and Oedipus. The chorus in each tragedy serves as an obvious internal audience. The theater spectators are encouraged to watch how the chorus reacts to the action on stage. While their frequently direct involvement in the action precludes members of the chorus from being the "idealized spectators" that Schlegel perceived,[10] they often serve as barometers for the theater audiences' response. As will be examined later, their language frequently contains an overtly performative vocabulary, which serves to alert the listener to their role as dancers or singers in the Theater of Dionysus.

Greek tragic metatheater avoids the overt kinds of enframement found in later plays like *Hamlet* or *A Midsummer Night's Dream*, wherein characters literally perform a dramatic presentation for other characters within the host play. Greek tragedy concerns itself with stories from a pretragic body of myth. The fifth-century Athenian audience knew the epic heroes of tragedy lived long before Thespis invented the tragic form and the playwrights appear to have avoided anachronistically incorporating postepic culture into their plays. In Greek tragedies, plays-within-plays are no less significant than in the Renaissance, but their presence is more covert. The Sophoclean corpus is filled with deceptive plots, quasi-theatrical processions and presentations that are usually orchestrated by an internal dramatist who endeavors to trick or otherwise manipulate another character or characters within the host play. Sophocles also displays theatrical self-consciousness through the use of words containing overt and subtle theatrical resonance. Messengers (*aggeloi*) speak of "messengering" (*aggellein*) and choruses (*choroi*) sing about "chorusing" (*choreuein*), to mention only two, particularly obvious examples. This is metatheatrical language because the words in question contain theatrical meanings that recall the theater and its conventions to the minds of an audience. Examples of this metatheatrical language permeate Sophocles' text, attesting to the poet's pronounced aesthetic self-awareness.

In a metatheatrical examination of a play, it is vital to bear in mind the *performative* aspects of a dramatic text. A play can be fully comprehended only in performance with actors and audience. It is useful to speak of a play's performative text, the cumulative effect of this inter-action of author, actors, and audience. In this sense, text becomes performance and performance becomes *text*. A fundamental but usually ignored aspect of this performative text, which is still largely recoverable from the plays themselves, concerns the *literal* as opposed to metaphoric role playing within the Theater of Dionysus. Sophocles' theater allowed the dramatist only three actors to undertake all of the roles in a given tragedy.[11] As observed earlier, Sophocles himself was credited by Aristotle with the institution of the third actor.[12] The three-actor rule has profound impact on the dramatic structure of Greek tragedy. To put it simply, the plays are designed as they are to accommodate gracefully only three actors. It is evident that, at least until the end of the fifth century, actors did not share roles. The only Sophoclean tragedy to require role sharing is *Oedipus at Colonus* from 406 B.C. and that for specific performative reasons, which will be examined later. In addition to the three actor/competitors (*agonists*) and the chorus, the Greek theater could utilize an apparently unlimited number of supernumeraries (*kopha prosopa*, literally "silent masks"), who, though masked and costumed, could not take part in spoken dialogue. In each of Sophocles' tragedies, the available casting configurations must be examined for what they reveal about the playwright's methods of "scoring" a play for three voices and the often self-conscious performative irony that these role assignments suggest. Although nothing will ever be known of the first actor to play Euripides' Pentheus, the dramatist is clearly making a point by structuring the entrances and exits in the *Bacchae* in such a way that the Pentheus actor must also play his mother Agave. The "Agave" actor enters the play carrying as the head of "her" son the very mask he had worn earlier in the tragedy. The actor of Dionysus in that play enjoys a similarly appropriate double with the prophet Teiresias. An awareness of role doubling under the three-actor rule not only heightens appreciation of the playwright's ingenuity but also reveals the playwright's perception of specifically *performative* ironies.

Many philologists, unfamiliar with the phenomenology of theatrical performance, may feel skeptical about discussion of a subject that has received so little direct attention in traditional scholarship, and one that must at times be conjectural. But the reality of role doubling in the ancient theater was as fundamental to how Greeks regarded tragedy as were the masks worn by the actors and chorus. The masking conventions of the ancient theater and the nonnaturalistic delivery of the lines assisted the actors in transforming themselves into numerous roles during a single play. It is one of the many features that separate ancient Greek aesthetic sensibility from the more realistic performance styles of most contemporary theater. Role doubling—and its implications for these plays in performance—constitutes a vital element in the plays' effect in the theater. An awareness of this practice will lead the reader to both a new and better perception of the realities of performance within the Theater of Dionysus and a deepened appreciation of Sophocles' intensely self-conscious craftsmanship.

Metatheatrical criticism forms an important aspect of contemporary dramatic theory, with strong ties to semiotic and phenomenological writing. While work utilizing metatheatrical awareness continues to appear, the critical approach is often unjustly subsumed into the rather overwhelming plethora of postmodern interpretive strategies. An attempt should be made to outline its initial development and the ways its ideas have nourished dramatic criticism, making inroads into performance criticism of ancient drama. Initially, metadramatic criticism focused on Shakespeare, his contemporaries, and the overtly self-conscious theatrical forms of the twentieth century. While the greater part of metadramatic studies continues to be occupied with these inexhaustible fields, steadily increasing attention is being given to the ancient theater. It is ironic that ancient drama, tragedy in particular, was originally considered to be a species of theater impervious to aesthetic self-awareness. The term metatheater was coined by the critic and playwright Lionel Abel in his innovative book, *Metatheatre: A New View of Dramatic Form* (1963). In Abel's view, metatheater is a kind of theatrical antiform filling the void left after the collapse of humankind's faith in an ordered universe. Bereft of comforting moral absolutes, Abel perceives that modern playwrights *and characters within plays* are faced with a dilemma best articulated in the drama of Pirandello and Beckett. These modern playwrights and their characters feel compelled to question every assumption. Characters query not only the fate assigned them by their playwrights, but even the genres of the plays in which they find themselves trapped. Hamlet is Abel's ultimate metatheatrical hero, a character who curses his fate in being forced to play a role he finds anathema to his nature. In the modern (meta)theater, "only that life which has acknowledged its inherent theatricality can be made interesting on the stage."[13] Abel recognizes characters who have become playwrights within the artifice of their plays and who manipulate the other characters to achieve their ends. This notion of an "internal dramatist" or "playwright-within-the-play" figures strongly in later studies of Shakespeare and other playwrights. Abel's major contribution is to induce the reader or audience member to look beyond the "play-within-the-play" and begin the exploration of theatrical self-consciousness within an entire dramatic work. Abel, along with other critics, has interpreted the presence of aesthetic self-consciousness as a symptom of a playwright's "sophisticated disillusionment" with both mimetic representation and ultimately life itself.[14]

Anne Righter's *Shakespeare and the Idea of the Play* (1962) set the pace for much Shakespearean metadramatic criticism. Her book outlines the enormous power of theatrical metaphor throughout Shakespeare's plays. Shakespeare obsessively uses words such as "art," "scene," "tragedy," "perform," "part," and "play," words "which possess in ordering usage both a non-dramatic and a specifically theatrical meaning." In Righter's view, Elizabethan playwrights utilized theatrical self-consciousness to achieve three specific objectives: it served to express the depth of the play world; it defined the relationship of that world with the reality represented by the audience; and, finally, this self-referential art allowed members of the audience to recognize the elements of illusion present in their daily lives.[15] Like Abel, Righter finds theatrical self-consciousness to be the product of a social malaise. The Elizabethan world, with its turbulent religious and political climate, engendered a feeling of disillusionment. The self-awareness of Shakespeare's art reflects a deep-seated disenchantment with reality. Righter also recognizes the strong tradition of audience response and flexible illusion found in the medieval English theater.[16]

From the early 1970s onward, James Calderwood has emerged as a leading figure in the metatheatrical approach to Shakespeare. Calderwood gives a lucid definition of metatheater as "a kind of anti-form in which boundaries between the play as a work of self-contained art and life are dissolved." Calderwood successfully widens the examination of metatheater from the handful of plays "that make forays across or at least flirt around the borders between fiction and reality" to examine a more subtle metatheatrical dimension than those found by Abel or even Righter.

Calderwood's Shakespeare is constantly aware of the "in-and-outness" of the theatrical experience. At one moment, the play is "receding from him into its own seemingly autonomous fictive reality." At the next moment, it changes course "to present itself as his dependent, a tenuous extension of his own playwriting and directoral skills."[17] Calderwood sees the duality of the theatrical experience where action, props, and stage space stand in for character, objects, and setting.[18] In Shakespeare's (meta)theater, actors and props share the capacity to represent differing layers of identity, as in the cases of the joint stool (which "plays" a stool in Macbeth's castle on which Banquo's ghost sits) and the stool Lear arraigns in place of Regan. Calderwood believes that Shakespeare, who was capable "of adopting multiple perspectives toward anything, could hardly help thinking of, say, a character both as a realistic person in a realistic world and as a device fashioned by himself to insert into an artificial environment in such a way as to satisfy the necessities of a literary and theatrical structure."[19]

Since the publication of Abel's book, Shakespeare has been deemed the arch metadramatist. Richard Hornby has gone beyond the Shakespearean metatheatrical critics by asserting the presence of metatheater in *all* significant and thoughtful drama, as well as outlining a kind of "poetics" of metatheater. Hornby's metatheater occurs "whenever the subject of a play turns out to be, in some sense, drama itself."[20] In Hornby's view, this situation is facilitated by the fact that drama is ultimately always about itself and not about reality. Hornby describes five principal kinds of metatheater: the play-within-the-play, ceremonies-within-the-play, role-playing-within-the-role, literary and real-life reference, and direct self-reference.[21] Hornby also discerns a sixth type: drama that makes "perception" its theme. This perceptual variety of metatheater occurs in a large number of classic plays. "The serious playwright in particular moves toward perception as an overt theme, making explicit what is always implicitly in the background. Drama which is a *means* of perception, turns upon itself and becomes *about* perception." While admittedly more generalized than the five previous types of metadrama, and less estranging upon the audience, it is still of equal importance to the other forms.

Hornby attempts to describe the effect of metatheater upon the audience:

> The metadramatic experience for the audience is one of unease, a dislocation of perception. It is possible to talk about the degree of intensity of metadrama which varies from very mild to an extreme

disruption. At times, metadrama can yield the most exquisite of aesthetic insights, which theorists have spoken of as "estrangement" or "alienation." This "seeing double" is the true source and significance of metadrama.[22]

Bruce Wilshire, a phenomenological critic, has also written on the theatrical experience in ways that strengthen understanding of the metatheatrical. In his book *Role Playing and Identity: The Limits of Theatre as Metaphor*, Wilshire depicts theater as a process primarily concerned with the phenomenon of "standing in," one person or object taking the place of another before an audience. Wilshire views theater as "the art of involvement and standing in, [which] involves us most intensely and enduringly when it deals explicitly with problems of standing in and involvement." While Wilshire avoids overt metatheatrical terminology, his book casts light upon the metatheatrical themes of role playing, recognition, and masking.[23]

Almost all of the critics studying the phenomenon of theatrical performance postulate a complex form of seeing on the audience's part. In an article on theatrical perception, Bernard Beckerman makes an analogy between theater and technology: "To use a term from television technology and information theory, we scan the dramatic object. That is, perceptually we travel over the presented object with our alerted sense systems, probing and testing the material. From time to time we temporarily and provisionally surrender ourselves to the impact of the object." Beckerman's explanation of how an audience processes and interprets what it sees is relevant to modern as well as ancient theater. His observations on Kabuki draw analogies between that highly stylized art form and other theater genres. "In a highly traditional and articulate theatre such as Kabuki," Beckerman writes, "audiences tend to be more cognizant of the performing features or surface." Audiences of these "traditional and articulate" theaters, which include the classical Greek, are capable of enjoying performances on multiple levels. In these "articulate" theaters, "a dramatic object [is] opaque to the degree that we are aware of its sensuous surface. To the degree that we see through the phenomenal object to the fictional content, we can speak of the object's transparency. Both opacity and transparency are properties of the dramatic performance, though not equally present at all times."[24]

Performance criticism began to enter the study of Greek tragedy with the work of Oliver Taplin, who has done much to articulate a "grammar" of Greek tragedy's dramatic technique.[25] Taplin's *The Stagecraft of Aeschylus: The Dramatic Use of Exits and Entrances in Greek Tragedy* (1977) and *Greek Tragedy in Action* (1978) have put needed emphasis on the "spectacle" or ὄψις of ancient stagecraft and have helped to make classicists aware of the visual as well as the literary "text" of Greek drama. David Bain is another performance critic pioneer in classics. Bain has made observations on issues of self-reference in drama and its presence in Greek tragedy. Although Bain acknowledges a metatheatrical dimension to Greek tragedy, he contrasts its use to that found in more modern dramatic genres. Bain delineates historical reasons for the Greek tragedians' avoidance of direct reference to the theater. Overt theatrical imagery would be out of place in the Homeric world the tragic poets were trying to create on stage. This leads Bain to admit, "though the Greek poet frequently makes reference to his art, he does so obliquely by referring to song and dance, age-old activities that are amply attested in Homer."[26] A handy example of this "oblique" reference is Hecuba's lines in Euripides' *Trojan Women* (1242–45): "But if god had not / overturned us, overwhelmed us beneath the earth, / we would be *unseen* and without a *hymn* by the *Muses*, we would give no *song* for mankind to come" (emphasis added). Most of the time, Bain argues, the Greeks treated mythic material as historically as they could, avoiding anachronistic mention of such later developments as books and the art of theater itself. Self-referentiality is present in the "oblique" ways Bain suggests. These references are "oblique" or "cryptic" because metatheatrical reference is far subtler in Greek tragedy (at least as those tragedies appear on the printed page) than in probably any other significant era of playwriting.

Other classicists have followed the lead of Taplin and Bain and expanded the library of performance criticism. Michael R. Halleran's *Stagecraft in Euripides*, like Taplin's Aeschylus study, is concerned with the dramaturgical strategies of entrances and exits. Peter D. Arnott, a rare combination of Greek scholar and theater practitioner, produced *Public and Performance in the Greek Theatre*. Arnott's book is particularly valuable for its appreciation of the give-and-take of the performance experience. His book offers much stimulating speculation on the interaction of actors, text, and performance. The work of J. Michael Walton is similarly informed by classical scholarship and a vital sense of performance.[27]

Both Simon Goldhill and Rush Rehm have given attention to tragic performance as part of a wider civic performance, the Festival of Dionysus.[28] The idea of integrating the civic and artistic elements of tragedy is explored in the articles that compose *Nothing to Do with Dionysos?*, edited by John Winkler and Froma Zeitlin. A. F. Bierl's work endeavors to answer the ancient question posed by the Zeitlin and Winkler collection. Bierl's *Dionysos und die griechische Tragödie: Politische und "metatheatralische" Aspekte im Text* examines the self-referential qualities of the theater god's latent presence on the tragic stage. Important work has also been done exploring individual plays and playwrights. Old comedy, with its numerous examples of paratragedy and audience address, has long been the subject of examination based on rupturing of the dramatic illusion and artistic self-consciousness.[29] Renewed interest in New Comedy has increased awareness of the self-conscious craftsmanship of the ancient theater. Several books have appeared on Menander, analyzing his stagecraft in a manner similar to Taplin's pathbreaking books.[30] Increased knowledge of Greek New Comedy has focused attention on Roman comedy and the often denigrated skills of Plautus and Terence, who adapted Greek plays for the Latin stage.

Bruno Gentili has used this phenomenon of adaptation to broaden the definition of metatheater to encompass any play that is "constructed from previously existing plays."[31] Using Gentili's observation on metaplays generating themselves out of preexistent texts, Niall Slater sees "the Plautine process of composition as the very paradigm of metatheatre: he imitates not life but a previous text. Plautine theatre, then, is not mimetic in nature but metatheatric."[32] The notion of texts feeding off each other finds a responsive chord in the plays of Sophocles and Euripides, frequently constructed out of familiar myths that had received previous stage treatment. Strangely enough, New Comedy begins to teach us about "old" tragedy.

Slater utilizes Abel's "play-within-the-play" model and the idea of the "inner playwright" in ways that both elucidate Plautine comedy and relate to the metatheatrical trickery in Sophocles.[33] "Play-within-the-play is a . . . term that I use for a scheme or trick which is controlled by a character of the outer play and behaves as a conventional play plot would. The controlling character is the playwright of the play-within-the-play."[34] One may easily project Slater's description of Plautus' clever slaves (*servi callidi*) upon the deadly servant in Sophocles' *Electra* with his frequent "scripting" of the plot and his virtuosic performance in his false messenger speech. We are even allowed to see the Sophoclean inner playwright improvise and revise as Electra is made a part of the scheme, seamlessly entering their charade upon the appearance of Aegisthus.

Froma Zeitlin has explored Euripides' *Orestes* as a work of theatrical self-consciousness. Zeitlin writes, "The repertory of tragedy and epic provides, as it were, a closet of masks for the actors to raid at will, characters in search of an identity, of a part to play." The title role in this play becomes, "in absence of the god, the director of the play," usurping the familiar pattern of his myth to achieve the results he desires.[35] Zeitlin's essay reveals the astonishing modernity of Euripidean drama.[36] Charles Segal has occasionally utilized the metatheatrical concept in his work. His essay "Visual Symbolism and Visual Effect in Sophocles" has some observations on the use of the urn in the *Electra*. Segal links the empty prop, which is paradoxically full of meaning, with the empty mask probably carried on by Agave in Euripides' *Bacchae* to represent Pentheus' head. Both urn and mask are "metatragic" objects, Segal believes, which reflect upon the experience of tragic drama.[37] In his monograph on the *Bacchae*, Segal has a chapter entitled "Metatragedy: Art, Illusion, Imitation." In Segal's ancient theater, the boundaries of illusion and reality are fluid and flexible. Segal writes:

> Dionysus is the god not only of wine, madness and religious ecstasy, but also of the drama, of the mask. His worship breaks down the barriers not only between god and beast and between man and wild nature, but also between reality and illusion. In the tragic theatre, or in the Bacchic ecstasy, the participant "stands outside" of himself: he temporarily relinquishes the safe limits of personal identity in order to extend himself sympathetically to other dimensions of experience.

Like Calderwood and Hornby, Segal perceives a doubleness or duality to the subjects of metadrama. "The stage business calls attention to the sign-systems, the conventions of illusion, of the theatre itself, and thereby calls them into question. Once we are made to feel that a mask is a mask, that a character before us is an actor, not 'Pentheus,' 'Agave,' or 'Dionysus,' we exchange the sense of pure presence for a double vision." Later Segal writes: "The mirroring, masking-unmasking effect of [the *Bacchae*'s] metatragic aspect allows no meaning to be final. The Dionysiac poetics opens every meaning to its counter meaning. Meaning emerges as process rather than crystalline structure."[38] While Segal addresses himself to the *Bacchae*, his comments are equally applicable to Sophoclean tragedy. Sophocles was as proficient as Euripides in producing plays that convey the same disturbing sense of indeterminacy. After all, his art served to worship the same god.

Sophoclean scholars are beginning to admit this notion of indeterminacy and theatrical self-consciousness to their author's work. David Seale's *Vision and Stagecraft in Sophocles* represents "an attempt to show the distinctiveness of Sophocles' stagecraft."[39] Seale focuses on the omnipresent vocabulary of "seeing" and "revelation" that permeates the Sophoclean plays, making many successful attempts to visualize the stage pictures implicit in the text. Seale's book is rich in insight, though he does not draw the logical conclusion that obsessive "visual" language (that is, words denoting sight and revelation) uttered in the "seeing place" or *theatron*, constitutes a kind of metatheatrical vocabulary akin to Shakespeare's performative metaphors. Perception and vision are basic components of drama. When a drama makes them the self-conscious focus of its operation, it creates a metatheatrical effect. We are dealing then with a drama that is, in an important measure, *about* drama.[40] Ann G. Batchelder's *The Seal of Orestes: Self-Reference and Authority in Sophocles' Electra* develops a metatheatrical interpretation of that play, focusing on the playwright/actor "roles" played by Orestes and the Paedagogus. Her study concentrates on the framework of the deception speech but does not place the play's central character within this self-referential framework. She views the play as an assertion of the Homeric view of the Orestes story. Lowell Edmunds' *Theatrical Space and Historical Place in Sophocles' Oedipus at Colonus* makes helpful observations regarding self-reference in the playwright's last tragedy.

As can be seen, scholarship is slowly but steadily moving away from the rigid view of Sophocles as an enlightened bishop and the Greek tragic theater as a site of fourth-wall theatrical illusion. The scholarship discussed here is necessarily a tiny sampling of a rich field in dramatic criticism and a developing area of classical studies. The next chapter will explore aspects of Sophocles' own environment and the ways in which the duality implicit in aesthetic self-consciousness permeated the culture that hosted the tragic competitions.

Thucydides, Pisistratus, and Solon

Metatheater implies any of a large variety of possible mimetic muta-
tions within the design of a particular play. A character's use of disguise
or role playing within the role carries metatheatrical implications if
such a phenomenon seems to acknowledge the condition of deception
inherent in the theatrical medium itself. A disguise and deception
scene like the "Mufti" charade at the close of Molière's *Le bourgeois
gentilhomme* stands as a handy example of such an occurrence. Clé-
onte's disguise and ritual not only win him his bride but also allow
Molière to send up the unreal, theatrical world of social pretense,
which Monsieur Jourdan so uncritically accepts. Plays like Sophocles'
tragedies, however, present not only grimmer views of existence but,

21

paradoxically, far deeper layers of play and illusion within the larger context of the theatrical performance. In the *Philoctetes* and *Electra* in particular, disguise, deception, and internal role playing seem to metastasize, threatening the logical progression of the dramas. The society that Sophocles' tragedies often present to the audience is theatricalized to the point where truth and illusion seem hopelessly blurred.

Except for *Ajax*, *Trachiniae*, and *Antigone*, Sophocles' works were created under the shadow of the Peloponnesian War. These turbulent years were a fitting period for such plays to be written, since theatrical self-consciousness tends to emerge during periods of cynicism.[1] Thucydides has described the Peloponnesian War's brutalizing effect on ethics and the attendant blurring of the boundaries between good and evil actions. His famous account of growing moral decay described the social background for *Oedipus Tyrannus*, *Electra*, *Philoctetes*, and *Oedipus at Colonus*.

Thucydides' description of the revolutions of 427 B.C. is particularly relevant. After remarking that war is "a stern teacher," capable of denigrating the character of individuals and cities by depriving people of the most basic necessities, he describes the changes brought about by a succession of violent revolutions, which rocked the Athenian Empire shortly after the war's outbreak.

To fit in with the change of events, words, too, had to change their usual meanings. What used to be described as a thoughtless act of aggression was now regarded as the courage one would expect to find in a party member; to think of the future and wait was merely another way of saying one was a coward; any idea of moderation was just an attempt to disguise one's unmanly character; ability to understand a question from all sides meant that one was totally unfitted for action. Fanatical enthusiasm was the mark of a real man, and to plot against an enemy behind his back was perfectly legitimate self-defense. Anyone who held violent opinions could always be trusted, and anyone who objected to them became a suspect. To plot successfully was a sign of intelligence, but it was still cleverer to see that a plot was hatching. If one attempted to provide against having to do either, one was disrupting the unity of the party and acting out of fear of the opposition. In short it was equally praiseworthy to get one's blow in first against someone who was going to do wrong, and to denounce someone who had no intention of doing any wrong at all. . . .

Revenge was more important than self-preservation and if pacts of mutual security were made, they were entered into by the two parties only in order to meet some temporary difficulty, and remained in force only so long as there was no other weapon available. When the chance came, the one who first seized it boldly, catching his enemy off his guard, enjoyed a revenge that was all the sweeter from having been taken, not openly, but because of a breach of faith. It was safer that way, it was considered, and at the same time a victory won by treachery gave one a title for superior intelligence. . . . Thus neither side had any use for conscientious motives; more interest was shown in those who could produce attractive arguments to justify some disgraceful action. As for the citizens who held moderate views, they were destroyed by both the extreme parties, either for not taking part in the struggle or in envy at the possibility that they might survive.[2]

Thucydides is describing an epistemological chaos where all signifiers are violently disconnected from their referents. Names become hollow masks or convey the opposite of their "real" meaning. Thucydides implies that the violence wrought upon language both mirrors and encourages violence between human beings.[3] Felix Wasserman draws a powerful analogy between theatrical genre and the linguistic changes in the Athenian Empire. Thucydides' postrevolutionary world is one in which "the fight of the Ἄδικος Λόγος (Unjust Logos) against the Δίκαιος Λόγος (Just Logos) has turned from a piece of comedy [as it is in the *agon* scene of Aristophanes' *Clouds*] into tragic reality."[4]

It is difficult to read Sophocles' later plays without this Thucydidean passage resonating in the memory. In *Electra*, trickery (δόλος) takes over the entire play, oaths are callously sworn for strategical advantage, and even the heroine's heroic resolve may be seen as an empty construct of a devastating nihilism. Thucydides describes a theatricalized world where deception rules the day, and those unwilling to separate their outer actions from their inner convictions are rooted out or rendered politically impotent. By the later years of the fifth century, a generation of young people would mature and "mistake the war for life."[5] The historian portrays a society that cannibalistically attacks itself, just as the elements of theater seem to militate within the *Electra* or *Philoctetes* and threaten to derail the action from its expected outcome.

Sophocles' prewar plays reveal a markedly metatheatrical dimension as well. From its very inception, Athenian tragedy had existed in a society where the boundaries of truth and fiction, being and playacting, were dangerously easy to breach. Tragedy received its official state sanction during a tyranny, which already had confused illusion and reality in order to solidify its power. Herodotus describes the rise of Pisistratus, the future tyrant of Athens, who would establish the dramatic competition at the City Dionysia in 534 B.C. Pisistratus, according to Herodotus, would stoop to the most ludicrous charades to consolidate his political power. "Wounding himself and his mules, he drove his carriage into the market place with a tale that he had escaped from his enemies, who would have slain him (so he said) as he was driving into the country. . . . Thus deceived [ἐξαπατηθεῖς], the Athenian people gave him a chosen guard of citizens. . . . Pisistratus rose and took the Acropolis; and Pisistratus ruled the Athenians."[6]

Later, Pisistratus was toppled in a coup but soon returned to rule in Athens. For his return to power, the tyrant devised a scheme to deceive the Athenians yet again. He secured the services of a particularly statuesque woman,

> equipped her in full armor, and put her in a chariot, giving her all such appurtenances as would make the seemliest show [εὐπρεπέστατον φανέεσθαι], and so drove into the city; heralds ran before them, and when they came into the town made proclamation as they were charged, bidding the Athenians "to give a hearty welcome to Pisistratus, whom Athena herself honored beyond all men and was bringing back to her own citadel." The townsfolk were duly persuaded [πειθόμενοι] that the woman was indeed the goddess, [and they] worshipped this human creature and welcomed Pisistratus.[7]

It is obvious that Pisistratus appreciated the effectiveness of costumes, playacting, and some of the rudiments of playwriting and directing, as in the case of the heralds and their important delivery of rehearsed text. In this context of theatricalized politics, it seems quite fitting that Pisistratus is credited with instituting the tragic competition in sixth-century Athens.

Plutarch, writing five centuries after Herodotus, would give an even stronger theatrical accent to Pisistratus' behavior. "Even those virtues which nature had denied [Pisistratus] were imitated [μιμούμενος] by him so successfully that he won more confidence than those who actually possessed them. . . . On these points, indeed, he completely deceived [ἐξηπάτα] most people."[8] Plutarch draws a distinction between the tyrant and his democratic opponent Solon by attributing to the latter a distinctively antimimetic, antitheatrical turn of mind. After Pisistratus has presented himself to the populace with the self-inflicted wounds described earlier in the Herodotus passage, Plutarch's Solon calls the would-be tyrant's bluff. When Pisistratus denounced his enemies for their alleged assault, "Solon drew near and accosted him, saying: 'O son of Hippocrates, you are playing (or "acting," ὑποκρίνῃ) the Homeric Odysseus badly; for when he disfigured himself it was to deceive his enemies, but you do it to mislead your fellow citizens.' "[9]

Plutarch also records another striking anecdote regarding Solon's alleged antitheatrical prejudice. In the midst of his description of Pisistratus' manipulative playacting, Plutarch remarks on Thespis and the emergence of tragedy. After viewing an early tragic performance by Thespis, Solon "accosted Thespis, and asked him if he was not ashamed to tell such lies in the presence of so many people. Thespis answered that there was no harm in talking and acting that way in play [μετὰ παιδιᾶς], whereupon Solon smote the ground sharply with his staff and said: 'Soon, however, if we give play of this sort [τὴν παιδιάν . . . ταύτην] so much praise and honor, we shall find it in our solemn contracts.' "[10] By placing this alleged exchange between the actor and the statesman in the midst of his account of Pisistratus' "acting," Plutarch firmly associates the theater itself with the politics of tyranny. Like Plato, Plutarch's Solon views the theater as a dangerous influence on public morality. Solon attacks the corrupting effects of mimesis in both its purely theatrical and real life political manifestations.

For all his allegedly antimimetic prejudice, Solon's own political and literary activities may be seen in a prototragic light. Gerald Else cites Solon's remarkable self-confessional poetry as perhaps the direct model used by Thespis in the creation of tragic speech and style. Else interprets Solon's self-presentation in his poetry as a prototype of tragic heroism. In Else's view, Solon's poetry affords a vision of "an individual relating himself to other individuals."[11] Many of Solon's self-presentational poems are composed in iambic trimeter, chosen presumably for its relatively conversational rhythm. This choice may well have suggested to Thespis the meter for "conversational" tragic speech.

Plutarch relates an incident from early in Solon's career, which, for its mixture of politics, poetry, and performance, rivals any of the stories concerning Pisistratus. After Athens had failed to recapture the island of Salamis from the Megarians, a law was passed making it a capital crime to propose a resumption of the war.

> Solon could not endure the disgrace of this, and when he saw that many of the young men wanted steps taken to bring on the war, but did not dare to take those steps themselves on account of the law, he pretended to be out of his head, a report was given out to the city by his family that he showed signs of madness. He then secretly composed some elegiac verses, and after rehearsing them so that he could say them by rote, he sallied out into the market-place of a sudden, with a cap upon his head. After a large crowd had collected there, he got upon the herald's stone and recited the poem which begins: "Behold in me a herald come from lovely Salamis, / With a song in ordered verse [κόσμον ἐπέων ᾠδὴν] instead of a harangue."[12]

Solon's ruse proved successful, the law was revoked, and Solon himself led the renewed military effort. Else cites this incident as the beginning of a "histrionic period" in Athenian history. These elements of disguise and recited poetry, "involving *impersonating another man in a public situation*," present a clear foretaste of tragedy.[13]

The Athenian lawcourts provide another intriguing prototheatrical model.[14] The inherently theatrical nature of court speeches written by master orators for delivery by their clients is an area deserving of attention. The Athenian juryman of the late fifth century must have developed a divided consciousness similar to that of an audience member in the theater. Even while sympathizing with the defendant speaking before him in the court, at least a part of the juror's mind must have been aware of the absent orator's craft. The courtroom presentation of a defendant, speaking from a script prepared by a master orator, shares much the effect of actors and chorus, enacting the words written and taught to them by the tragic dramatist.

The stories and observations concerning Solon and Pisistratus illuminate something of the political environment that nurtured the beginnings of tragic art in Athens. They indicate that Greeks of the sixth century were fully cognizant of how theater may penetrate the real world which surrounds it. Just as Herodotus could appreciate the layering of fiction upon fact in the political maneuvers of Pisistratus, the more sophisticated theatergoers in the age of Socrates and the young Plato appreciated the layers of deception that a poet like Sophocles applied onto the mythic "truth" portrayed in his dramas.

Gorgias

Plutarch's moral essay *De Gloria Atheniensium* affords a brief passage associating tragedy with one of the most important intellectuals in late fifth-century Athens, Gorgias the Sophist. Born around 485 B.C., he lived well into the fourth century. His direct influence on Athenian intellectual life began with his famous embassy to that city from his native Leontini in 427 B.C. His reported remarks on tragedy must date from sometime after his arrival in Athens; possibly during the closing years of Sophocles' career.

> Tragedy blossomed forth and won great acclaim, becoming a wondrous entertainment for the ears and eyes of the men of that age, and, by the mythological character of its plots, and the vicissitudes which its characters undergo, it effected a deception [ἀπάτην] wherein, as Gorgias remarks, "he who deceives is more honest than he who does not deceive, and he who is deceived is wiser than he who is not deceived" [ἣν ὅ τ' ἀπατήσας δικαιότερος τοῦ μὴ ἀπατή-σαντος, καὶ ὁ ἀπατηθεὶς σοφώτερος τοῦ μὴ ἀπατηθέντος]. For he who deceives is more honest, because he has done what he promised to do; and he who is deceived is wiser, because the mind which is not insensible to fine perceptions is easily enthralled by the delights of language.[15]

How may a "deceiver" (ἀπατήσας) be "more honest" (δικαιότερος) than someone who does not deceive? How may the dupe of such a deception be "wiser" (σοφώτερος) than the one who is not tricked? Plutarch seems to have appreciated the cryptic difficulty of the Gorgian remark when he composed the final sentence of the passage quoted above. Taplin has viewed the passage as "a balanced paradox, typical of Gorgias' manner, that deceit should be the means of justice and wisdom. It is also a shrewd reply to all those moralists, above all Plato himself, who have complained that fiction is all lies. The deceit,

Gorgias implies, is temporary and beneficial."[16] The notion of the "temporary" nature of the deceit, however, does not cohere with the Gorgian view of the instability of words (λόγοι). Gorgias' remarks seem to confuse ethics with aesthetics in an unexpected and disturbing way. Such a confusion carries interesting implications for fifth-century tragedy.

Gorgias' principal means of income, as a sophist, was the teaching of rhetoric, enabling students to manipulate language or λόγοι for their best advantage. As rhetoric was a form of ordering language, tragedy was considered another branch of the larger art of rhetoric.[17] Consequently, Gorgias' opinions on rhetoric as a whole may reveal much about his thoughts concerning the art of tragedy. His treatise *On the Nonexistent, or On Nature*, probably written in the late 440s, sets forth several ideas with important ramifications for his remarks on tragedy.

In this treatise, Gorgias comes to three major conclusions: nothing exists; if it did exist, it would be inapprehensible to human beings; and even if it were apprehensible to one person, that person would be incapable of explaining it to another since λόγοι can do no more than approximate meaning and experience.[18] No single word (λόγος) means the same to any two people. Consequently, *all* techniques of ordering words (λόγοι) are forms of deception.[19] Seen in this light, persuasion (Πειθώ) becomes a process of deceiving (ἀπατάσθαι) an audience.

Gorgias' statement about the inherently deceptive nature of λόγοι places humankind, in W. J. Verdenius's phrase, within "an entangled world of seeming." Verdenius writes that λόγος, for Gorgias, "is autonomous; it cannot be a reflection of things, and this makes it its own master."[20] Gorgias equated the power of λόγος, its ability to work upon human emotions, with the power of drugs upon the body. Gorgias writes: "For just as different drugs dispel different secretions from the body, and some bring an end to disease and others to life, so also in the case of speeches, some distress, others delight, some cause fear, others make the hearers bold, and some drug and bewitch the soul with a kind of evil persuasion."[21] The accomplished speaker can manipulate λόγοι so as to "mold the soul" of his audience as he wishes, despite the fact that all his arguments are inherently fictitious.[22] With all λόγοι equated with fiction, Gorgias' endeavor to ornament prose with the "poetic" devices of metaphor and elaborate antitheses comes into clearer focus.

Gorgias insisted that prose, the orator's medium, was identical with verse in many important respects. "I both deem and define all poetry as speech with meter," he remarked in his famous *Encomium of Helen*.[23] Since all λόγοι are incapable of communicating truth, all literary forms are equally fictitious and subject to similar rules of aesthetic style. Under this assumption, any prepared speech is to be considered an artistic creation, wrought with the goal of persuading an audience to believe an inherent falsehood. Gorgian prose makes use of poetic devices not merely for the sake of embellishment but, as Verdenius observes, for "the very practical purpose of making the audience more easily inclined to accept the persuasive tricks by heightening the pleasure of listening."[24] Speeches regarding "real" issues must be just as entertaining as speeches spoken as part of a play.

Gorgian speech is an interpenetration of poetry and prose, a heady mixture of λόγοι spun to win the credulity of an audience. The Gorgian orator is a kind of playwright and actor rolled into one. Like a playwright, he carefully crafts his deceptive speech to relate stories and ideas, even false ones, in the most convincing manner possible. He then must recite his literary creation to an audience, presumably with the gestures and vocal inflections that will aid the process of persuasion. His sole criterion of success is whether his act of aesthetic ἀπάτη has won the belief of his auditors. Gorgias' idea about the indeterminacy of λόγοι was applied to poetry and its interpretation. In the *Protagoras*, Socrates notes the confusing plurality of interpretations that emerge when poetry is discussed.[25] Another sophistic concern of particular interest to Gorgias involved the appreciation of καιρός ("the ripe / opportune moment," "good timing"). The poised and successful speaker must have a keen appreciation of timing—when to use his most effective devices and turns of speech to persuade the audience. Gorgias wrote an entire treatise (now lost) on the subject of καιρός.[26] Καιρός and the notions surrounding it fit in with the ruthless, goal-oriented atmosphere of late fifth-century Athenian society. It is no accident that words like καιρός and the associated sophistic notions of opportunism figure prominently in Sophocles' later plays.

Gorgias' use of language, like that of the later deconstructionists, is both playful and terrifying.[27] Gorgias proposes a world of moral relativism, where victory rests with those who can best manipulate verbal structures for their own advantage. Traces of such a relativism are to be seen in the passage from Thucydides examined earlier. The historian suggests that when the meaning or the valuation of words has been altered, a kind of moral free-for-all sets in. Words are ruthlessly manipulated to achieve immediate self-gratification. Language is "theatricalized," in that words are cleverly used as substitutes for what had formerly been their antonyms.

Something of this relativism is reflected in Gorgias' remarks about tragedy recorded by Plutarch. There, the word δικαιότερος seems to have suffered an ethical degeneration from its original meaning of "more just" or "more honest" to something closer to "more successful." The "more successful" tragedian is the one who "deceives" the most—that is, the one who creates the most persuasive or captivating stage illusion. In Gorgias' view, "deception" is the goal of tragedy, just as it is of all rhetoric.

The effect of sophism on the plays of Euripides has long been observed. In recent years classicists have begun to explore Euripides for rhetorical and aesthetic self-consciousness that indicates the influence of contemporary sophistic teaching. Sophocles is seldom seen by critics in a similar light. But Sophocles reveals a fascination with role-playing-within-the-role and other self-referential aesthetic devices that are akin to the self-awareness of sophistic, particularly Gorgian, aesthetic ideas. Sophoclean tragedy partakes of this sophistic kind of game playing with its peculiar blend of deadly playfulness. In elucidating the recurrent tension between "play" (*paidia*) and "earnestness" (*spoude*) in the *Bacchae*, Charles Segal observes that "play may be deadly yet still remain play. . . . The more the play element in culture is repressed, the greater the risk that its creative energies will re-emerge as destructive abandon, madness."[28]

This brief examination of some of the theatrical elements of sophism and Athenian politics suggests ways in which a metatheatrical exploration of Sophocles will uncover an aesthetic attitude that has its roots deep in the culture that produced those texts.

3 | *Ajax* | The Staging of a Hero

Ajax is generally considered the earliest of the seven surviving Sophoclean tragedies, probably composed sometime between the 450s to mid 440s. Whatever its actual date of composition, it is arguably Sophocles' most original work, a construct of dazzling ingenuity. Dramatic suspense is created and sustained through the subtle manipulation of tragic convention and from several almost unparalleled violations of expected dramaturgical practice. Above all, *Ajax* is a profoundly metatheatrical work, often calling attention to its own status as a tragedy performed in the Theater of Dionysus. This vital metatheatrical dimension forms an insufficiently understood aspect of the play. It reminds us of the ephemeral state of human happiness and its disturbing similarity to theatrical illusion.

The prologue of the tragedy creates a performative scheme, which is periodically reenacted throughout the play. As in his later works, meta-theatrical effects assist in portraying a world where sign and signifier are dangerously confused. In the prologue (1–133), Sophocles creates an image of the "great stage of the world," which bears a striking affinity with the metatheatrical visions of Calderón and Shakespeare. The prologue serves as a self-conscious theatrical metaphor. Sopho-cles utilizes his performance space with the utmost virtuosity. The complex effect of this prologue must be examined as well as the way in which the staging may support and underscore its meaning.

Ajax commences with a strange pantomime, which only becomes intelligible when the dialogue begins.[1] Entering from one of the par-odoi, Odysseus warily scours the floor of the orchestra, approaching the skene that represents the tent or hut of Ajax at "the extreme edge of the camp" (4). He is silently watched by Athena. The goddess's speech to her favorite (1–13) suggests that Odysseus has been searching around the skene for some time ('Ἀεὶ, 1),[2] obviously covering a substantial segment of the orchestra. Athena's lines indicate that Odysseus' ges-tures and movements have imparted a strong sense of expectancy con-cerning the skene and what its doors may conceal from view. Ajax' eventual entrance with bloodied hands will use the skene to its max-imum effect as the focal point of dramatic revelation. The skene repre-sents Ajax' hut, and Sophocles takes advantage of the fact that the word σκηνή could mean both the scene building in the theater and a tent or hut. The duality of the word infuses Athena's interrogation of Odysseus when she asks him why he is searching near Ajax' "skene" (σκηναῖς, 3). Athena appears on the theologeion, her elevated physical presence giving a clear expression of both her omniscience and her psychologi-cal distance from the mortals she controls. Skene, theologeion, par-odos, and orchestra are all utilized. As one scholar has observed, the *Ajax* prologue "has everything for the eye and ear."[3] It is fitting that all of the theater's physical potential be utilized for this remarkable open-ing scene, which creates a paradigm of tragedy itself, a tragedy in little which is over before the Chorus even enters.[4]

Athena asks Odysseus why he eagerly hunts after Ajax "like a keen-scenting Laconian hound" (8). Odysseus adopts Athena's bestial imag-ery. A witness to the slaughter of the cattle alerted him, he explains, and "I immediately rushed upon his track" (31–32). The prologue presents a world of inversion and substitution, which has resonance in the phenomenon of theater itself. Men hunt their fellows like animals and kill animals as though they were humans. This aspect of mimesis, of one thing "standing in" for another, points toward the theatrical humiliation Ajax is about to suffer. He will be disgraced not so much for his homicidal fury against the Greek host as for his being witnessed by the army/audience committing a grotesque act of substitution: Ajax has tortured and killed animals in place of the Greek host.[5]

With the exception of the demigod Heracles, who appears in *Philoctetes*, Athena is the only divinity portrayed in Sophocles' surviving work. She functions as the first of Sophocles' playwright/directors-within-the-play, her relationship to Ajax and Odysseus being analogous to the relationship of the tragic dramatist to his characters and public. She has created a bestial mimesis or *Verfremdungseffekt* out of Ajax' homicidal fury. Animals represent or substitute for men in his butcheries. Within the hero's tent, Tecmessa is witnessing the bloody spectacle soon to emerge through the skene doors. Tecmessa will later remark to the Chorus that Ajax was "uttering foul curses taught him by no human but by some divinity" (κακὰ δεννάζων ῥήμαθ', ἃ δαίμων / κοὐδεὶς ἀνδρῶν ἐδίδαξεν, 243–44). The prologue has already identified the δαίμων and shows the goddess coaching her unwitting actor. In like manner, tragic poets were regarded as the "teachers" or διδασκάλοι of Athenian society; these playwright/directors were also understood to "teach" their plays to their casts of actors and chorus members.

Athena takes apparent delight in displaying her handiwork to her onstage audience, Odysseus. Like a didactic tragic poet, she takes care to underline the moral of the spectacle she has created. Laying special emphasis on the act of presentation, she prepares Odysseus for Ajax' grotesque "performance."

δείξω δὲ καὶ σοὶ τήνδε περιφανῆ νόσον,
ὡς πᾶσιν Ἀργείοισιν εἰσιδὼν θροῇς.
θαρσῶν δὲ μίμνε, μηδὲ συμφορὰν δέχου,
τὸν ἄνδρ'· ἐγώ γὰρ ὀμμάτων ἀποστρόφους
αὐγὰς ἀπείρξω σὴν πρόσοψιν εἰσιδεῖν.

But I will *show* this sickness [of his] to you also
so that *having seen* it, you can proclaim it to all the Argives.
And you be steadfast and have no fear of receiving any
harm from the man. For, turning away the vision of his eyes,
I shall prevent him from seeing your face.

(66–70)

Ajax is to be made a spectatorial object both within the world of the play and in the Theater of Dionysus. Seale has noted the great emphasis placed on Ajax' entrance as a "visual event." Athena "speaks not of disclosure but of an exhibition. She is about 'to display the madness in full sight' (*periphane*, 66), to put Ajax on show."[6] Ajax is positioned to become the performer in Athena's grotesque play-within-the-play, and Odysseus becomes that play's inner audience.

While Odysseus knows that the flocks and their guardians have been slaughtered and that someone has seen Ajax bounding across the plain with a bloody sword, he says, "we know nothing certain, rather we are floundering" (23). Odysseus' information is perhaps not much fuller than that of the average Athenian audience member who may well be familiar with some version of the Ajax myth but is as uncertain as Odysseus how the fragments of the story are going to be pieced together.[7] His lack of information is a convenient device for relaying exposition and a subtle way of putting Odysseus on the audience's perceptual level. Like Odysseus, the audience lacks Athena's omniscient knowledge and control of the situation. Sophocles has constructed the prologue so that the immediately ensuing action is seen through Odysseus' eyes. Odysseus is made into the audience's surrogate onstage, an "audience-within-the-play." This unique status will serve him well when he returns to resolve the bitter conflicts at the close of the play.

Odysseus' reluctance to view the insane Ajax, even while magically protected by Athena's veritable "fourth wall" of invisibility, prepares the theater audience for a shocking visual revelation. The goddess cannot understand why her favorite should shrink from witnessing his archenemy's degradation.

> *Athena*: Isn't the sweetest laughter to laugh at your enemies?
> *Odysseus*: It's enough for me if he stays within doors.
>
> (79–80)

Odysseus' reluctance to join in the derision of Ajax conditions the audience to view Ajax' brief performance in the prologue (91–117) in a complex way.[8] Odysseus' reactions prepare the audience to find terror as well as pity in the grotesque spectacle it is about to witness (74, 76, 88). It also serves to put the character of Athena in an unusually troubling light. The patron goddess of Athens, the divinity whose sacred precinct stood overlooking the theater was often seen as a benign and mediating presence, as in Aeschylus' *Eumenides*.[9] Here she appears as a terrifying daemonic force, implacably intent on vengeance—a being more like the Eumenides she tames in Aeschylus' tragedy than a divine conciliator.

Athena summons the hero from the skene. This display of the protagonist orchestrated by the "playwright" Athena pushes the tragedy dangerously close to the ridiculous. We see the mighty hero covered with the blood of livestock, exulting in their mutilation. At the end of his brief interview with Athena, Ajax tells the goddess he must "get back to work" (χωρῶ πρὸς ἔργον, 116), a shockingly casual, almost slang expression whose absurdity could easily draw a laugh from the audience. Ajax' exchange with the goddess (91–117) forms a remarkable play-within-the-play. Athena has arranged for Odysseus to stand within a charmed spot in the orchestra where he will not be recognized by the "performing" Ajax. This standing place is a specific location for viewing the spectacle from which he must not stray; nor should he interrupt the proceedings with interjections. "Stand silent now and stay where you are," Athena tells her favorite (87). The spectators in the theater also enjoy a vantage point where they may witness and hear the madman without danger of his entering their charmed space, a magic maintained by their repose and attention.

Ajax' violence is set within a triple theatrical frame. He is exhibited both within the Theater of Dionysus and within the self-conscious play created by Athena. His murderous activity is made into a kind of mimesis within the greater mimesis of the tragedy itself. His brutalities, unbeknownst to him, are mere imitations of genuine homicide, with animals standing in for human beings.[10] When Ajax finally comes to his senses, his *seeming* triumph over the men who dishonored him will gall him more than the exposure of his murderous intentions. Ajax' metatheatrical enframement in the prologue sets up a pattern for Sophocles' presentation of the character throughout the play. The imaginary inner stage on which Ajax is placed within this tragedy isolates him from all the other characters in the play. The substitution and enframement create a remarkably ambiguous effect. G. H. Gellie has observed, "The more terrible Ajax appears, the more ridiculous and therefore pathetic he becomes." In the prologue, Ajax appears "foolish," and his crime has been "turned into a farce."[11]

Gellie interprets this "farcical" aspect of the situation as an attempt on Sophocles' part to soften Ajax' criminality, enabling the audience to sympathize with the hero once his sanity returns. Joe Park Poe goes a step further, viewing Ajax' first entrance as a daring mixture of tragic and comic genre, which pushes at the limits of tragic decorum and threatens to "cheat [tragedy] of its full impact." Poe's vision of Ajax is of a "hero who is both laughable and horrible." The extremes of Ajax' nature turn the prologue into "a parody of the tragic situation."[12] Odysseus' position as an audience member during the prologue establishes a rapport with the audience in the theater. Poe writes: "As an unwilling spectator, Odysseus expresses an ambivalence of feeling not perfectly similar to that felt by the audience but certainly analogous to it. He is repulsed by Ajax' madness and fears it (74–82). But he does not react in a predictable way, with indignation and rancor to Ajax' avowed intent to murder him. Instead, he maintains the distance of a spectator after the brief farce is over, expressing a mixture of distaste and pity (121–22) which must be shared by all who have observed Ajax' disgrace."[13]

"Do you see, Odysseus, how great is the power of the gods?" (118) Athena asks her favorite, and, by extension, the theater audience itself, which has just witnessed her grotesque presentation of Ajax. Odysseus responds.

> But all the same, I pity him [ἐποικτίρω]
> for his misfortune, even though he is my enemy,
> because he is yoked to a horrible ruin,
> I think of myself no less than of him.
> For I see that we, all of us that live, are nothing
> more than phantoms [εἴδωλ'], or fleeting shadows [κούφην
> σκιάν].
>
> (121–26)

Ajax' mad delusions are visual testimony to the instability of human existence. Watching Ajax has awakened pity (121) and fear in Odysseus, the principal emotions stimulated by the experience of tragic drama. Like Shakespeare's Prospero, Odysseus reflects that "we are such stuff as dreams are made on." Human existence is as transitory as the mad shapes or εἴδωλα clouding Ajax' vision. Odysseus' view of mankind as a "shadow" (σκιάν, 126), the melancholy insight gleaned from Athena's cruel show, is ironically echoed much later in the play. When Agamemnon enters and delivers his tirade against Teucer and his fallen brother, the general's words unconsciously echo Odysseus' speech at 126. "That man [Ajax] is no longer living, rather he is a shadow [σκιᾶς] now" (1257). This verbal reminiscence, with its striking use of σκιά, calls to mind Odysseus' insight and shows Agamemnon's failure to understand the instability of the human condition. Sophocles is preparing the way for Odysseus' reentrance to resolve the dispute, guided by the insights that the play-within-the-play has taught him.[14]

The prologue ends with Athena's proclamation of the moral of her little play.

> Therefore, having beheld such arrogance
> never speak a word against the gods,
> nor assume any pomp, if you exceed another
> in power of hand or depth of great riches.
> For a day can push down or up
> everything human; but gods love
> the wise and hate the bad.
>
> (127–33)

Stanford has noted that Athena's parting words are "the kind of moral lesson which more usually comes at the end of a Greek tragedy" than near its beginning.[15] With its gnomic closure, the prologue shows itself to be not so much a parody of tragedy, as Poe suggests, but rather an intense distillation of the genre. The prologue and the lessons Odysseus has learned as "audience member" will help impart closure to the latter half of the play.

Throughout the tragedy, Ajax remains alienated from the characters surrounding him. He is constantly enframed by the onstage environment. The Chorus of Salaminian sailors takes Odysseus' place as onstage audience to Ajax' humiliation when Tecmessa enters to report the hero's behavior. Her speeches (232–44, 284–328) to the Chorus serve as a mirror image of what the prologue has just shown the theater audience. Her description serves to reveal the horrible inner scene concealed within the skene, a scene soon to be substantiated by the opening of the doors and an evident use of the eccyclema. Tecmessa would have been portrayed by an actor who, a little over sixty lines earlier, had played either Odysseus or Athena. Tecmessa's lines as she orders the opening of the hut put emphasis on the acts of revelation, witnessing and judging the spectacle inside: "Look, I'm opening [the door]; and it's possible for you to see / both this man's deeds, and his condition" (ἰδού, διοίγω· προσβλέπειν δ' ἔξεστί σοι / τὰ τοῦδε πράγη, καὐτὸς ὡς ἔχων κυρεῖ, 346–47). Tecmessa inherits Athena's dramaturgical function as a revealer of Ajax' downfall, giving us another perspective on the prologue. Like Athena, Tecmessa is a female figure whose advice or help Ajax has brusquely rejected (288–94).[16] This fateful rejection will be reenacted when Ajax brutally orders Tecmessa away (369–70).

Unlike the implacable goddess, however, Tecmessa has the deepest empathy with Ajax. As the prologue has shown, even Odysseus pities Ajax in his present state. Tecmessa's character, performed by either the Athena or the Odysseus actor, represents a subtle amalgamation of these two earlier roles. She is both sympathizer and revealer of Ajax, presenting the fallen hero to the Chorus, the already empathetic onstage audience. As may be seen, *either* the "Odysseus" or "Athena" actor in the role of Tecmessa would create fascinating and telling resonances when that actor's voice and physicality were recycled by Sophocles in the part of Tecmessa. The prologue foreshadows one of the major themes that returns later in this play and throughout the rest of the Sophoclean corpus: the notion of the instability of human relationships under the onslaught of time. Friendships turn to enmity and enemies become friends. When either the "Athena" or "Odysseus" actor enters the theater as Tecmessa, Sophocles uses tragic performative conventions to underscore this theme. An enemy of Ajax has "become" a friend. The process of performance in the Theater of Dionysus becomes part of the play's meaning. Life outside of the theater is as mutable as that of the three *agonists* changing identity within the skene.

Tecmessa reports the action of the prologue from her perspective inside the skene. "He finally darted through the doors, dragging up words / *directed toward some shadow* [σκιᾷ τινι] concerning the Atreidae . . ." (301–2). From Tecmessa's vantage point within the skene, the imposing goddess Athena was no more than a σκιά, a shadow or phantom of Ajax' imagination. To Tecmessa, the great goddess is as illusory as the human being itself, a thing no better than an εἴδωλον or σκιά, as Odysseus grimly remarked only a few minutes earlier (125–26). The irony is intensified when we realize that lines 301–2 are being spoken by one of the actors who created the scene Tecmessa could not fully hear or see. On a linguistic level at least, not even the Olympians are free from the unstable, transitory condition afflicting beleaguered humanity. For a brief moment, both humanity and divinity seem as insubstantial as the fragile tragic mimesis that gives them life in the Theater of Dionysus.

Ajax presents fundamental conflicts between human and divine spheres and between the worlds of Homeric heroism and the mid fifth century. While the prologue blatantly embodies the human-divine dimension, the second conflict is absorbed into the relationships between Ajax, Tecmessa, and Odysseus. The heroic world of Achilles and Ajax was far removed from the Athens of the mid fifth century, a period whose political convulsions resonate in such dramas as the *Oresteia* and *Prometheus Bound*. *Ajax* presents a world that has transformed itself literally overnight from the distant Homeric world of *geras* (honor gift) and *arete* (heroic excellence) into the far more ambiguous world of mid-fifth-century politics. The brutal but magnificent Ajax has been maddened by the skullduggery of petty figures like Menelaus who can, in Teucer's words, make "many evil deeds appear good through crafty deception" (1137). Ajax can no longer navigate though an environment of illusion and subterfuge. His madness manifests itself in his confusion of animals and men, a grim confusion of being and representation. This misunderstanding of symbol and substance and of language itself continues to isolate and enframe Ajax throughout the play. Ajax and his concubine almost speak a different language from each other. There could be no clearer indication of the gulf that separates Ajax from the world surrounding him than the different meanings he and Tecmessa give to the word εὐγενής. To Ajax, a man must live nobly or nobly die if he is to be regarded as "nobly born" (εὐγενῆ, 480). Tecmessa argues that a man who forgets a kindness done him may no longer be called "nobly born" (εὐγενὴς, 524). These differences in meaning seem to articulate the shifting values from a heroic to a mid-fifth-century moral universe. Ajax is made to appear a relic of some distant past, alienated from surrounding characters and stage environment. Words have become displaced from the concepts they represent. Nobility signifies different things to Ajax and those surrounding him. Animals may stand in for humans.

When he is revealed by the eccyclema at line 348, Ajax is a man trapped and isolated within his own stage setting. As his young son Eurysaces is brought to him, Ajax directs the servant leading the boy to

αἶρ᾽ αὐτόν, αἶρε δεῦρο. ταρβήσει γὰρ οὔ
νεοσφαγῆ τοῦτόν γε προσλεύσσων φόνον,
εἴπερ δικαίως ἔστ᾽ ἐμὸς τὰ πατρόθεν.

(545–47)

Lift him, lift him here; for he will not be afraid
even looking at this newly shed blood,
not if he really is my true-born son.

The bloodied carcasses literally and figuratively cut him off from, and paradoxically elevate him over, his fellow men. This isolation was probably physicalized by the actor maintaining his place upon the eccyclema or standing on steps leading to the skene.[17]

Ajax slowly begins to take command of his situation. His means of control is overt manipulation of his theatricalized environment. Bent upon suicide, he orders that the skene doors be closed, concealing himself and the inner scene from the audience onstage and in the auditorium. "Won't you quickly shut the door?" he asks some unspecified character, perhaps the same mute supernumerary who opened the doors at Tecmessa's demand (593). In the following scenes, Ajax will restage or rewrite his own character within the play. He will reveal a quasi-theatrical talent for utilizing properties, speech, and movement to deceive his onstage audience. His new behavior will ultimately lead to the Chorus's vacating the orchestra, barely halfway through the play. Ajax will then in effect start the play over again, ending his life nobly before the deceived Chorus reemerges from the side entries in a "second parodos."

After the Chorus's stasimon (596–645), Ajax reemerges from the skene carrying a sword. Even without the tableau of carnage surrounding him, his entrance at 645 finds the protagonist again enframed. The anxious Chorus and Tecmessa form an onstage audience, hanging upon every word uttered by the armed man who has so recently threatened suicide. Ajax' opening words (646–53) are a stark contrast from anything he has said before. Both the onstage and the theater audiences are drawn into his speech as he seems to play a freshly created role.

His new tone of cosmic acceptance has led some scholars to view this speech as evidence that Ajax is actually sincere in his apparent resolve to change his stubborn ways.[18] Scholars espousing this interpretive line are faced with explaining Ajax' impending suicide speech (814–65) as representing an offstage regression to his old bloody-mindedness. This interpretation is a contrived strategy, which seeks to reconcile the stubborn, archaic hero of the earlier scenes with the remarkable volte-face presented by the great speech at 646–92.

Gellie is surely closer to the truth when he writes, "We must accept the fact that the Ajax of this play is capable of an ironic understanding of his world and of a very clever piece of deception."[19] Tecmessa herself refers to the speech as "deceiving" (ἠπατημένη, 807), once the true situation has dawned on her. The word she uses at 807 derives from ἀπάτη, the noun used by Gorgias in his fragmentary discussion of the "deceptive" powers of (tragic) poetry (see Chapter 2). The deception or ἀπάτη that is evident in this speech is a complex phenomenon suggesting contradictory layers of meaning. Ajax' entire speech is a lie in which he does not tell a single untruth.

Ajax muses on the power of time to give birth to all things and then hide them forever. Any change, any transformation is possible (646–49). His own tongue, once as inflexible as a dipped sword, has been made effeminately soft on account of the woman Tecmessa. He pities his widow and orphan, left among his enemies (650–53). He says he is going to a meadow by the sea to cleanse away the goddess's heavy wrath. In this deserted place he will hide his sword for Night and the god of death (654–60). Night is an appropriate guardian since the preceding night proved his destroyer. For a telling moment, Ajax' sword possesses metatheatrical resonance. It becomes a prop within both the Theater of Dionysus and the fictive world of Sophocles' play. Of course Ajax needs the weapon to commit suicide. In order to escape with it, Ajax gives the sword a seemingly harmless "role" to play: it will be a symbol of appeasement. Ajax has chosen the weapon carefully. The sword, he tells us, has an important history. It was a gift from his enemy, Hector. As long as he has possessed it, the Argives, his supposed friends, have shown him no respect. Now he understands the proverb that *a gift* from an enemy is *no gift* (ἄδωρα δῶρα, 665). Ajax resolves that for the rest of his life he will yield to the gods and show reverence to the Atreidae. He has come to understand that enemies may become friends and friends will turn into enemies. These reflections on the instability of friendship and enmity have already been revealed in Odysseus' unexpected reactions during the prologue and by the performative necessity of the Athena or Odysseus actor inhabiting the character of Tecmessa, Ajax' dearest supporter. The sword, the ἄδωρα δῶρα, inhabits a mimetic field similar to that of the actor. Ajax' prop plays a role in his tragedy. In this regard it may be compared with Philoctetes' bow and Electra's urn. It will deceive his followers as much as do his own words and actions.

Ajax must escape from his family and friends in order to die nobly by his own hand. Segal writes: "To assert his heroic greatness, he must momentarily assume the traditional role of his enemy and opposite (cf. 187–89): he plays Odysseus to be more deeply Ajax." Since the great speech "hovers between concealing and revealing," the audience is positioned to appreciate Ajax' remarkably self-conscious rhetorical performance.[20] Ajax has learned how to act. With this speech he creates two contrasting images of himself for his two audiences. For his fellow characters within the play, his words and gestures of sublime resignation create a "new" Ajax, capable of an almost Odyssean adaptability in the face of necessity. This perceived change of heart allows Ajax to slip through the Chorus's guard and commit suicide. The other "new" Ajax is created for the theater audience. This Ajax is just as committed as ever to the code of Homeric warrior ἀρετή, but is capable of a new ironic perception of his place in the world.[21] Before the madness descended on the hero, confusing the roles of animals and humans, the mighty warrior would presumably have been incapable of the striking oxymoron at 665. Ajax' appreciation of the sword's duality, literally the "gift-no-gift," points to his newly developed ironic perception. The sword appears to be a deadly weapon, and of course Ajax intends to use it as such. Nevertheless, his words and gestures make it appear harmless and unthreatening, a symbol of peaceful reconciliation and atonement between himself and the gods and not a means of self-destruction.

This remarkable double presentation is a product of Ajax' isolation and enframement, the way he and those around him, both mortal and divine, "stage" him within his tragedy both for their view and that of the theater audience. The hero's enframement is instrumental in making his great speech both an address to the Chorus and Tecmessa and a soliloquy for the theater audience alone. Reinhardt alludes to the phenomenon when he observes that Ajax' words, "instead of remaining within the play, break right through its framework and address the audience."[22]

The great speech of Ajax exists in an ambiguous moral territory close to that of the deceptive (ἀπατή) art of tragedy itself. His words are crafted to simultaneously reveal and conceal his innermost nature. It is a brilliantly executed strategy of rhetorical self-presentation. By opposing his heroism to the superhuman power of time, Ajax becomes a paradigm of the contradictions implicit in the art of tragedy. His self-conscious performance-within-the-role reveals a liar who tells the truth, an act of deception committed to reassert a higher notion of reality. His speech is a fitting stratagem within the larger game of tragedy, a rigorously organized form of human play that utilizes play-acting and ἀπατή to beguile an audience into a deeper understanding of the human condition.

Ajax' deception leads the Chorus into its euphoric second stasimon expressing its relief at the hero's apparent change. This stasimon represents a dramaturgical sleight of hand, which will recur often in the latter tragedies. In comparable moments in *Trachiniae* (633–62), *Antigone* (1115–50), and *Oedipus Tyrannus* (1086–1109), the Chorus will mistake an approaching catastrophe for a happy resolution and sing and dance ecstatically, often with overt reference to its primary performative task, dancing. Choric language in each of these instances is metatheatrical, in that it is calling direct attention to the dancing (χορεύειν) of the Chorus (Χορός). The audience in the theater, expecting the myth's established outcome, probably knows better and may appreciate these moments of dramatic irony. The present stasimon (693–718) presents the Salaminian sailors rejoicing and calling direct attention to their dramatic function as a Chorus. Within fifteen lines they make three pointed references to the act of dancing (χοροποί᾽ . . . ὀρχήματ᾽ . . . χορεῦσαι, 698–701), thus striking an artificial note, signaling to the audience that the rejoicing is premature.[23]

All of these instances of self-referential choral language will be examined in their contexts. *Oedipus Tyrannus* will add interesting variations on this theme in that play's second stasimon (864–910). The last use of this device appears in the second stasimon of *Electra* (1059–97). The *Electra* example reveals a fascinating reversal of this formula when the Chorus, falsely believing *bad* news about Orestes' death, deems the present situation a subject *unfit* for dancing. Dancing and singing were performance modes that were inseparable from poetry in the Greek imagination. The epic poets make frequent reference to singing and storytelling. The Pindaric Epinecian odes make reference to the arts of dancing and singing as do several Aeschylean and Euripidean choruses. But Sophocles' use of this self-referential choric language marking "false" turns in the action of his plays displays a consistent awareness of performative irony.

After the Chorus's references to dancing, the Messenger's entrance line contains a similarly self-referential description of his character's dramaturgical function. "Friends, gentlemen, first of all I wish *to announce* [ἀγγεῖλαι] the news / that Teucer is here, just back from the Mysian hills" (719–20). This overt reference to the function of the Messenger (Ἄγγελος) encourages the audience to assume that the Messenger has arrived to describe the protagonist's death, the messenger's usual function in tragedy.[24] The Messenger's opening remark that "the first news" (τὸ πρῶτον) he will report is Teucer's arrival heightens this expectation. If "the first" news regards Teucer, surely the next news will be a report of Ajax' suicide. The theater audience must wait twelve lines for a direct reference to the protagonist. Sophocles' manipulation of tragic convention leads us to expect to hear Ajax' name at any moment, and a long narrative description of his death. Instead, the Messenger, conventionally a character who has seen a decisive offstage event and can relate it to the theater audience, runs out of material in just a few lines. We hear Ajax' name at last but it comes in the form of a question. "But tell me, where is Ajax, so that I may report this to him?" (ἀλλ᾽ ἡμὶν Αἴας ποῦ 'στιν, ὡς φράσω τάδε; 733). The Messenger is even more ignorant of the protagonist's whereabouts than the Chorus. The subsequent exchange with the Chorus and Tecmessa leads the Messenger to reveal his true function within the scheme of Sophocles' plot. He enunciates Calchas' prophesy and the story of Ajax' hubristic affront to Athena.

The Messenger reports Calchas' warning to Teucer that Ajax, if he is to survive this day, must stay indoors. The Messenger's language gravitates repeatedly to the metatheatrical description of Ajax' hut as a σκηνή. Calchas had warned Teucer to use "every strategy" (παντοίᾳ τέχνῃ, 752) to keep Ajax inside his hut (ὑπὸ σκηναῖσι, 754). The Messenger reiterates this warning to Tecmessa: Ajax must be kept inside the hut (σκηνῆς, 796) and must not be allowed beyond the doors (θυραῖος, 793). We are reminded that the σκηνή before our eyes on the outer edge of the orchestra "plays" a σκηνή (hut) within the artifice of the play and is, of course, a σκηνή in the real world of the theater. Sophocles' metatheatrical language reminds us we are in a theater beholding a tragic performance. As with the Chorus's premature celebration in the second stasimon utilizing choric language, the dramatist is forcing his audience to confront the nature of theatrical illusion by reminding us how the tragic illusion works. Choruses remind us they are "chorusing," messengers that they are "messengers," and we hear the warning that a character who has recently left the skene or scene building is doomed. If no protagonist (be he Ajax, Oedipus, or Pentheus) ever came out of the skene during his "day" of tragic presentation, tragedy would cease to function and choruses would stop dancing. The conventional messenger speech describing the protagonist's suicide will be rendered superfluous by Ajax' onstage death. After Ajax' passing, Sophocles will give lines describing the hero's wounds, lines traditionally handled by a messenger, to Tecmessa in her dialogue with the Chorus (917–19).

The report of Calchas' warning galvanizes Tecmessa and the Chorus into action. Ajax has made his fateful exit from the skene out one of the two parodoi. Tecmessa commands the Chorus to divide into two groups and exit out both parodoi.

> Ah me, friends, protect me from destined misfortune,
> and hurry, some of you get Teucer to come as fast as you can,
> some to the western [ἑσπέρους], others to the eastern [ἀντηλίους]
> bends of the shore seeking the man's ill-stared going forth [ἔξοδον
> κακὴν].
>
> (803–6)

Tecmessa's words rouse a tragic chorus to do the extraordinary—it leaves the orchestra before the play is half over. The Chorus must leave via the two parodoi, half to the west (ἑσπέρους) and half to the east (ἀντηλίους), seeking the man who has made the fateful exit (ἔξοδον). The Chorus eagerly responds to her request.

> χωρεῖν ἑτοῖμος, κοὐ λόγῳ δείξω μόνον.
> τάχος γὰρ ἔργου καὶ ποδῶν ἅμ' ἕψεται.
>
> (813–14)

> I'm ready to go, and I shall *show* it not *by words* alone.
> Rather swift *deeds* and *footwork* shall follow.

The Chorus will theatrically realize Tecmessa's request, revealing (δείξω) a unity of word (λόγῳ), action (ἔργου), and the exertion of foot (ποδῶν), which one expects of a chorus. With this exchange, the Chorus leaves the stage in a kind of "false exodos" similar to the Chorus's surprising midpoint exit in Aeschylus' *Eumenides*.[25]

After all of the performers have left the playing area, Ajax emerges alone to commit suicide. His deception speech has effectively shut the tragedy down and started it over again on his own terms. His suicide speech serves as a "false prologue," in that it enables him to take charge of his destiny without the enframement or manipulation of other characters. He is at last able to present himself before the theater audience, free of Athena's stage managing and free of the onstage audience of his followers. The tragic theater is seldom so starkly empty during the duration of a performance as in Ajax' suicide speech (815–65). Now the hero may address the theater audience without the interference of onstage auditors.

Alone, preparing to fall on his sword, Ajax says farewell to his parents, his homeland Salamis, and the city of Athens (859–63). The reference to Athens does not grow logically out of Ajax' list of beloved persons and places. Sophocles is using Salamis' relative proximity to Athens to heighten the pathos of Ajax' final speech. For a fleeting moment, the theater audience on the slope of the Acropolis is drawn almost directly into the action. This moment of unusually intimate contact makes Ajax more sympathetic and surely must help in preparing a negative reception for the blustering Atreidae. The effect is repeated when, just before Agamemnon's entrance, the Chorus sings of greeting Athens on its return to Salamis (1222). Segal perceives the references to Athens (860–61, 1222) as evidence of "Ajax' special connection with Athens through his hero cult in that city."[26]

Dolores O'Higgins has written about Ajax' rhetorical re-creation of his heroic persona in the suicide speech. The suicide scene, performed by one actor on a remarkably empty stage, presents Ajax' attempt to "write his own death," making his suicide stand "for the completed combat promised and denied him in the *Iliad*." O'Higgins is referring to the duel between Ajax and Hector in book 7 of the *Iliad*, which ends in an unsatisfactory stalemate. Sophocles, O'Higgins believes, has used all of his poetic skill to create a kind of "disinvention" of the *Iliad*, where Ajax is repeatedly damned with faint praise as "the second best of the Achaeans."[27] In *Ajax*, the hero is given magnificent language, particularly in the suicide speech. He reveals a certain flair for self-dramatization, which creates a more striking figure for himself than the one allotted him in Homer.[28]

Ajax' fall onto his sword represents the only onstage death in extant fifth-century tragedy. Consequently, this scene shatters one of the most firmly established conventions of ancient stagecraft. While our surviving evidence is admittedly scanty, onstage death scenes must have been extremely rare, if not unprecedented. One can imagine the original audiences' stunned reaction when, after virtually starting the play over again by giving the Chorus a false exodos, Sophocles has the audacity to stage his protagonist's suicide before their eyes. *Ajax* repeatedly turns convention on its head.

After Ajax' death, a divided Chorus begins to reenter the performance space, creating a veritable "second parodos." The Chorus's second entrance, searching for the hero, also serves a practical dramaturgical objective. The entrances from both parodoi and the search of the orchestra area would afford an excellent opportunity for the Ajax actor to exit unobserved into the skene to assume the mask and costume of his second character, Ajax' brother Teucer. There is much sense in the Ajax actor doubling as Teucer. Besides having the inevitable "family" resemblance such a doubling would foster, Teucer is the character who most directly represents Ajax' interests after his death. It is striking to note that Teucer enters the play in a manner reminiscent of his brother's reemergence from insanity. Teucer's first words repeat the first offstage cries of the sane Ajax (ἰώ μοί μοι, 333, 974). Such a verbal reminiscence builds an additional link between the two brothers. Teucer's appropriation of Ajax' earlier cry occurs directly after Tecmessa's remark that Ajax no longer exists (972). (By this point in the performance, he has been replaced by a dummy or some other form of representation and the actor who had portrayed him is awaiting his entrance as Teucer.) When Teucer at last beholds his brother's "body" he declares that "now, by seeing him, I am myself destroyed" (1001). The actor is beholding an image of his former character.

The following role allocations seem likely. The protagonist doubled Ajax and Teucer, while the deuteragonist played Odysseus and, probably, Tecmessa, the two characters whom, aside from the Chorus, express the deepest empathy with Ajax. The patterning of exits and entrances from Tecmessa's exit at 989 to the reentrance of Odysseus at 1316 suggests that the deuteragonist also undertook the role of Menelaus. This extra role makes the balance of parts between the three actors more equal. It also affords a nice contrasting part for the second actor: one "anti-Ajax" role to balance the two "pro-Ajax" parts. The third actor probably played Athena, the Messenger, and Agamemnon. While the Messenger is sympathetic to Ajax and his followers, he delivers the belated explanation for the goddess's wrath, describing Ajax' fateful rejection of Athena (770–77).

In any casting scheme, the "Athena" actor has to play Agamemnon.

This casting detail has profound resonance in the play's final scene. Teucer, the former "Ajax" actor, serves as the advocate for his fallen brother. He engages in a confrontation with Agamemnon, the most powerful of Ajax' human enemies who is played by the "Athena" actor. The ensuing stalemate is resolved by the return of the "Odysseus" actor, reprising his first role, linking the play's prologue with its concluding scene. This casting of the final scene, the only viable way the last scene can be staged utilizing three actors who do not share roles, allows the three performers to reprise and ultimately resolve the bitter conflict portrayed in the prologue. The structuring of the casting reveals the striking unity of the *Ajax* as a performance piece in the fifth-century theater, a unity that is obscured when the play is read or acted with modern theater conventions unconsciously intruding upon the play.

While the above scheme is highly likely, it is admittedly conjectural. Other readers or producers may attempt to adjust the scheme and this is healthy as it compels us to grapple with vital performative realities, which confronted the playwright as he sculpted his tragedy for performance at the City Dionysia. As in the modern performance of baroque music on "authentic" instruments, any attempt to come closer to the realities of a lost performance tradition entails conjecture. That conjecture, if it is based on informed opinion, brings us closer to appreciating the realities of a bygone aesthetic.

The reentrance of Odysseus to resolve the controversy between Teucer and the Atreidae derives its dramatic power and meaning from the unique status Odysseus has acquired through the metadrama that opened the tragedy. The last scene (1316–1420) rephrases the prologue. The "Ajax" actor playing Teucer is in conflict with his archenemy, the "Athena" actor who is playing another powerful antagonist, Agamemnon. Odysseus, enlightened by what he witnessed during the prologue, enters to resolve the action. The theater audience hears the same voices now resolving the conflict in which they were engaged at the start of the tragedy. The prologue's play-within-the-play is the vehicle that makes the reconciliation at the end of the tragedy possible. Those in the theater audience, in Poe's words, "are drawn into the reconciliation by their identification with Odysseus, so that when Teucer, at the processional exodos, calls upon φίλος ὅστις ἀνὴρ / φησὶ παρεῖναι [Whoever is here who calls themselves the friend of this man] (1413–14) to join in honoring Ajax, they receive this as a call directed to themselves."[29] Odysseus' role as audience surrogate has enabled him to resolve the mighty conflicts that continue to surround Ajax, even in death.

Ajax is a drama that continually makes the impossible possible. Athena, goddess of wisdom and patron of Athens, is presented as a pitiless daemonic force, closely linked to the Atreidae. Odysseus, often portrayed as a slippery opportunist, becomes, by the play's end, a kind of ethical hero embodying a code far in advance of conventional mortal, or Olympian, morality. The Chorus leaves the orchestra halfway through the play, facilitating a shift of scene and an unprecedented onstage suicide. The power of (meta)theater has allowed Odysseus and the theater audience to see beyond the narrow and divisive conflict that separates one human being from another. The audiences, both in the theater and on the stage, have come to view the complex, often repellent hero as more than a mere personal enemy or danger to civilization. Ajax has become, through his theatrical presentation, a paradigm of the human creature itself: a mysterious combination of creative and destructive passions and of tenderness and cruelty; a victim of its own shortsightedness, yet preserved from total annihilation by its ineffable sense of dignity.

4 | *Trachiniae* | Staging a Double Hero

Trachiniae has long been the most neglected of the seven tragedies, but it has never been without its advocates. Ezra Pound, in the preface to his outrageous but often imaginative translation, extolled the play as the closest of the surviving tragedies to "the original form of the God-dance." *Trachiniae* is indeed a play that has much to do with Dionysus, and much to do with theatrical self-reference. The self-conscious devices that made such an impact in *Ajax* are used with heightened sophistication and sublimation. *Trachiniae* concerns itself equally with Deianeira and Heracles, with the mythic subject and its self-consciously theatrical representation. Theater is a medium that exists by simultaneously creating and dissolving boundaries. These unstable boundaries are between author and actor, and performer and audience. Within the performative context of *Trachiniae*, beautiful youth dissolves into loveless age, gender boundaries collapse, and a human being (perhaps) advances toward divinity. Like *Ajax*, *Trachiniae* explores the instability of identity under the corrosive impress of time. Seeming opposites are reconciled and Sophocles explores, even more fully than in *Ajax*, the tragic discrepancy between intention and result, illusion and reality.

The structure of the play calls for the protagonist to undertake the roles of both Deianeira and Heracles. This performative fact contains much of the play's thematic import. Like *Ajax* and *Antigone*, *Trachiniae* has been referred to as a "diptych" structure, which breaks into two parts at the point of the main character's death. The realities of role doubling in the Theater of Dionysus imparts a performative unity, which many scholars have ignored. Deianeira exits the play at line 812 both to die and to "become" her husband Heracles. Sophocles is portraying the tragedy of a doomed marriage, and *Trachiniae* gains both expressive power and structural cohesion by its adherence to Greek theatrical convention. By assigning the role of both Deianeira and her husband to the same actor, the playwright suggests through theatrical convention the dysfunctional nature of their relationship. The husband and wife never meet on stage but still share a common fate, as well as the Dionysian body of the same actor.

Along with the protagonist's doubling of wife and husband, the remaining two actors were kept predictably busy. One of the actors probably doubled as Hyllus and Lichas. This double contains its own ironic implications when it is considered that the audience would have beheld the "Lichas" actor exiting at line 632 with the deadly robe to reemerge as Hyllus at line 734, describing his previous character's death as well as the effects of Deianeira's gift. The third actor would have doubled as the Nurse with the Messenger and the Old Man attending Heracles. This last double allows the same actor to play three contrasting roles that resemble each other, in that they are all sympathetic or subordinate to Deianeira and Heracles. The "Nurse" actor moves from describing Deianeira on her deathbed to playing the Old Man attending the prostrate Heracles. The transformation of female into male servant underscores the translation of mistress of the house into the returning master. In the ancient theater, these role changes are as ironic and unexpected as the tragic discrepancy between Deianeira's intention and its disastrous result. The instability of life and the void separating intention and action are given a potent and theatrically self-conscious dimension. Throughout the play, Sophocles toys with dramatic convention and audience expectation in ways that call attention to the medium of performance in the Theater of Dionysus. This manipulation of dramaturgical convention underscores the disturbing, open-ended nature of *Trachiniae*. These striking metatheatrical ripples on the surface of the play need to be examined sequentially.

The play begins with Deianeira's expository speech detailing her present circumstances (1–48). It is unclear from the text if the Nurse enters with Deianeira at the opening of the tragedy, though she must be onstage and ready to speak at line 49. Deianeira is disengaged from the Nurse, if that supporting character is present, in a way that sets this play's opening apart from other Sophoclean prologues. Deianeira seems to address the theater audience itself. It is interesting to compare this speech with the dialogue of the two sisters that starts *Antigone*. The heroic isolation of Antigone manifests itself gradually in the prologue of that play as it becomes evident that Ismene will not help her with the clandestine burial. We see Antigone interacting with someone else before she assumes her lonely position within her play. Deianeira's "initial relationship," however, "is with the spectators," as Seale observes.[1] Her first speech is a virtual soliloquy delivered to the audience which establishes her character and relationship with the spectators. Until her final exit from the play at line 812, the theater audience will behold the unfolding events through her eyes. Like Odysseus in *Ajax*, Deianeira functions as an audience-within-the-play. But her first speech signals that this device, used so effectively in *Ajax*, is going to be problematized.

Deianeira starts the play with a homely old maxim: one cannot know a person's fortune until he is dead. Even with this saying fresh in her mind, she proceeds to make pronouncements about her life. This immediately establishes an ironic perspective for the theater audience.

> There is a saying [Λόγος] among men that came to light [φανεὶς] long ago,
> that you cannot learn about [ἐκμάθοις] a man's life, whether
> it has been a good or bad existence, until a man is dead.
>
> (1–3)

These lines are perhaps the most striking opening words of any Sophoclean play. At first the words impress the hearer as a casual, rather banal observation proffering a piece of folk wisdom. In retrospect, the lines self-consciously enunciate the entire action of *Trachiniae*, a play where learning or understanding comes too late, a world dominated by an ancient *logos* (a word admitting of a surprisingly wide realm of senses in the present context, from "word," "saying," "logic," even "truth" itself), which is brought into the light or made manifest (φανείς) within the theater.

While Deianeira acts as an audience surrogate throughout her presence in the play, unlike Odysseus in *Ajax* she is an imperfect audience. Without an omniscient divinity like Athena to direct her view, Deianeira is prone to stumble disastrously as she attempts to read the world's deceptive presentations. At times Deianeira's audience skills are so wanting that she cannot bear to look at what confronts her. The battle between Heracles and Acheloüs for her hand was so horrible that she was compelled to look away. "I cannot tell / the manner of the struggle, for I know nothing of it; rather whoever was / *sitting* [θακῶν] there unafraid *at the sight* [τῆς θέας], he could *tell* [λέγοι]. / For my part I *sat* [ἥμην] dumbstruck with fear / lest my beauty might bring me pain at last" (21–25). The emphasis on Deianeira's position as a sitting (θακῶν . . . ἥμην) observer of the spectacle (θέας) and her inability to recreate the sight through speech (λέγοι) points to the behavior of both theater spectator and actor: neither theatrical task does she accomplish. She fails as an audience when she looks away from the violent *agon* before her view and consequently cannot relay the details to the theater audience through speech. Throughout the play, Deianeira will fail in her role as a metaphoric audience to the sights and words presented to her. Her character serves as both principal actor and audience-within-the-play, a forerunner of the title character in *Oedipus Tyrannus*.

The Chorus, in its parodos, calls attention to the performative realities of the drama with its sonorous invocation to the sun, Ἅλιον Ἅλιον (94–102). These young Trachinian women call on the sun to reveal the whereabouts of Heracles to the audience, those sitting in the theater and that most important audience-member-within-the-play, Deianeira. The sun was one of the most prominent features of performance within the Theater of Dionysus. It blazed down on the orchestra, illuminating and uniting actors, audience, and performance space. The play will enable the sun to "reveal" Heracles. Before the tragic day has ended, Heracles will be brought into the orchestra. Natural sunlight will both activate and reveal the ravages of the burning robe that consumes his body and brings the prophesies of Zeus to fulfillment (693–704). The sun is evoked as the ultimate spectator for the events unfolding in the *theatron* or "seeing place." Of all the spectators in the Theater of Dionysus, the sun has "the strongest eye" (κρατιστεύων κατ᾽ ὄμμα, 102).

The Trachinian maidens of the Chorus, who sympathize so strongly with Deianeira, all wear the masks and costumes of young women. Deianeira, Seale observes, "is isolated visibly by her age and by the attendant suffering and understanding," which forms so stark a contrast to the Chorus's "joy and optimism."[2] While Deianeira's position is far removed from the heroic world of Ajax, she suffers a similar isolation within her play. As in *Ajax*, the chorus of well-wishers paradoxically acts as a frame around the character of Deianeira, putting her "onstage" within the greater artifice of the play. Deianeira's first speech to the Trachinian women establishes the Chorus as, among other things, a metatheatrical framing device for the protagonist.

> You are here, so it seems, in the knowledge that I am *suffering*
>   [πάθημα τοὐμόν];
> but may you never *learn to know* [ἐκμάθοις] through suffering such
>   agony of heart as mine,
> of which you now have no experience.
>
> (141–43)

The Chorus will watch her suffering and learn about a pain outside of its own experience. The entrance of the Messenger (178) begins an extraordinary scene, which utilizes virtually all of the resources of the ancient theater. This sequence also creates a unique opposition between the "true" and "false" messengers with their destabilizing effect upon the status of reportage within this play. The Messenger announces himself as "the first messenger [πρῶτος ἀγγέλων] to free [Deianeira] from fear" (180–81). Indeed he will be the "first" of the play's messengers, preceding the herald Lichas who acts as this self-proclaimed Messenger's foil. There is a degree of artistic self-consciousness in the Messenger's use of ἄγγελος, which describes his actual role within the tragedy, an effect similar to the use of the word in *Ajax* (719) and *Electra* (47, 1443).

The Messenger relates his news gleaned from overhearing Lichas' report of Heracles' victory to "the whole citizenry of Malis" crowding around him (194). It is worth noting that the Messenger, who makes a point of his desire to win favor with Deianeira (190–91), tells her a heavily censored version of Lichas' report. While the Messenger reassures the queen of Heracles' military triumph, he omits details of the story, particularly Heracles' lust for Iole, which motivated the hero's destruction of her homeland. The Messenger tells only as much of the truth as will please Deianeira. While he tells no direct lies, as Lichas will do, the Messenger's ethical standards are hardly superior to the herald's. Both the Messenger and Lichas' accounts of the sack of Oechalia are made especially ambiguous by the varying ways they learned the "facts" about Heracles' actions. The Messenger claims to have learned about Heracles from listening to Lichas' speech in the Malian field before a huge crowd. The description of the audience circle that surrounds Lichas, preventing him from leaving, reminds the spectators of their own presence before the actors and Chorus. Lichas, as herald, is giving a performance for the Malians. The news Lichas reports, while including more information than he dares at first to pass on to Deianeira, is at least in part inflated by the lies and trumped-up excuses devised by Heracles himself (361) to justify his aggression against Eurytus' city. The deliberate withholding of the truth about Heracles' latest conquest makes the ensuing procession of captive women a complex interplay of appearance versus reality.

Just before the entry of Lichas and the captive women, the Chorus sings an ecstatic stasimon anticipating the herald's full report of Heracles' victory and imminent return. The Chorus's joy is exuberant, premature, and (as almost always in such situations in Sophoclean tragedy) self-referential (*Ajax* 693–705, *Antigone* 1146–52, *Oedipus Tyrannus* 1086–97).[3]

> I am lifted up [with joy], nor shall I reject
> the pipe [τὸν αὐλόν], oh, master of my mind,
> see, the ivy [ὁ κισσὸς] shakes me up
> euoi!
> whirling me round now
> in the Bacchic contest [Βακχίαν ... ἄμιλλαν].
> Io, io, paian!
>
> (216–22)

The Chorus describes its own performative behavior within the play. While they may not be literally decked with the ivy sacred to Dionysus, the maidens are dancing with leaps and exuberant movement to the accompaniment of the aulos player (τὸν αὐλόν) in the theater. As in the instances mentioned above, this self-reference reminds the theater audience of the mimetic nature of the performance. This reminder serves to accent not only the way in which tragic performance as a whole serves as a reflection and imitation of reality, but also the audience's position of omnipotence within the theater. By creating a *Verfremdungseffekt* at this moment of premature rejoicing, Sophocles is encouraging the theater audience to appreciate his craftsmanship and the doubly artificial aspect of a fictional situation infused with unsubstantiated optimism. This device of choral self-reference will recur at a similar moment of false optimism when the Chorus happily anticipates Heracles' homecoming after Deianeira has sent the fatal robe. The Chorus's lyric at this point refers again to the sound of the aulos (αὐλὸς), the instrument that accompanied tragic performances as rising "not in hateful / strain of sorrow, but responding / to the Muse divine!" (640–42). Again, the Chorus is functioning under an illusion of an imminent happiness, and its language touches on the theatrical illusion in which it participates.

The Messenger and Deianeira remain onstage throughout the earlier stasimon (205–21), preparing to receive Lichas. "See, dear lady, / this is face-to-face with you now, / present and plain to see" (222–24). The next several hundred lines will reveal just what "this" (τάδ᾽, 223) is opposite Deianeira. The entrance and procession of the slave women compose one of Sophocles' most striking ceremonial presentations. The silent captive women, headed by Iole, make their entrance into the orchestra space to a virtual barrage of visual or spectatorial language from Deianeira.

> ὁρῶ, φίλαι γυναῖκες, οὐδέ μ᾽ ὄμματος
> φρουρὰν παρῆλθε, τόνδε μὴ λεύσσειν στόλον·
> $$(225–26)$$

I *see*, dear ladies, nor does the *sight*
of this procession escape my *watchful eye*.

Deianeira asserts her role as spectator within the "seeing place" of the theater. She watches and listens as insistently as the auditors sitting within the theater. Unlike the theater audience, however, Deianeira lacks the spectator's godlike omniscience. Trapped within her play, deprived full knowledge of the objects and people brought to her perception, she strives to interpret her world. The visual/spectatorial language returns as Lichas refers to the procession as "these women whom you *see* with your *eyes*" (241), driving home the theme of vision and interpretation, which concerns all audience members in the theater and so many Sophoclean characters.

Deianeira remarks that the women "are pitiable [οἰκτραὶ] if their misfortune does not deceive me" (243). This line is ironic on several levels. Of course, Deianeira *is* deceived by the women's misfortune, since she does not understand the actual reason why their town has been razed. The women, Iole in particular, represent the spoils of Heracles' violent lust. Iole will replace Deianeira in Heracles' bed. But on another, equally important plane, the women, too stunned or cowed to speak before their captors, are deserving of the greatest pity, even from Deianeira. Deianeira, as audience-within-the-play, "reads" their appearance in the orchestra as a symbol of all human suffering. Like Odysseus in the *Ajax* prologue, she can infer from the lot of particular mortals the condition of all people. The captive women's subjection to male violence represents a vivid counterpart to Deianeira's own experiences of sexual anxiety and (potential) violence as recounted in her prologue speech. Like an audience member in the theater, Deianeira experiences a temporary displacement of her individual concerns. She sees for a moment the general state of humankind reflected in the particular. The procession images the kinds of sorrows she has either known or feared and represents a projection of potential future disasters awaiting her or her children (303–6). She is filled with fear (δέδοικα, 306) and a terrible pity (οἶκτος δεινὸς, 298) at the sight (ὁρωμένη, 306).

The ceremony-within-the-play stimulates the fundamental "tragic" emotions in Deianeira that Aristotle expected of the theater audience. Her "tragic audience" response is slightly different in effect from Odysseus' musings on Ajax' downfall. Deianeira does not realize she is pitying a rival for her husband's love and her response is further colored by the exaggerations and probable lies of Lichas, who self-consciously promises that he will please Deianeira with a "speech" (λόγου) that will be "delightful to hear" (ἥδιστον κλύειν, 290).[4] Like Odysseus in *Ajax*, Deianeira is capable of pitying those who should be her enemies when their defeat and misery are staged for her eyes. Ironically, the enemy slave women's misery, which moves her to compassion, is the image of her own. Gellie observes, "Iole, as prize of

Heracles, as woman-chattel, is only another rendering of Deianeira herself, and that is how Deianeira first sees her."[5]

Lichas presents Deianeira with the slave women and gives his highly modified and selective view of the events leading to their capture (248–90). The Messenger later explains that the causes Lichas gives for the sack of Oechalia were Heracles' "trumped-up petty accusations" (361) used to justify his assault on the city. Lichas will pay a horrible price for his lies about Heracles' hurling Iphitus from the walls of Tiryns (269–73) when he himself is hurled to a grisly death by the dying Heracles (777–80).

Deianeira asks Lichas for information on the captive girl who, of all the slave women, most deeply stirs her pity.

Speak; for I pity [ᾤκτισα] her more than all the others,
when I saw her, she is the only one who knows how to feel.
(312–13)

When Lichas denies that he knows the girl's identity, Deianeira turns to Iole herself for an answer.

Then tell us yourself, poor creature; for it would be
a misfortune not to at least know who you are.
(320–21)

Lichas immediately interjects, bringing the inquiry to a temporary halt.

It would not be anything like her former behavior
if she starts talking now, I can assure you, for she
has not made an utterance either big or little,
but rather is always suffering birth pangs of heavy sorrow,
weeping, poor girl, ever since she left her windy
fatherland. It is certainly her misfortune that
she cannot speak, but forgive her all the same.
(322–28)

The moment when Deianeira asks Iole to identify herself is fraught with tension, built not only from the dramatic situation (Iole is, of course, Heracles' mistress who is being made a permanent fixture in Deianeira's household) but from the conventions of the dramatic medium itself. There are three speaking actors on stage at the moment: Deianeira, Lichas, and the Messenger who is silently watching the present exchange. With all of the available speaking actors engaged at this moment in the play, the captive women are played by mute extras. An attentive audience member, aware of the three-actor convention, must assume that the figure of Iole would remain mute, at least for the duration of this scene. Deianeira's asking Iole for a verbal reply pushes the conventions of Greek tragedy close to the breaking point. Lichas' response (322–28) rescues the dramaturgical/social crisis. By asking the mute actor to speak, Deianeira draws attention, however briefly, to the unreality of the situation, with its procession of silent women who simultaneously represent both her own past and present misfortunes.[6] The agony that makes Iole a nonspeaking supernumerary will later overcome the protagonist who has been gently interrogating her. Deianeira will make her exit in silence to commit suicide within the house while the Chorus demands, "Why are you going in silence? Don't you know that / your silence seconds your accuser?" (813–14). It is a silence that will soon be replaced by the same actor's bellowing as the dying Heracles.

After Lichas' exit with the captives, the Messenger corners Deianeira and begins to reveal the full nature of Heracles' sack of Oechalia and Iole's identity.

> That man just now has not said anything in accordance with
> the straight rule of honesty; either he was false now
> or he was not a true messenger [δίκαιος ἄγγελος] before.
>
> (346–48)

The interrogation of Lichas ensues with its *agon* of the self-styled "true" Messenger and the "false" herald (401–35). One critic has dubbed this scene, with the two characters presenting different narratives, each vying for dominance, as "one of the strangest sequences in Greek tragedy."[7] The Messenger assaults Lichas' credibility in heated, rapid-fire exchanges until Deianeira finally demands the truth from the herald in a speech of awesome rhetorical force, "No, by the high glen of Oeta, struck / by the lightning of Zeus, do not rob me of the truth!" (436–37). She portrays herself to Lichas as a person capable of accepting the power of Eros and of comprehending the whole truth about her husband's infidelities (438–69). Lichas relents and tells her the "whole truth," now that he has perceived by her words that she "sees things as we mortals must" (472–74). Deianeira assures Lichas that she will not add to her troubles by waging a "hopeless battle against the gods" (491–92). She promises to give the herald gifts to take to her husband (494–95), and the three actors exit into the skene (496).

Whitman has interpreted Deianeira's speech (436–69) as the high-water mark of her particular ἀρετή, her Oedipus-like insistence on knowing the truth whatever the cost.[8] Her rhetoric is overwhelming, but that should not dull appreciation of the irony that undercuts her act of seeming self-abnegation. Within minutes, the theater audience will learn that Deianeira *cannot* endure the truth: her protestations to the contrary were either a deliberate ruse to gain the last shred of information or a desperate attempt to talk herself into an acceptance alien to her nature. Her offer to have Lichas transport a gift to her husband suggests that the plan to use the blood of Nessus is already forming in her mind. Again Sophocles has used deception and rhetorical self-presentation to create a situation where word and deed have become separated and the audience must interpret what is seen and heard for clues about a character's inner motivation.

At least one ancient critic, an anonymous scholiast, has noted a provocative similarity between Deianeira's speech (436–69), asserting her ability to bear the disclosure of the truth, and Ajax' great speech (*Ajax* 646–92), professing his acceptance of the onslaught of time.[9] This interpretation of Deianeira's speech as an enacted falsehood comparable with the rhetorical tour de force in *Ajax* has found surprisingly few modern adherents.[10] Reinhardt is perhaps the most important Sophoclean critic to capitalize on the similarities of the two speeches. "The disguise that the character [both Ajax and Deianeira] assumes makes it clear what he should have been like in order to escape his fate—and that he could never be like that," observes Reinhardt. "Thus the speech of deception itself becomes one of the protean forms which the character's basic daimon assumes, only to come upon him in ways which despite their strangeness and variety leave it essentially the same."[11] Reinhardt's description of the respective speeches as "disguises" donned by Deianeira and Ajax is particularly interesting, with its intimation of role-playing-within-the-role.

After the exit of the three characters into the palace, the Chorus sings a narration (497–530) describing Heracles and Acheloüs' battle for the young Deianeira's bed. The Chorus's narration, with its attendant dancing and mimetic gesture, allows Deianeira's youth to be enacted for the audience in a manner analogous to a flashback sequence in a motion picture. The brutal struggle between the river monster and the demigod is superimposed upon our knowledge of Heracles' recent warfare, both actions having been stirred by Eros. Sophocles' poetry unites the old story related by the Chorus with the action unfolding in the present. The image of the captive, helpless Iole, the innocent object of Heracles' violent lust, stands in for the younger Deianeira recalled by the stasimon. This choral song creates a mimesis of the young Deianeira's capture by Heracles that mirrors the abduction of Iole previously enacted in the procession.

Deianeira reenters to talk furtively with the Chorus. She asks the Trachinian women for their "pity for her sorrows" (πάσχω συγκα-τοικτιουμένη, 535). Heiden notes that Deianeira's asking for pity "indicates that her [ensuing] speech will have a theatrical character, like the tragic performance which itself aims at exciting pity in the audience."[12] She goes on to broach her plan to recapture Heracles' love by anointing a robe with the Centaur's blood. The Chorus responds in language that hints at the theatricality of the situation.

If the action [τοῖς δρωμένοις] is trustworthy,
you don't seem [δοκεῖς] to be badly counseled.
(588–89)

"Action" and "seeming" inform this critical moment of dramatic choice. Like Oedipus in the *Tyrannus* play, Deianeira is engulfed by a deceptive world where the best intentions end in disaster. The ensuing scenes of *Trachiniae* are among the most troubling and ambiguous in Greek tragedy. Almost as soon as Lichas has departed with the robe anointed with Nessus' blood, Deianeira has misgivings which she shares with the Chorus (663–722). She describes the terrifying disintegration of the tuft of wool she had used to anoint the robe.

And when I was going out I saw an unspeakable
sight, beyond human understanding.
I happened to have thrown the piece of wool
with which I had rubbed the ointment onto the hot floor,
in the rays of the sun. And as it warmed
it melted into nothing and crumbled on the ground,
looking most like the sawdust you see
when someone cuts wood.
So it lay, where it fell, and from the ground
where it lay clotted foam boiled up,

just as when the rich liquid from the blue-green fruit
is poured on the ground from Bacchus' vine.

(693–704)

The Centaur's blood works as a deadly melting agent, triggered by the sun, which hovers over actors and audience alike. A ruinous melting begins which contains Dionysian properties. Dionysus, the theater god, blurs and dissolves boundaries. His powers extend from the vine harvest to forces of madness and familial destruction. A Bacchic force in the deadly blood will melt the distinctions between demigod and mortal. The boundaries will be dissolved between man and wife through the performance of the protagonist playing both Deianeira and Heracles, fusing the estranged couple in a deadly union in the Theater of Dionysus.

Soon Hyllus enters to relate the horrifying effect the robe is having upon his father and to accuse Deianeira of deliberately poisoning Heracles with the robe (734–812). After her son's denunciation, Deianeira leaves the stage in silence to take her life within the palace (812). The Nurse emerges from the house to relate to the Chorus and audience the last image the play will afford us of Deianeira, lying dead upon her bridal bed (899–946). The Nurse's verbal image merges into the concrete image of Deianeira's husband, played by the same actor, borne onstage in a deathlike stupor. The wife, in effect, turns into her husband. In his agony Heracles will exclaim to his son,

Come on, son, take courage; and show pity [οἴκτιρόν] for me
whom many would find pitiful [οἰκτρόν], moaning and crying
like a girl. And there is not one man who could say
that he ever saw me crying before;
rather without complaining I submitted to bad things.
Having been such a man, now I am found to be a woman.

(1070–75)

Heracles' "womanly" crying and the emasculation inflicted upon him by the poisoned robe hint of some parity between the wife and husband, both enacted by the same actor. The gentle Deianeira has used a sword to die in a surprisingly masculine manner (923–31) and now the supermasculine Heracles feels himself robbed of his virility by the effects of Nessus' poison. Deianeira's womanly role merges into the part of Heracles with deadly consequences. Just as Deianeira had requested pity from the Chorus (συγκατοικτιουμένη, 535) and, by extension, the theater audience, the same actor presents himself in his new character of Heracles as a figure also worthy of tragic pity (οἰκτρόν, 1070, 1071). The deaths of husband and wife, two irreconcilable figures, become literally one calamity, one tragedy, through the skillful use of fifth-century dramatic convention.[13]

The play draws to a close with Heracles' grisly display of his ravaged body (1076–80), the brutal demands he lays upon Hyllus, and the procession leading out of the theater, bearing the hero up to Mount Oeta to be incinerated alive.[14] The closing lines are spoken by Hyllus as a bitter denunciation of Zeus and the other gods for the gratuitous suffering their children are allowed to endure.[15]

> Behold the cruelty of the gods
> in the deeds that are being done.
> They beget children and are called
> fathers and they look upon such sufferings.
> No one can see the future;
> but the present is pitiable for us
> and shameful for the gods.
> But hardest of all
> for him who undergoes this disaster.
> Come, maidens, do not be left behind at the house;
> you have recently seen an awful death,
> along with many griefs and uncanny suffering,
> and there is nothing here that is not Zeus.
>
> (1266–78)

Hyllus puts the play's closing situation into visual terms that have strong associations with the theater experience. He creates an image of the gods, and Zeus in particular, as beings who sit outside, watching the destruction of Heracles' family. The gods' attitude is not far removed from that of a tragic playwright viewing his completed work from the auditorium.

The last speech of Hyllus in *Trachiniae* represents the only surviving example of a Sophoclean play closing with lines not delivered by the chorus.[16] This speech allows Hyllus to become a spokesman for the entire dramatis personae of the tragedy. His denunciation of the gods' treatment of their "children" is also a character's denunciation of a playwright. The tragic dramatist has breathed eloquent life into his dramatic figures and then ruthlessly maltreated them, leaving both the characters and the theater audience without a reassuring moral lesson or coherent reason for the suffering. The playwright, mirroring the father of gods himself, has created a kind of world within the orchestra circle. Like Zeus, Sophocles must take responsibility for all that is included and all that is excluded from that world. Like Zeus, he is both present and absent from his creation. This playwright is, like Zeus, under no compulsion to justify his actions.

Sophocles has closed his drama just before Heracles is to be incinerated alive on Mount Oeta. According to myth, Heracles experienced an apotheosis, becoming a kind of god or semidivine, immortal figure. This deification of Heracles was one of the few examples in the Greek tradition of a human transcending his own mortality. The action of *Trachiniae* has led up to Hyllus' concluding speech without any mention of this redeeming deification. Many scholars, understandably uncomfortable with this inconsistency between the myth and the play, assume that the audience, familiar with Heracles' story, would fill in the gaps left by the playwright. This argument assumes that Sophocles was under no obligation to include any reference or premonition of the apotheosis, since the part of the story he had chosen to dramatize took place before it. It may be argued that any reference to Oeta (the place of the apotheosis) or to fire is a hint at the hero's impending transcendence.

Both Jebb and Easterling take the view that Hyllus' line 1270 ("No one can see the future") alludes, however vaguely, to a coming apotheosis.[17] If such an allusion is Sophocles' intention, it hardly relieves the cumulative impact of the speech, which focuses on the family's present agony, a moment of devastating pain frozen forever in the audience's mind by the striking tableau. If present, the allusion remains a surprisingly tepid hint to the future, hardly as defined as are Aegisthus' premonitions of the future at the end of *Electra* (1497–98). Gellie has reasonably argued that "If apotheosis is hinted at, and then the hint is not made good, we are surely being asked to observe the gap, not to fill it in."[18]

The omission of the apotheosis leaves Sophocles' play to be completed in the minds of the theater audience. The play's conclusion is profoundly unsettling, however one chooses to interpret it. If the audience is being asked to fill in the gaps in the myth to give the story a reassuring closure, the situation is hardly comforting. The tragic playwrights freely added and excluded material in creating their versions of the mythic stories. Sophocles would consequently be asking his audience to add back into the story all that he has carefully excluded. An analogous situation might be a medieval mystery play depicting Christ's crucifixion with all reference to the resurrection scrupulously excluded. While a good, churchgoing medieval audience could be counted on to fill in that gap, it is not difficult to imagine such an audience resenting the author's omissions, sensing that a denial of the resurrection is somehow being implied. This hypothetical medieval playwright would probably arouse a degree of anger in his audience for his failure to meet its expectations, for not "doing his job." Sophocles, by excluding the apotheosis, may be seen in much the same light.

While line 1270 may be a feeble premonition of Heracles' transcendence, the reference serves to direct focus less on the delayed, though redeeming, blessings of a beneficent deity than on the power of the playwright, who selects and discards mythic detail to create an artistic vision that may frustrate his audience's hunger for pious religious formula. The play ends at a moment of crisis without imposing any real closure on the story. The audience is compelled to grapple with the play, to interact with it. In this way, Sophocles' world of illusion insidiously enters the audience's world.[19]

In *Trachiniae* we see Sophocles utilizing several metatheatrical devices that he had already used with such consummate skill in *Ajax*. For all the horror of Athena's cruel "demonstration" of the insane Ajax, her presentation affords both Odysseus and the theater audience the opportunity to gain a greater perspective on Ajax and the human condition itself. *Trachiniae*, however, presents a tragic vision that will allow for little or no comfort or reflection. It is a world permeated by senseless cruelty and suffering. In giving expression to this vision of senselessness, Sophocles presents us with a *theatrum mundi* that stubbornly refuses to "work." Though revealing a humanity much like that of Odysseus in *Ajax*, Deianeira is incapable of transcending her limited, but touchingly human, perception of the world. In this regard she fails in her role as an internal audience to the procession of captive women and to Lichas' final revelations. Enacted deceptions have become more numerous and more difficult to identify than in *Ajax*. Finally, *Trachiniae* comes to an unforgettable conclusion with one of its characters coming forward to condemn the arbitrary cruelty that Zeus (and the playwright) has inflicted upon him and his fellow characters.

All of Sophocles' tragedies engage the spectator in the fundamental metatheatrical problem of appearance versus reality. The dichotomy of appearance and essence is one of the favorite subjects of serious drama. By its very nature, drama deals in illusion, in the creative tension of one person or object standing in for or representing something else. As one of the masters of dramatic irony, Sophocles exhibits the keenest appreciation of the often invisible gulf that separates deeds from words and perception from reality. It is natural that someone so attuned to these fissures in experience would want to explore thoroughly the boundaries of his aesthetic medium. This exploration often calls attention to the irony of a character's situation in the story as well as the irony of the theatrical situation itself, the flickering "in and out"

of illusion that is repeatedly created and destroyed in the course of a performance.

The so-called Theban Plays, *Antigone*, *Oedipus Tyrannus*, and *Oedipus at Colonus*, were not viewed by Sophocles as a deliberate cycle or trilogy. *Oedipus at Colonus* may be securely dated around 406, at the very end of the poet's long life; the other two plays came from earlier in Sophocles' career. There is evidence that *Antigone* dates from around 442, and *Oedipus Tyrannus* may have appeared between 429 and 425.[1] While Sophocles was not the only tragedian to return to a particular myth at different stages of his career, the story of Oedipus' family obviously held a special fascination for him, drawing the enormous concentration of his powers in these three plays. In varying degrees, Sophocles' three most famous tragedies represent drama about drama.

Antigone

All three Theban Plays use the illusion-versus-reality motif as a major component of their thematics. *Antigone*, the earliest of the three tragedies, is built on two contrasting visions of reality: the brutal, corporal world of the literalist Creon and the invisible world of the dead, which Antigone seeks to honor. One critic observes that during the course of the play, "Death will finally reveal the true *apolis* [cityless one] and the true *hypsipolis* [person held in high esteem by the city] and separate the illusion from the reality."[2] These contrasting visions of reality are embodied by two characters who strive for dominance as playwrights-within-the-play.

Sophocles was elected as a general in 441/40. One of the ancient hypotheses of *Antigone* claims that Sophocles won this post due to the popularity of this play. If true, this would place *Antigone* close to 442. Even if the anonymous author of the hypothesis is incorrect, it seems plausible that such a detail would not have been recorded unless it were at least chronologically possible. As a growing imperial power, Athens would have found particular resonance in a tragedy dealing with conflicts between state authority and private or local traditions and beliefs. Few surviving tragedies suggest the notion of the poet as διδάσκαλος or "teacher of the polis" as clearly as does *Antigone*. The verb derived from διδάσκαλος serves literally as the play's last word (γήρᾳ τὸ φρονεῖν ἐδίδαξαν: "The old are taught wisdom," 1353). The tragedy serves as an object lesson in the dangers of tyrannical power—the kind of power that has come to the untested Creon and the expanding Athenian Empire.

Antigone is one of the few Sophoclean heroines who unequivocally sustains the weight of Cedric Whitman's vision of ἀρετή. Her self-image never suffers the kind of compromises that either threaten, injure, or overtake characters like Ajax or Electra. With Antigone, word and deed are never separate. Creon, on the other hand, offers a fine example of just such a fragmentation. The play ruthlessly exposes the dichotomy of Creon's noble-sounding speeches and sentiments and the hollowness that lies beneath them, a hollowness comparable with that of an egocentric actor.

It does not minimize Antigone's radiant moral purpose that the brunt of the dialogue and stage time is given to the character of Creon. *Antigone*, during the course of its action, strips away the illusion of Creon's integrity as a ruler, while affirming the real integrity of the heroine. The perception of his true identity as a petty, empty figure grows and develops throughout the play. In Creon's first appearance, his "ship of state" speech (162–210) is an impressive piece of self-representation. There is evidence that this speech was regarded in antiquity as a model of statesmanship. Demosthenes' great rival, Aeschines, had been an actor before turning to oratory; and one of his more notable roles had been Creon in *Antigone*. In order to bait his opponent about his deficiencies in citizenship, Demosthenes ordered that the "ship of state" speech be read over to Aeschines to remind him of the duties of a true statesman. Demosthenes' tactic would lack point unless Creon's speech were regarded by the average fourth-century audience as an idealistic statement of principle. In ridiculing the former actor, Demosthenes refers to him as "Creon-Aeschines" and berates him for not "repeating [the speech] over to himself to guide him as an ambassador." Demosthenes might even have seen a deeper similarity between Sophocles' tyrant and "Creon-Aeschines": both the dramatic character and the ex-actor have a fine patriotic speech in their "repertory" that only serves to illustrate their inner hollowness as politicians and as men.[3]

Sophocles' Creon provides his audience with the necessary criteria to appreciate how far he falls from his own standard for the ideal ruler and citizen. The play's central development takes this exemplary speech of Creon's as a starting point, then steadily reveals his actual character through his ensuing actions. On a metatheatrical plane, Creon sets himself a noble role to play but fails to live up to the part. His selfish and cruel deeds (ἔργα) jar with his noble sounding words (λόγοι). His failure as a ruler and as a man is a kind of theatrical-performative failure. His blustering tirades and posturing disintegrate his own family, revealing him to be "one who does not exist, equal to nothing" (1325). The "big words of the excessively boastful are punished with great blows" (μεγάλοι δὲ λόγοι / μεγάλας πληγὰς τῶν ὑπεραύχων / ἀποτείσαντες, 1350–53).

While *Ajax* afforded examples of stage tyranny in the bullying figures of Menelaus and Agamemnon (who, like Creon, concern themselves with obstructing a burial), Creon's tyranny is made all the more memorable for its added metatheatrical dimension. During his confrontation with the captured Antigone, the princess remarks that "tyranny is happy in many things / particularly in being able *to do and say whatever it wants* [δρᾶν λέγειν θ᾽ ἃ βούλεται]" (506–7). Creon's power is theatrically or performatively defined throughout *Antigone*. Like an egotistical actor/playwright, he controls what may be done (δρᾶν) or said (λέγειν) as well as what may be seen and heard. He even endeavors to control other characters' exits and entrances. His attempts at being the only actor or speaker within the theater meet with opposition and failure from early on in the tragedy. By the end of the play, Creon has lost all of his "theatrical" control. Other voices successfully contend with his. He ends the tragedy not as the master of what may be shown or discussed but as a spectatorial object standing amid the ruins of his own family.

Creon will deliver his first public address as ruler as a kind of self-styled herald or κηρύξ. Antigone warns Ismene that he is about to come "here [δεῦρο] and make proclamation [προκηρύξοντα] to those who do not know his rulings" (33–34). Creon himself uses the same language of heralding in respect to his proclamation: "I make proclamation [κηρύξας] to the citizens [αστοῖσι]" (192–93). Creon's authority as herald is challenged when Antigone tells him, "It was not Zeus who made *this proclamation* [ὁ κηρύξας τάδε]" (450). Creon's authority as a "speaker" or "announcer to all" is directly threatened.

The exposure of Polyneices' corpse is referred to as a kind of ghastly act of showmanship. The body is left "to be seen [ἰδεῖν] as a feast for dogs and birds" (206). This same presentational or spectatorial language is adopted by the Sentry, who describes the mysterious first burial of the body as causing the corpse to "vanish" (ἠφάνιστο, 255). Creon, the cruel showman, is incensed that the grotesque spectacle might be taken from the gaze of his captive audience, the Theban citizens. The worst extremes of Creon's hubris are attained when the king orders Antigone to be brought onstage so that she may be killed "right in front of her bridegroom" (760–61). Haemon averts this ghastly spectacle by leaving the stage.

As ruler, Creon views himself as the ultimate speaker or doer. The burial is referred to repeatedly as "the deed," that action which the chief "actor" will not allow (252, 262, 273). The presence of the comic Sentry serves to highlight the disparity between Creon's self-image and his real nature. The Sentry allows us to examine, in Reinhardt's words, "the mighty man . . . seen by a creature who shrieks and shakes, is chosen by lot, dilly-dallies, and comforts himself tragically with 'fate.'"[4] David Grene has described the role of the Sentry as "a remarkable experiment in Greek tragedy in the direction of naturalism of speech."[5] Grene seems to have mistaken the most remarkable aspect of the Sentry's words: his speech is notable not so much for "naturalism," an effect difficult to achieve in Greek tragic verse, as for the character's use of an inflated, pseudotragic tone (223–24, 235–36). The Sentry speaks as a comic figure, aware that he has been thrust into a tragic setting. He self-consciously views himself as a messenger (ἄγγελον) bearing bad news (ἐπῶν, 277). His self-conscious status as a messenger puts him in contention with Creon who quickly tries to control this "rival" performer, angrily ordering him to say his piece and leave quickly (244). But the Sentry cannot be controlled so easily. The Sentry's ability to share and dominate stage time helps to undermine Creon's authority on stage. Clearly Creon is not the only doer and speaker. In fact, he is powerless to silence even this lowliest of characters and drive him from the stage before the Sentry establishes an easy rapport with the theater audience. The Sentry also displays an ability to "stage" his arguments with himself for the audience's benefit.

> Often I was halted by my thoughts,
> making me turn myself around in circles.
> For my soul [ψυχὴ] found a voice, speaking many things to me:
> "Wretch, why go where you'll pay the price on arrival?"

"Poor one, stalling again? And if Creon learns this
from another man, how could you not suffer for it?"
Revolving like this, I made a short journey long . . .

(225–31)

His description of "revolving," "turning in circles," and the reported
speech of his "soul" suggests rich mimetic possibilities for the actor. For
the passage to be effective, the contrast between the Sentry's persona
and his "soul" needs to be strongly highlighted by the actor. This
reenacted self-interrogation is full of comic potential and prefigures the
self-interrogation performed by slave characters in Plautine comedy.[6]

By his words and body language, the lowly comic character calls
attention to playacting. We see an actor playing a character who suddenly fragments into several "characters," all aspects of the same theatrically represented figure. The Sentry's tendency to "fragment" into
different voices makes him appear a character of less dramatic integrity
than Creon, with whom he shares the stage. But the Sentry's brief,
comic role playing momentarily destabilizes Creon's illusory sense of
power; and his ludicrous cringing before Creon somehow makes
Creon share in his ridiculousness.

The Sentry's inept use of a tragic-style gnome ("For I come with a
firm grasp on the hope / that one cannot suffer anything other than
what is fated," 235–36) along with his explanation of his breathless
entry ("My lord, I will not say that I have arrived breathless / due to
speed, plying a nimble foot," 223–24) have a touch of the metatheatrical. They all suggest a consciousness of theatrical convention.[7] Speech
and action (λόγος καὶ ἔργα) are the principal building blocks of all
drama, and they are the things Creon most wants to monopolize and
control. The Sentry's talkative personality is an affront to Creon's stage
management. "You are a chatterer by nature, it is clear," the tyrant
proclaims. Picking up on Creon's need for control, the Sentry responds, "Yes, but at least I'm not the one who *did this deed* [ἔργον
τοῦτο ποιήσας]" (320–21). Another speaker is exasperating enough for
Creon in his theater/state, but not as exasperating as another "doer."

As the Sentry leaves the stage under Creon's bitter mandate to find
the criminal, he bids farewell to his monarch.

Well, may [the criminal] be found, that's most important. But
whether he is caught or not, for fortune will decide that,
you shall certainly not see me coming here again.

As it is, I have been saved beyond hope and my own
expectation, and owe the gods much thanks.

(327–31)

The force of these lines is directed not at Creon but to the audience.
The Sentry's entertaining performance and his incongruous presence
have undermined Creon's authority before the eyes of the theater
spectators. His promise never to return "here" (δεῦρ', 329) is the remark not only of a character leaving the stage but of a comic actor self-
consciously saying good-bye to his audience.

The Sentry's later reentry reminds the audience of his earlier
promise.

My lord, men should never swear an oath not to do something.
Afterthought belies intention. I could have sworn that
it would be long before I came here again because of
your threats which lashed at me.

(388–91)

The comedy in the Sentry's reentrance is muted by the fact that he is
bearing Antigone to her doom. It is typical of his ambiguous placement within the tragedy that, while offering momentary diversion from
the rising tensions of the action, this peripheral figure hints so suc-
cinctly at the serious issue of Creon's dangerous stubbornness: unlike
the Sentry, Creon will *not* learn to change his mind before it is too late.

The question of who is the central character of the play, Antigone or
Creon, would probably have been of little interest to an ancient audience. Modern criticism has exerted much energy on this vexed question, which arises from Antigone's disappearance from the stage in the
middle of the play and Creon's control of the rest of the tragedy. This
structural feature has led the play to be termed a "diptych," the result of
Sophocles' relative immaturity as a dramatist, before achieving structural perfection in his later plays. The same charge has been brought
against *Ajax* and *Trachiniae*. These concerns vanish when the performance conditions of the ancient theater are taken into account in all
three of these allegedly "diptych" dramatic structures. The allocation
of roles between the three actors is particularly evocative in *Antigone*.
One actor doubled as Antigone with Teiresias and either Eurydice
or the Messenger. A second actor doubled as Ismene, the Sentry,
Haemon, and either the Messenger or Eurydice. One actor played

Creon only. The voice and physical presence which brought Antigone to life before the ancient audience would go on to assume the role of Teiresias, the seer who reveals the Gods' anger and leads Creon to yield belatedly to their will (and Antigone's). The same "Antigone" actor would also impersonate either the Messenger, who relates the heroine's fate, or Eurydice, whose brief appearance signals the final destruction of Creon's family wrought by his opposition to Antigone. The "Ismene" actor would enjoy a similar association with his later roles. The Sentry and Haemon represent sympathetic figures who, for all their many contrasts, are both falsely accused by Creon.[8]

These probable role assignments point to an aesthetic unity attained by the act of ancient theatrical performance. Viewed in this light, the tragedy is no longer a diptych when we can hear and see the "Antigone" actor absorbed into other characters who maintain the conflict "she" had instigated with Creon. Creon's function as a solo role defines that character's position in the play. He is isolated both by his extreme political stance and by the physical realities of performance within the Theater of Dionysus. His role is played by a single actor surrounded by colleagues who continually change their roles. As Creon is isolated from his surrounding actors, so too is he isolated from the polis of Thebes and the polis represented by the theater audience. The play makes frequent reference to the ruler and the polis, often contrasting the populous city-state and the isolated nature of the tyrant. This contrast contains a latent theatrical corollary, the opposition of a crowded *theatron* and a single actor performing before it.

The tragedy opens with Antigone and Ismene furtively entering from the skene door to discuss what Antigone has learned about Creon's decree. The skene becomes the Theban royal palace, and the two women see their situation as one that will potentially isolate them from their polis. That polis, the citizens who make up Thebes, is inescapably equated with the polis that fills the theater auditorium. Ismene balks at setting herself against the overwhelming force of Creon and the city. "What, you intend to bury [the corpse] when the polis has forbidden it?" (44). Ismene tells Antigone she is incapable of defying the citizens (πολιτῶν, 79). The performative implications of these two theatrical figures, caught between the skene and the vast auditorium containing thousands of Athenian citizens, resonates throughout these lines.

Antigone proposes the clandestine burial to her sister as a kind of action which will reveal Ismene's inner nature. "You will show [δείξεις] / whether your nature is noble or if you are a coward sprung from a noble line" (37–38). Ismene refuses "to act against the citizens" (πολιτῶν δρᾶν, 79). She argues that she is weak and incapable of defying those in power. While she may be as appalled as Antigone by the proclamation, Ismene counsels that the sisters keep their feelings to themselves and endure this and whatever worse may follow (61–64). Antigone's rage against her sister is charged with the performative language of action and deeds. "I would not tell you to do it, even if you were / willing to act [πράσσειν] after all, nor would I be content for you to act [δρῴης] with me. / Rather you be [ἴσθ'] the sort of person that you decide, but for my part / I shall bury him. It's noble for me to do [ποιούσῃ] this and die" (69–72). Antigone refuses to separate her inner and outer nature. She insists on acting or doing the deed dictated by her inherent nobility. By her insistence on action, she irrevocably breaks from her sister and sets in motion her challenge to Creon's political and performative authority. The tyrant's rule necessitates subjects who will be too intimidated to speak or act against the ruler. For Antigone, action and intention are inseparable. She will not be the fragmented, doubly theatrical figure her sister has become. When Ismene attempts to share her sister's punishment, Antigone rejects her. "I don't tolerate a loved one who only loves *in words* [λόγοις]" (543). Unlike Ismene or the Sentry, both of whom were undertaken by the same actor, Antigone is unafraid to link deed with word in challenging Creon's autocratic rule. "Did you do this deed?" (δεδρακέναι τάδε;), Creon demands when she is brought before him. "I *say* that I *did* it and I do not deny it" (καὶ φημὶ δρᾶσαι κοὐκ ἀπαρνοῦμαι τὸ μή, 442–43). This conflict of inner and outer nature, of word and action, will be developed further by Sophocles in the relationship between Electra, Chrysothemis, and Clytemnestra.

Antigone will make frequent reference to the phenomenon of the single individual (or performer) opposing the will of a vast polis (or audience). At first it is Antigone who is portrayed as the lone outsider. But as the play progresses, Creon is presented increasingly as the lone individual whose folly leads him to oppose the polis and the gods. Antigone's arraignment before Creon marks a turning point in the audience's perception of the outsider or "cityless one," as well as a development of the conceit of the audience standing in for the Theban polis. Antigone says:

How could I have achieved more glory
Than by burying my brother?
These here all [τούτοις ... πᾶσιν] would
Say this if fear didn't seal their mouths.
But tyranny is happy in many things,
Particularly in doing and saying whatever it wants.
Creon: You alone [σὺ ... μούνη] among these Cadmeans see this.
Antigone: They [χοῦτοι] see it *too*; but *they* keep their mouths
   shut because of you.

(502–9)

The "Theban citizens" or "polis" now becomes the Chorus and the theater audience as well. The theater audience's silence and attentiveness to the "actor" Creon blend into the stage illusion of the Chorus, the onstage audience. This passage begins Creon's isolation from all other stage figures, an isolation that will increase with Creon's condemnation of Antigone. The rhetorical figure of the single person opposing the polis, as enunciated by the Chorus's preceding songs (106, 370), now seems to be identified as Creon alone. In his argument with his father, Haemon cautions Creon: "I can hear in the dark how the city mourns for this girl" (692–93). Creon has replaced Antigone as the figure isolated from the audience and surrounding theatrical environment, the on- and offstage cities.

Haemon: No city [πόλις] belongs to one man.
Creon: Isn't the city considered to belong to its rulers?
Haemon: You would be an excellent monarch for a desert.

(737–39)

Sophocles signals Creon's final collapse as the playwright/director-within-the-play when he crumbles before the Chorus and asks "What must I do then? Tell me, and I will obey" (τί δῆτα χρὴ δρᾶν; φράζε· πείσομαι δ᾽ ἐγώ, 1099). Even after Creon learns his mistake and rushes to undo his error, the polis-audience relationship is maintained. When Eurydice silently exits to commit suicide after the Messenger's speech, the Messenger reasons that she does not think it proper to utter laments before the city (1246–50). The last scene, when Creon bears Haemon's body into the theater, is charged with the language of revelation and visual presentation. Creon, the arch realist, has come to acknowledge the unseen forces that drove Antigone. His folly is manifested in the dead son he bears and the dead wife revealed to him on the eccyclema. He and the characters on stage with him regard him and the carnage surrounding him as spectatorial objects or theatrical symbols exemplifying a moral lesson (1263–64, 1270, 1279–80, 1293–95, 1297–99).[9]

Twice during the course of the tragedy, the Chorus makes direct reference to the god of theater.[10] During the parodos celebrating the defeat of the Argive forces, the Chorus calls on Bacchus to be its leader in night-long celebratory dances at the gods' temples (θεῶν δὲ ναοὺς χοροῖς / παννύχοις πάντας ἐπέλ- / θωμεν, ὁ Θήβας δ' ἐλελί-/ χθων Βάκχιος ἄρχοι, 152–55). This passage is interesting not only for its references to the god but for the self-reflexive device of the Chorus discussing its primary performative function (χοροῖς). This image of Bacchus leading his dancing Theban countrymen is soon contrasted with Creon's first entrance and his proclamation. After Teiresias' warnings have finally prevailed upon Creon and he leaves to release Antigone, the Chorus bursts into an excited hymn to Dionysus (1115–52). As in comparable moments in *Ajax*, *Trachiniae*, and *Oedipus Tyrannus*, the Chorus prematurely predicts a happy resolution to the play's action. Dionysus, the "dance leader of the fire-breathing stars" (πῦρ πνεόντων / χοράγ' ἄστρων, 1146–47) is urged to appear "with cleansing foot" (1144).

These two references to Dionysus are rich in suggestiveness. Each is placed at a deciding moment in the drama: before Creon proclaims his fateful edict and after he has renounced his stance against Antigone. The passages encourage the listener to look for the theater god's literal or figurative manifestation on stage. After the parodos, Creon symbolically renounces Dionysus in his insistence upon punishing the dead Polyneices. Two of Dionysus' greatest attributes were as a dissolver of boundaries and as a god of ecstatic release. Creon's autocratic rule, with its insistence on male prerogative, stands opposed to any Dionysian impulse. Like Pentheus in the *Bacchae*, Creon refuses to be bested by a woman, lest he relinquish his masculine authority (484–85). Unlike the god who "makes no distinction of ages" (*Bacchae* 204–9), Creon refuses to learn from the ideas of the young (726–27). The god of role playing and masks forsakes the actor playing Creon, allowing him only the one role to play, while the other two actors are constantly changing characters.

By the time the Chorus pleads for Dionysus to appear as a redeemer (1115–54), it is already too late. The god's presence *is* felt in the closing scenes of *Antigone*, but it is in his role as destroyer and god of destructive madness. Dionysus, through his servant Sophocles, has attempted to teach Creon and the Athenian audience the limits of mortal power and masculine prerogative. By electing Sophocles to the generalship in 441/40, the Athenian audience signaled the playwright that, unlike Creon, it had grasped his lesson, at least for the moment.

Oedipus Tyrannus

One can imagine the disturbing effect of *Oedipus Tyrannus* upon its original audience, if the consensus of scholarly opinion is correct in dating the play to the early or mid 420s. This period saw Athens, already enmeshed in the Peloponnesian War, undergoing bouts of plague that wiped out hundreds of citizens, including Sophocles' friend Pericles. Sophocles seems to have originated the plotting device of the Theban plague as the motivation behind Oedipus' fateful investigation. The Athenians wanted their tragic playwrights to create distance between the contemporary polis and the catastrophes represented in the theater. With their own plague fresh in the collective memory, the Theban plague would have reminded the Athenians of one of their worst civic calamities. Perhaps this is one of the reasons this play, so often regarded as the highest achievement of the ancient theater, only won second place.

In addition to its startling connection to contemporary events, the play harks back to the earlier *Antigone*. Jebb perceived an analogy between the first entrance of Creon in *Antigone* with the proclamation delivered by his ill-fated nephew near the beginning of *Oedipus Tyrannus* (216–75). "In each case a Theban king addresses Theban elders, announcing a stern decree, adopted in reliance on his own wisdom, and promulgated with haughty consciousness of power; the elders receive the decree with a submissive deference under which we can perceive traces of misgiving; and as the drama proceeds, the elders become spectators of calamities occasioned by the decree, while its author turns to them for comfort."[11] Both *tyrannoi* engage in similar arguments with Teiresias. Both learn harsh lessons concerning the limitations of human power and the unseen forces that move below the surface of nature. Like Creon in *Antigone*, Oedipus is a ruler described as a "*tyrannos*," a word with associations of nonhereditary kingship and the pejorative sense of "tyranny." Both tragedies seem to play with the double implications of this word. Like the Creon in *Antigone*, King Oedipus can be rash and destructive when opposed; and his stubborn determination forces the action of the play to its horrible conclusion. But Oedipus is a far more complex figure than the earlier tyrant. It is as if Sophocles had fused elements of Antigone's character, particularly her propensity to sacrifice herself for a higher cause, with that of her uncle.

Even more than the Creon of *Antigone*, the protagonist of *Oedipus Tyrannus* possesses qualities that are analogous to those of a theater artist. Oedipus is a dramatic figure obsessed with performing actions and speeches and revealing truths for the entire polis before his palace/skene. Oedipus promises his citizens and the theater audience that he "shall make manifest" (φανῶ, 132) the mystery threatening his polis. Ironically, he himself becomes the object revealed (πέφασμαι, 1184). His relentless search for the truth about the past ultimately exposes the searcher, much as a finished artwork reveals as much about its artificer as about its subject matter. Oedipus is presented as a master of action and deeds and a genius at the decipherment and manipulation of language. He attained his kingship after engaging in a deadly competition of quasi-literary and performative dimensions. Unaided by gods or men, Oedipus answered the riddle of the Sphinx, described as "the rhapsode hound" (ἡ ῥαψῳδὸς . . . κύων, 391). This curious image of the Sphinx as "rhapsode" makes their encounter an *agon* not only between human being and monster but between two verbal and performative artists.

After his true parentage has been revealed, Oedipus asks the Shepherd why he had spared the crippled infant's life so many years before. The old man responds, "I pitied it, my lord" (κατοικτίσας, ὦ δέσποθ᾽, 1178). From the beginning, Oedipus has been an object of pity, either for the few who were aware of his cursed birth and subsequent mutilation or for the theater audience viewing a man who is blind to the horrid circumstances of his life. Pity, one of the cardinal tragic emotions in Aristotelian literary theory, is at the core of Oedipus' dramatic situation. The Shepherd's line at 1178 reveals that "pity" is, ironically enough, the reason Oedipus survived to experience the present catastrophe. Part of the irony rests in the self-reflexive nature of the Shepherd's "pity." Oedipus is the ultimate subject for tragedy. He stimulates pity in the theater audience and owes his existence to the pity he generated in the Shepherd.

After the Shepherd's final revelations, the Chorus literally refers to Oedipus as possessing a fate that is a "paradigm" (παράδειγμ') of humanity's unhappiness (1193). The Second Messenger's first lines, which introduce the tragedy's final revelation, are striking for their explicitly metatheatrical language. "O you who are held in greatest honor in this land, / what deeds you shall hear of, what deeds you shall see, and what / grief you shall endure [οἷ' ἔργ' ἀκούσεσθ', οἷα δ' εἰσόψεσθ', ὅσον δ' / ἀρεῖσθε πένθος], if you still have a kinsmen's regard for the house of Labdacus" (1223–25). These words prepare the audience to view Oedipus' imminent reentry, stumbling and blinded, as a *theatrical* experience.[12] The Messenger will refer to him as a "sight" (θέαμα) the "beholding" (εἰσόψῃ) of which will lead to "pity" (ἐποιτίσαι, 1295–96).

Like *Antigone*'s Creon, Oedipus is used to "doing and saying whatever he wants" which, as Antigone observed, is the prerogative of the *tyrannos* (*Ant.* 506–7). Like the earlier Creon, Oedipus is a playwright/director-within-the-play who displays formidable powers in controlling the stage space and other characters' performative behavior, as well as correctly perceiving a challenge to his dramaturgical authority. But in this later, far more ironic work, Oedipus misinterprets the source of this metatheatrical challenge. Oedipus wrongly perceives his rival dramatist to be Creon, who, in Oedipus' view, is scripting and directing subordinates like Teiresias to set the groundwork for a political coup.

After the scene with Teiresias, Oedipus suspects an insurrection is underway. It is particularly ironic that Oedipus, now in Creon's position in *Antigone*, suspects Creon as the instigator of the alleged plot. Creon, Oedipus charges, is a man with a "daring face" (τόλμης πρόσωπον, 533). The theatrical nature of Creon's alleged duplicity (his deceptive behavior and stage management of others) is registered by Oedipus' use of πρόσωπον, a word that means both "face" and the actor's "mask." Oedipus charges Creon with behaving like a malevolent dramatist. Unlike Antigone's direct challenge to Creon in her play, utilizing defiant words and actions to subvert her uncle's authority, Oedipus perceives a subtler metatheatrical game. Creon, according to Oedipus, is disguising his handiwork and scripting others to do his dirty work for him. Oedipus asks Creon, "Did you think that I would not recognize the act [τοὔργον] as yours?" (538). Oedipus is accusing his brother-in-law of dramatist-like behavior, sending (ἐσπέμψας, 705) the "actor" Teiresias into the theater after "persuading him by speeches to tell lying words" (πεισθεὶς . . . τούς λόγους ψευδεῖς λέγοι, 526). Creon has allegedly used Teiresias as a mouthpiece for slanderous accusations, which would have tainted his own lips had he spoken them directly (706). Teiresias has served Creon much as an actor serves his playwright. Even the reverend prophet's elderly behavior is challenged as a sham or "seeming" by Oedipus. The prophet will not be physically harmed, Oedipus reasons, because he "seems old" ('δόκεις γέρων, 402). Oedipus' position *is* under threat, but the threat does not come from any of his fellow characters within the play, as Creon had experienced in *Antigone*. In *Oedipus Tyrannus*, the threat to the *tyrannos*'s autonomy as playwright/director-within-the-play comes from outside the mimetic world of the tragedy. The challenge resides with the gods and with Sophocles.

Like Shakespeare's Hamlet, Sophocles' Oedipus is a character who has rejected the role thrust upon him by divine (or authorial) prophecy. Oedipus has endeavored to ward off the disasters predicted for him and to script his life in his own way. Oedipus is a character who discovers himself trapped within a play he does not want to write or act in. For all his eagerness to solve Laius' murder and discover his own identity, Oedipus has been "found out, unwillingly, by time, the all seeing" (ἐφηῦρέ σ' ἄκονθ' ὁ πάνθ' ὁρῶν χρόνος, 1214). The true metatheatrical rivalry is between Oedipus, the playwright-within-the-play, who fulfills his traditional role "unwillingly" (ἄκονθ') as incest and parricide, and Sophocles, who enjoys omniscient power over his creations who are striving within the orchestra circle. Something of this character-author conflict has been observed in the frustrating closure of *Trachiniae*. The idea of a character in conflict with his or her prescribed role has grown in complexity since Hyllus challenged the gods and the playwright for their treatment of their "children" on stage. Sophocles' metadramatic irony has deepened in the time since *Trachiniae* and *Antigone*.

As in *Antigone*, the part of the *tyrannos* serves as the protagonist's only role in the play, accenting Oedipus' position as the unambiguous focal point of the tragedy. A second actor played the Priest, Jocasta, and the Shepherd. The second actor's parts share interesting resonances. It is fitting that the "Jocasta" actor also plays the Shepherd who received the infant Oedipus from her so many years before (1173). The casting presents Oedipus with the missing link with his mysterious past. It is a piece of extraordinary performative irony that the Priest who represents religious orthodoxy within the play literally speaks with the same voice as Jocasta, the religious skeptic. The third actor played Creon and the Corinthian Messenger, a fitting arrangement since both characters bring misleading "good" news to Oedipus.

The role of Teiresias could have been played by either the second or the third actor. Either assignment contains interesting performative resonances. If Teiresias is played by the "Creon" actor, the irony of Oedipus' accusations against Creon would be intensified. Teiresias would literally be speaking from the same "mouth" (705–6) as Creon. This theatrical situation would give Oedipus' mistaken accusations a delightfully paradoxical dimension. The other possibility, that the "Priest/Jocasta/Shepherd" actor plays Teiresias, is more likely. It is equally attractive in terms of ironic implications and appears more aesthetically elegant in terms of theatrical applicability. If the "Priest" actor plays the prophet, the tritagonist avoids having to rapidly change back and forth between Creon and Teiresias within a little over 350 lines (150–512), certainly a possible feat, but an awkward and unnecessary one, considering the availability of the deuteragonist, who has 480 lines between the Priest's exit and Jocasta's emergence from the skene (150–630). This latter schematic allows for a more equal allotment of acting responsibilities between deuteragonist and tritagonist in the first half of the play. In performative terms, it creates the effect of both the Priest and Teiresias, the two symbols of religious orthodoxy, inhabiting the body and voice of the "Jocasta" actor. Jocasta is the character whose disbelief in oracles and in any middlemen between humans and divinity will so scandalize the Chorus.

The Second Messenger also could have been played by either the second or third actor. Assigning the role to the third actor is attractive for reasons of balance, making his responsibilities more equal to the second in amount of lines and stage time. It also allows one actor to handle all of the messenger roles, a configuration encountered in the tritagonist's doubling of both messenger parts in Euripides' *Bacchae*.

Oedipus' character suggests the poet's refining vision of the Creon-Antigone opposition of some dozen years earlier; the play also affords a second glimpse of Creon himself. The Creon of this play is hardly the bully of the *Antigone*, but much of his presence in this later play carries intertextual, metatheatrical associations with the earlier character. Creon's speech about the disadvantages of kingly power (583–602) contains strong irony in light of his royal performance in *Antigone*. Creon's argument with Oedipus recalls the *agon* between Creon and Haemon. Stichomythic exchanges like

> *Oedipus*: I must be ruler.
> *Creon*: Not if you rule badly.
> (*OT* 628–29)

or Creon's remark "I have a share in the city too, it's not yours alone" (630) could easily find a place in the *agon* scenes of *Antigone*. The audience member familiar with *Antigone* would appreciate the ironic role reversal in Creon's position. In Oedipus' tragedy, Creon seems to play Haemon's role by arguing with a tyrannical ruler. For all of Creon's protestations that kingship holds no attractions for him, he assumes kingly responsibility with great alacrity after Oedipus' downfall. Creon's newfound power is manifested by his stage management of his nephew and his children during the exodos. Creon readily tells the blinded Oedipus when and where he may exit the theater space (1429, 1515, 1521). "Do not desire to have power in everything," Creon admonishes, "for power did not accompany you through all your life" (1522–23). When Oedipus blesses Creon for bringing Antigone and Ismene to their father, it is impossible not to register the irony of Oedipus' wish that better fortune may attend Creon than has overseen Oedipus' fate (1478–79). That wish resonates with the catastrophe of the *Antigone* play.

Oedipus Tyrannus borrows from situations and characters in *Antigone* but rephrases them into entirely new configurations. Both tragedies are concerned with the limitations of a ruler's vision. *Oedipus Tyrannus*, as Karl Reinhardt has written, is a play devoted to the "tragedy of human illusion." In this play, "the danger to man lies not in the *hubris* of human self-assertion but in the *hubris* of seeming as opposed to being."[13] Reinhardt's view, with its obvious analog to the conditions of theater itself, an art form created out of appearances and deception, has influenced many subsequent interpreters. Seale, admitting his debt to the German scholar, envisions "the very matter of the tragedy" resting upon the protagonist's perception of his world in the play.[14]

Creon's "ship of state" speech in *Antigone* (162–90) gains ironic power only when viewed against his later actions. The *Oedipus Tyrannus* begins with the tacit assumption that the theater audience is thoroughly aware of the title character's genuine identity as incestuous parricide. The rich, obsessive irony of Oedipus' words is present from the play's opening speech (1–13). The play strips away the layers of illusion that surround the protagonist until he perceives his true identity, the identity the theater audience was aware of from the beginning.

Ajax and *Trachiniae* have already afforded examples of one of Sophocles' favorite metatheatrical devices, the phenomenon of the audience-within-the-play. With this strategy, the playwright focuses the spectators' attention on a character whom they watch in order to gauge their own responses to what they see and hear. *Oedipus Tyrannus* is structured so as to focus attention on how Oedipus receives and processes information. The audience is fascinated to watch how he reacts to the events occurring around him. Near the beginning of the play, Oedipus remarks that no one suffers as much as he does for his dying city (59–61). He insists that the investigation be conducted before the suppliants (and theater audience) who have assembled before the palace door. "Speak before all" (ἐς πάντας αὔδα, 93), Oedipus urges, engaging both the characters surrounding him before the skene and the theater audience.[15] During much of the play's action, Oedipus self-consciously plays the part of the ideal monarch—a role he mistakenly believes he has won by merit rather than merely inherited. The suppliants, and, by extension, the theater audience, have come expecting him to act like a king, and his words and actions do not disappoint. He is an ideal audience and ideal actor, suffering with those he sees suffer and then offering himself as the agent and, ultimately, the scapegoat of his community. Throughout the play, the protagonist represents the ultimate actor, "the greatest in all men's eyes" (40).

When the final revelation occurs during the interrogation of the Shepherd, Oedipus turns from one who sees or reveals things for others (φανῶ, 132) into the thing seen, the person revealed (πέφασμαι, 1184). This new, terrible vision of himself as the most horrible of spectatorial objects paradoxically moves him out of the audience's sight with his exit into the skene. Once inside the palace/skene building, Oedipus destroys his eyes, the organs of Apollo and the principal means of perceiving theater, at least in the Greek imagination. The blinded Oedipus will later remark that he would have destroyed his hearing had that been possible (1386–89). Oedipus rejects the senses of sight and hearing, the two "theatrical" senses, ironically transforming himself into the most shocking of theatrical revelations. His self-conscious display of his own degradation at the end of the play is one of the most harrowing sequences in Western drama. Reinhardt observes: "Now there are no biers, no eccyclema, no apparatus. . . . instead of being brought in, put on show so that men can point him out, the victim is eager to put himself on show, to display the monstrous discovery that he has made in his search for himself: the blinded man he has been all along."[16] Oedipus is perhaps the greatest of Sophocles' internal director/playwrights. His final transformation into a blind pariah is the supreme example of the duality of human life, its dangerous instability, its ability to turn one being into its apparent opposite. Oedipus becomes the image of Teiresias, his former nemesis. The blinded king, once rooted in power and wealth, is reduced to "a voice" that "floats on the wings of the air" (φθογγὰ διαπωτᾶται φοράδαν, 1310). Just as disaster has brought Oedipus closer to his earlier opponent, Teiresias, the haunting image of the blinded Oedipus' "floating voice" suggests he has attained a mysterious parity with an even earlier enemy, the demonic, flying "rhapsode" (391) called the Sphinx.[17]

When Oedipus runs from the stage to confront Jocasta and blind himself, the Chorus sings its third stasimon, making Oedipus the "paradigm" of the tragedy of human "seeming."

ἰὼ γενεαὶ βροτῶν,
ὡς ὑμᾶς ἴσα καὶ τὸ μη-
δὲν ζώσας ἐναριθμῶ.
τίς γάρ, τίς ἀνὴρ πλέον
τᾶς εὐδαιμονίας φέρει
ἢ τοσοῦτον ὅσον δοκεῖν
καὶ δόξαντ᾽ ἀποκλῖναι;
τὸν σόν τοι παράδειγμ᾽ ἔχων,
τὸν σὸν δαίμονα, τὸν σόν, ὦ
τλᾶμον Οἰδιπόδα, βροτῶν
οὐδὲν μακαρίζω·

(1186–96)

O race of mortals,
I count your life as no more than nothing.
For what man, what man has
more of happiness
than so much as a seeming
and after the seeming a falling away?

As an example, you,
your fate, you, o wretched Oedipus,
I deem no mortal happy.

Illusion and seeming (δοκεῖν, δόξαντα) are the bane and basis of existence. The horror of life may be seen in its parity with the theatrical experience, where seeming and representation are the foundation of perception. In *Oedipus Tyrannus*, theatrical seeming is employed to reveal *all* seeming. By analogy, the theatrical deception is yet another form of the "seeming" of human life. Human happiness, the very will to live, is portrayed as an illusion, as ephemeral as Oedipus' triumph and the present enactment that has recounted his story. The play exists as a means of revealing Oedipus. It is an illusion dependent on the destruction of Oedipus' illusion. Even after the apparent destruction of all "seeming" with Oedipus' self-discovery and blinding, the seeming-versus-reality dichotomy remains. The blinded Oedipus begs Creon to let him touch his children again. "If I lay my hands on them I can seem [δοκοῖμ'] to have them with me, as when I could see" (1469–70).

Seeming and duality are at the core of the *Oedipus* world. When announcing to the citizens his investigation into Laius' death, Oedipus promises: "I shall speak these words as both a stranger to the story, / and as a stranger to the deed" (ἀγὼ ξένος μὲν τοῦ λόγου τοῦδ' ἐξερῶ, / ξένος δὲ τοῦ πραχθέντος, 219–20). Oedipus' relationship with the Laius story is as paradoxical as the relationship between the actor playing Oedipus and his role. The actor is a "stranger" to the words and deeds Sophocles has directed him to perform. Nevertheless, the actor says and does these things as if they were his own speeches and actions. Oedipus is actorlike in his taking upon himself words and deeds on the behalf of other characters. Of course, the audience enjoys an additional ironic perception that Oedipus is not a ξένος to either the Laius story or the Thebans surrounding him. Oedipus' ambiguous relationship to his theatrical environment is analogous to the theater audience's relationship to tragedy. In order to enjoy tragedy as an aesthetic experience, members of the audience must perceive the subject matter of tragedy as something strange (ξένος) or "other" than their personal lives or experiences. At the same time, tragedy must partake of the deepest fears and anxieties of its audience if it is to excite the pity, fear, and catharsis that Aristotle articulated as the primary results of the tragic experience in the theater. This implicit connection between the deception or ἀπάτη of life and the medium of theater works to remove the distance between the play and its audience. Segal has suggested the ways in which "Oedipus' fate in the orchestra mirrors back to the members of the audience." Their absorption in his tragedy causes them to "temporarily lose [their] identity, [their] secure definition by house, position, friends, and become, like Oedipus, nameless and placeless."[18]

Oedipus is in a dilemma similar to that of Ajax. Both characters perform disastrous acts while under a deluded notion of reality. Both men are destroyed by a hostile cosmos. In *Ajax* the audience actually sees the divine instigator of the hero's downfall in the character of Athena. But in *Oedipus Tyrannus*, the metatheatrical role of the god, a playwright-within-the-play, has been absorbed into the fabric of the tragedy with breathtaking subtlety. In *Oedipus Tyrannus*, Sophocles enjoys a parity with Apollo, the divine artificer of Oedipus' misfortunes. The human playwright's craft portrays the operation of the god's design. Both divine and human artificers are paradoxically omnipresent yet unseen. Apollo's inscrutability and distance from the human characters whose actions he has manipulated serve as metaphors of the playwright's art. Sophocles also maneuvers his subjects into the patterns he desires while remaining outside of his creation. The relationship of Apollo to the playwright and the art of tragedy is suggested by the Chorus in its second stasimon.

In order to calm her husband's mounting anxiety, Jocasta has cast doubt upon the truthfulness of oracles. After the exit of Jocasta and Oedipus, the Chorus sings an ode denouncing impiety. The second strophe of the stasimon must be quoted in full.

εἰ δέ τις ὑπέροπτα χερσὶν
    ἢ λόγῳ πορεύεται,
Δίκας ἀφόβητος, οὐδὲ
    δαιμόνων ἕδη σέβων,
κακά νιν ἕλοιτο μοῖρα,
    δυσπότμου χάριν χλιδᾶς,
εἰ μὴ τὸ κέρδος κερδανεῖ δικαίως
καὶ τῶν ἀσέπτων ἔρξεται,
ἢ τῶν ἀθίκτων θίξεται ματάζων.
τίς ἔτι ποτ' ἐν τοῖσδ' ἀνὴρ θυμοῦ βέλη
τεύξεται ψυχᾶς ἀμύνων;

εἰ γὰρ αἱ τοιαίδε πράξεις τίμιαι,
τί δεῖ με χορεύειν;

(883–96)

If someone walks with haughtiness
in deed or word,
unafraid of Justice and without
reverence for shrines of Gods,
may an evil fate seize on him,
for his unlucky pride,
if he will not gain advantage justly
and keep away from unholy things
or rashly touches what should not be touched.
Amid such things, what man shall contrive
to defend his life against angry arrows?
For if such deeds are honored
why should I be in a chorus?

In the antistrophe following, the Chorus remarks that it will no longer regard the important shrines of Delphi, Abae, or Olympia "unless these [oracles] do fit together / so as to be pointed at by all mortals" (902–3). Unless the oracles of Apollo are made manifest, an open, public spectacle which may be "pointed to" (χειρόδεικτα, 902), the Chorus will lose its sense of religion and, as it intimates in the preceding strophe, will literally stop "being a chorus" (χορεύειν, 896). If god (or the tragic dramatist) does not bring his prophecies to fruition, the Chorus will give up its principal function in the tragedy being enacted. The words are a challenge both to Apollo and to the playwright.

These lines from the second stasimon are among the most controversial in Sophocles, due to their metatheatrical implications. It has been argued that χορεύειν has no dramatic self-referentiality.[19] The overwhelming body of secondary literature, however, acknowledges the self-reflexivity of the ode.[20] Bernard Knox's summary of the parabasis-like effect of 896 eloquently states the implications of Sophocles' *trompe l'oeil*.

"Why should I dance?" With this phrase the situation is brought out of the past and the myth into the present moment in the Theatre of Dionysus. For these words of the Chorus were accompanied not only by music but, as the Chorus's very name reminds us, by dancing: this is the choral dance and song from which tragedy developed, and which is still what it was in the beginning, an act of religious worship. If the oracles and the truth do not coincide the very performance of the tragedy has no meaning, for tragedy is itself a form of worship of the gods. The phrase "Why should I dance?" is a *tour de force* which makes the validity of the performance itself depend on the *dénouement* of the play.[21]

The placement of the stasimon after Jocasta's rejection of oracular power is telling. Her denunciation of the oracles and the religious beliefs surrounding them is tantamount to her rejecting her place as a character within the play. She and Oedipus have no more freedom from the prophecy than they have from the dramatic script of which they are a part. Neither script nor prophecy may exist without the validation of a higher, divine order. The members of the Chorus intimate that their lives within Thebes and as characters within the present play are in jeopardy. The passage jolts the audience's perceptions by simultaneously calling attention to the Chorus and the play's double nature as story and performance of that story. The Sophoclean stasimon may be compared with an equally self-referential passage in twentieth-century drama. In Beckett's *Endgame*, Clove threatens that play's continuance in a manner similar to the defiant actions of Oedipus and Jocasta.

> Clove: I'll leave you.
> Hamm: No!
> Clove: What is there to keep me here?
> Hamm: The dialogue.[22]

The Chorus will again draw attention to its performative function when singing the ode to Mount Cithaeron (1086–1109). As so often in Sophoclean tragedy, the poet heightens the impact of the final calamity by having the Chorus prematurely celebrate a happy resolution. The direct reference to dancing (χορεύεσθαι) at 1092 bestows a self-conscious artificiality upon the Chorus's merrymaking. The Chorus is following its dramatic function—it is "dancing"—but the audience may realize that it is celebrating only because it remains incapable of penetrating the illusion of Oedipus' identity. It is intriguing that the Chorus theorizes that the foundling Oedipus may be the child of Dionysus himself (1105). Earlier, during the parodos, the Chorus had called upon Dionysus to redeem his suffering homeland (211). The wine god's presence is discernible throughout this play. Apollo's brother, a god of role playing and reversal, the patron of the tragic competition itself, Dionysus may be a spiritual father of Oedipus, if not a biological one. A god who often wreaks havoc on the family, who revels in duality and contradiction, is the appropriate force compelling Oedipus to discover his true identity.

Somewhat earlier in the play, Oedipus discussed the claims made by the lone survivor of the attack on Laius at the place where three roads met. The man claimed a troop of robbers committed the crime. Oedipus takes comfort in the alleged plurality of the attackers. "I was not the killer," he reasons, "for one [man] is not the same as many" (845). Oedipus finally learns how "one may equal many" (845). In the Theater of Dionysus, one man performing actions (τοὔργον, 847) may stand in for any or all of his fellow men. It is this "standing in" that allows the performer and the spectators the scope and resonance that make *Oedipus Tyrannus* one of the masterpieces of metatheater.[23]

Oedipus at Colonus

In *Oedipus at Colonus*, the relationship of the play's world to the world of the audience has changed drastically. The title of the play suggests something of what is unique and different in this final work, written at the close of the fifth century. Athens and its immediate environs figure comparatively rarely as a setting for fifth-century tragedy.[24] The Athenian tragedians preferred setting their plays in areas other than Athens to create a sense of distance and perspective for their audiences. Tragedy, with its malfunctioning families and governments, often carries by its very nature an implicit critique of the society in which its action is set. While much of Greek tragedy may be said to offer a critique of fifth-century Athens, it does so obliquely through the comfortably distant mirrors of places like Thebes, Trachis, and Troy. The festival presentation of tragedy, an important propaganda tool of the Athenian Empire, could ill afford to openly criticize its host city by using it as an example of a "tragic" society. It is also probable that Athenian audiences themselves enjoyed the aesthetic distance that a foreign setting brought with it.[25] From this perspective we may begin to appreciate Sophocles' boldness in giving his final play an Athenian setting.

Throughout his career, Sophocles devoted careful attention to the physical environments in which he set his plays. We may remember Ajax' solitary tent on the shore. The Paedagogus' opening lines in *Electra* create a brief but significant entry point to that play. *Philoctetes*, written only a few years before *Oedipus at Colonus*, gives significant attention to the depiction of Lemnos, whose desolate landscape carries significance both for the play's action and the nature of the title character. Colonus, however, is given the most detailed and thorough place description in Greek tragedy.

Knowledge of fifth-century skenographia is virtually nonexistent. It will never be known how detailed or schematic the actual stage setting or decoration would have been for this or any fifth-century play in the Theater of Dionysus. Whatever the means of scenic representation, Sophocles is taking a great risk in compelling his audience to compare the stage space representing Colonus with the real model. As one scholar notes, the fifth-century actors and audience "shared the very daylight of the grove one mile away."[26] Antigone, in describing the place to which she and her father have arrived, remarks that "the towers that / shield the city are, to judge by the eye, far off" (14–16). "The towers" are none other than the temples of the Athenian Acropolis, which stood behind the audience in the Theater of Dionysus.[27] Sophocles' choice of setting, whatever its physical representation on the ancient stage, displays his confidence in the power of his theater to withstand the comparison of his created scene with the genuine article.

The deme of Colonus and the city of Athens almost constitute dramatic characters within the play. Sophocles' choice of setting was probably influenced by events during the closing years of the Peloponnesian War. A troop of Boeotians was repulsed by Athenian soldiers near the grove of Colonus Hippios in 407 B.C., an action that may well have reminded Athenians of Oedipus' legendary powers within the grove.[28] Colonus, like the Theater of Dionysus, is a sacred place where humanity may intermingle with the gods. Both the theater and the grove are located near the very heart of Athenian society. Colonus was Sophocles' own deme. His use of Colonus represents an example of an ancient dramatist "staging" his home and polis, endeavoring to preserve it, through dramatic action and poetry, from the ravages of war and time.

Critics have remarked on the idealizing nature of Sophocles' praise of his homeland, particularly the sublime encomium for Colonus and

Athens contained within the first stasimon (668–719). It has been noted that many of the physical and moral features held up for admiration by the poet were already nearing destruction when Sophocles was writing the play. Kirkwood has compared the play's use of Athens with other near-contemporary texts such as Thucydides' version of Pericles' funeral oration and later fourth-century authors who would nostalgically describe the city as a utopia. Sophocles' emphasis on the "justness" or "fairness" (ἔπιεκες or ἐπεικῆς) of Athens represents the playwright's attempt to restore this lost trait to his crippled society.[29] Athens is the one place capable of receiving a hero such as Oedipus. While Thebes desires possession of his body as a powerful talisman, Athens can accept all of the hero with his strange mixture of blessings and curses. Athens is civilized enough to understand and accept the contradictions inherent in Oedipus, as the city has symbolically accepted so many other tragic heroes into its community during performances at the Theater of Dionysus.

Just as Sophocles shows great daring in his choice of scene, his dramaturgical structure puts unprecedented demands on his three actors. Virtually all fifth-century tragedy may be comfortably performed by three actors without the necessity of a single role being shared between actors. Before *Oedipus at Colonus*, only a late work by Euripides, the *Phoenician Women* (411–409 B.C.), required a role to be shared by two actors and this text may well have been substantially altered for performances during the fourth century. In *Oedipus at Colonus*, Sophocles requires his deuteragonist and tritagonist to share the role of Antigone, while all three actors share the part of Theseus. This doubling feat sustains Sophocles' extraordinarily fluid dramatic structure and stands as a testimony to the versatility of late fifth-century actors, as well as to the innovative courage of the octogenarian playwright. Sophocles obviously wanted his last play to stand as a repository of spiritual and poetic vision as well as a testament to his unsurpassed technical skill. As so often occurs, Sophocles' doubling of roles will carry thematic and structural resonances for the tragedy's performative meaning. The protagonist played Oedipus throughout the play, returning, appropriately enough, to narrate his previous character's death in the guise of the Messenger. As if this were not enough, Sophocles required the protagonist to be recycled as Theseus for that character's final entrance from line 1750 to the end of the play. The deuteragonist played Antigone from lines 1–847, Theseus in that character's second and third scenes (886–1210 and 1500–1555), Polyneices, and Antigone again, from line 1670 to the end. The tritagonist played the Citizen, Ismene, Theseus at that character's first appearance (551–667), Creon, Antigone (1099–1555), and resumed the role of Ismene from line 1670 to the end.

If this scheme of doubling seems wildly complex and challenging, even for a cast of accomplished actors, it is. Some scholars, including Jebb, have postulated that Sophocles must have composed the play with a fourth actor in mind, but there is no evidence of a fourth actor being used for fifth-century tragedy. No other tragedy requires it; and the availability of a fourth actor would obviate the play's carefully orchestrated patterns of entrances and exits. Furthermore, this remarkable pattern of role allocation strongly suggests performative meaning. All three actors are allowed to play members of the Theban royal family. The role of Antigone, already one of the most popular heroines of classical tragedy, journeys from the deuteragonist to the tritagonist and back again to the original actor. The role of Theseus undergoes a far more remarkable journey with the role being played by all three actors in succession from the third, to the second, to the first agonist. Brian Johnston has written that "Theseus' role gradually increases in mimetic authority" during the course of the tragedy until, with Oedipus' transfiguration, Theseus stands as the last living link with Oedipus' heroism and as the custodian of Oedipus' legacy for Athens. At this point, Oedipus' voice literally speaks through the mask of Theseus. Theseus, by the end of the play, "has earned the right, as it were, to be 'performed' by the Oedipus actor. He has become the closest to Oedipus, underscored by the fact that he alone, and not Antigone nor Ismene, is privileged to witness Oedipus' wonderful death. . . . [The protagonist's assumption of Theseus at 1750] is the *theatrical* manifestation of Oedipus' gift to Athens."[30]

Sophocles' virtuosity as a playwright and the virtuosity he demands of his cast illustrate the void separating modern, naturalistic acting and production styles from those of classical Athens. They also reveal a playwright capable of great technical daring, even at the end of an unusually long and successful career. Only Verdi's stylistic self-recreation in his late operas, *Otello* and *Falstaff*, seems a comparable example of octogenarian creativity. The doubling and tripling of roles also points to the self-consciousness of Sophocles' dramaturgy, the way dramatic convention becomes part of a play's very meaning.

Unlike the Oedipus character in the *Tyrannus* play, the aged Oedipus has had from the opening moments of *Oedipus at Colonus* a clear perception of his true status and relation to the stage world that surrounds him. The "Oedipus" actor has stood his ground while the deuteragonist and tritagonist have each played deceptive characters like Creon and Polyneices, figures whose crafty and duplicitous speeches serve to disguise their ulterior motives. In the play's concluding moments, Theseus replaces Oedipus in the body and voice of the protagonist, whose voice and stage presence have, through the roles of Oedipus and the Messenger, represented the spiritual "reality" and integrity that lie at the core of Sophocles' play.

Were intertextual reference to other dramatic texts the sole criterion of metatheatricality, *Oedipus at Colonus* would rank among the most metatheatrical of ancient tragedies.[31] While tragedy frequently carries allusions to earlier texts, tragic or epic, *Oedipus at Colonus* is particularly "bookish."[32] Sophocles adopted the pattern of earlier tragedies based on the theme of the suppliant. These "suppliant" plays, Aeschylus' *Suppliants*, Euripides' *Children of Heracles* and *Suppliants*, and many lost examples, served as the models for *Oedipus at Colonus*. Suppliant dramas are made up of a fairly traditional set of encounters: the suppliant meets and pleads with the host; an enemy seriously challenges the suppliant's security; the host encounters and defeats the enemy in a military action, winning security for the suppliant. In addition to the suppliant play schematic, *Oedipus at Colonus* presupposes an audience familiar with the two earlier Sophoclean Theban tragedies as well as Aeschylus' *Seven Against Thebes* and Euripides' *Phoenician Women*. The wrangling between Eteocles and Polyneices, described by Ismene (*OC* 336, 365–81), and the chillingly prophetic scene where Polyneices begs Antigone to give him burial, should he die in his campaign (*OC* 1399–1446), all suggest these earlier plays, which were already very famous when *Oedipus at Colonus* was written. Echoes of the *Antigone* prologue are evident in the brief exchange between the two grieving sisters, when Ismene sensibly tries to restrain the impulsive Antigone from visiting her father's mysterious burial place (*OC* 1724–36). Creon's seizure of Oedipus' daughters and their eventual restoration by Theseus rephrases and resolves the wrenching exodos of *Oedipus Tyrannus*, where the blind Oedipus is presented with his children and then is forcibly parted from them by Creon. Sophocles is compelling us to look not only beyond the closure of the present play into an uncertain future: he is compelling us to look into *other plays* as well; plays by himself and by other poets.

Sophocles devotes much important stage time in *Oedipus at Colonus* to debating issues raised by *Oedipus Tyrannus*, particularly Oedipus' speeches of self-defense before the ghoulishly inquisitive Chorus of Colonian elders and, later, his enemy Creon (510–48, 960–1000). The present play functions as a belated sequel to the earlier tragedy. Like the *Eumenides*, which closed Aeschylus' *Oresteia* by bringing the action to an Athenian setting, *Oedipus at Colonus* uses its Athenian locale as a site of final consummation both for Oedipus and, by extension, for Attic tragedy itself. By absorbing the contradictions inherent in Oedipus (and in tragedy), Athens reaps the benefit of a mysterious protective power.

In *Oedipus at Colonus*, Sophocles reverses the structure of dramatic irony that he used to such great effect in *Antigone* and *Oedipus Tyrannus*. In those earlier plays the audience beheld the struggle of two rulers, Creon and Oedipus, who each attempt to maintain a vision of the world based either on misapprehension or illusion. By the end of each tragedy, the rulers meet their downfall after finally seeing the truth of their situation, a truth that the audience has either known all along or has realized long before the character. In *Oedipus at Colonus* the protagonist moves from the lowest fortune to a state of deification. This last Sophoclean tragedy serves as a kind of "antitragedy," a work that self-consciously reverses the tragic pattern of earlier plays. The *Colonus* play begins with an Oedipus who seems in some ways similar to the figure who exits the stage at the end of the *Tyrannus*. Like the earlier rendering of the character, the aged Oedipus has a habit of blundering upon places that are not to be touched by ordinary humans. Soon after Oedipus' first entrance in the orchestra, the Chorus describes him as "Terrible to see, terrible to hear" (δεινὸς μὲν ὁρᾶν, δεινὸς δὲ κλύειν, 141). These theatrically charged words are reminiscent of the description given the newly blinded Oedipus by the Second Messenger in *Oedipus Tyrannus*: "what deeds you shall hear of, what deeds you shall see, and what / grief you shall endure" (οἷ᾽ ἔργ᾽ ἀκούσεσθ᾽, οἷα δ᾽ εἰσόψεσθ᾽, ὅσον δ᾽ / ἀρεῖσθε πένθος, OT 1224–25). At the start of Sophocles' last play, Oedipus remains the paradigm of theatrical suffering and misfortune. But this similarity to his earlier self is superficial. The Chorus is soon won over by the old man's suffering. Antigone pleads for the Chorus and, by extension, the theater audience, to view the aged wanderer with "pity" (οἰκτίραθ᾽, 242). This "pity" will move the Colonians to sympathize with Oedipus to the point that they accept him into their community. The ambivalent ξένος of the earlier play finds a home. Ismene will wonder "when will the gods take pity [κατοικτιοῦσιν] on [Oedipus'] sorrows?" (383–84). By the end of the play, even these distant, mysterious beings, Oedipus' cosmic audience, "take pity" and accept the old man into their company.

In Sophocles' last tragedy, the spectators and the protagonist share a "conspiracy of knowledge" from the opening moments of the play.[33] The audience is assured of the "reality" of Oedipus' ultimate destiny, and the assurance is maintained throughout all of the challenges that face the protagonist before his final apotheosis. As Peter Burian has shown, the play follows a pattern, discernible in other suppliant dramas, that helps to assure the audience of Oedipus' ultimate victory.[34]

The protagonist now represents a kind of "truth," while all the obstacles he faces (the initial rejection by the Chorus, the evil machinations of Creon, the pleas of Polyneices) almost seem illusory, since they "are waged against [the certain] knowledge" of Oedipus' redemption.[35] Oedipus' security seems so assured that the numerous threats posed to his position in the grove have about them the air of dramaturgical contrivance. Reinhardt notes the "baroque" tendencies of this final Sophoclean play with its fascination for minute detail representing a "struggle to create drama within drama itself." Reinhardt describes Ismene's arrival as "a whole recognition scene in miniature," as Antigone painstakingly describes her sister's distant approach from the parodos (310–21).[36]

Oedipus' certainty concerning his destiny and rightful place within the Eumenides' grove protects his character from the ironic separation of word and action that occurs so frequently in Sophoclean drama. Oedipus and Athens itself, as personified by Theseus and the Chorus, are incapable of subterfuge and are able to see through the hypocritical "performances" of outsiders such as Creon and the Theban government he represents. Oedipus, the last of the tragic protagonists of fifth-century drama, is accepted into a society where word and action go hand in hand. This helps to make Oedipus at Colonus into a "tragedy to end tragedy," a deliberate resolution of the nagging ambiguities at the core of so much fifth-century drama. Both Creon and the polis he represents reveal a false, "theatricalized" nature, in which appearance is more important than essence and where human beings are exploited as empty material objects. This is exemplified by Creon's scheme to force Oedipus back to Thebes, where he will live a prisoner outside the city perimeter. This cruel plot will enable Thebes to reap the benefit of Oedipus' physical presence while protecting the city from actual contact with the pariah. It may now be seen why Sophocles gives Ismene the grand entrance, which Reinhardt described as a "miniature recognition scene." Ismene reports the oracle, enabling Oedipus to unmask Creon even before he enters the stage and begins his elaborate "performance" of sympathy with his wretched cousin. This oracle will prove the final salvation for both Oedipus and Athens.

Eteocles and Polyneices share a good part of Creon's "theatrical" perfidy. For the sons of Oedipus, Reinhardt observes, "action has parted company with meaning," as has "the appearance of justice with its reality."[37] Athens represents a place where word and action exist in harmony, a place that can accept the paradox of Oedipus and, by extension, the paradox of tragic drama itself, which uses masks to "unmask truth." Segal has argued that the character of Oedipus in this last play may be equated symbolically with the entire genre of tragedy. "By returning to this figure whose life contains the most extreme of tragic reversals, Sophocles seems to be consciously reflecting upon and transcending the tragic pattern which he did so much to develop."[38]

Just as Oedipus may be equated with the performative genre in which he appears, so too may the aged playwright be found reflected in his title character. In no other Greek tragedy is it so natural to speak of a personal identification between a character and a playwright. Like Oedipus and the Chorus, Sophocles was an old man by the time he wrote his last play. That Sophocles was held as a symbol of veneration during the latter stages of his life may be inferred by the fact that he was given the cult name of *Dexion* ("Receiver," or "Hospitable One") after his death and was worshiped as a beneficent deity (*Vita* 17). This curious historical fact unavoidably reminds the reader of the more spectacular deification that Oedipus undergoes in Sophocles' final play.

Several Greek and Roman sources preserve an anecdote that the octogenarian Sophocles was brought before a lawcourt by his middle-aged sons, who hoped to have the old man declared senile so that they might take control of his property. By way of self-defense, Sophocles was said to have read the jury the first stasimon of the play he was currently writing, *Oedipus at Colonus* (668–719), comprising the ode to

Colonus and Athens. Sophocles won his case and "was escorted from the court as if from the theater [ὥσπερ᾽ ἐκ θεάτρου], with the applause and shouts of those present."[39] While such a story cannot be verified, its very existence suggests something of the remarkable personal identification perceived in the ancient world between *Oedipus at Colonus* and its creator. Whatever the reality of Sophocles' domestic situation in his last years, Oedipus' expression of love for Athens and his terrifying revilement of his son have encouraged ancient as well as modern readers to read an autobiographical element into the character. While this is a dubious practice at best, it would be impossible as well as absurd to attempt it with any other character from Greek tragedy.

Sophocles did not live to see the final capitulation of Athens to Sparta. His final play allows the playwright, through the voice of his protagonist, to utter a lasting benediction for his homeland. A conspiracy of knowledge has been forged between Oedipus and the spectators from the very first moments of the drama. The audience has been allowed to share with the aging hero a sure knowledge of his destiny. Now with his daughters and Theseus at his side, Oedipus hears the sound of thunder that presages his passing from this world.

> I will teach you, Aegeus' son, something which shall
> be a treasure for your city that age cannot hurt.
>
> (1518–19)

Oedipus commands Theseus not to describe his final moments to anyone, neither "to these citizens" (ἀστῶν τῶνδ᾽, 1528), nor "to my own children, though they are dear all the same" (1529). By "citizens" Oedipus is ostensibly referring to the Chorus, but his words must surely carry to the theater full of Athenian citizens who, until this moment, have enjoyed their position as Oedipus' passive confidant. Oedipus is now passing into a stage of his journey that may be neither seen nor spoken about. It is impossible not to hear in Oedipus' final lines, before his onstage audience, the aged poet's farewell to his theater audience and to his city.[40]

> Come, dearest of friends,
> may you yourself and this land and your helpers
> be blessed, and in that prosperous state remember
> me, one of the dead, and be fortunate forever.
>
> (1552–55)

Oedipus at Colonus was first performed in 401 B.C., some four years after the death of Sophocles (406/5) and three years after the capitulation of Athens (404). Contemporary audiences must have been keenly aware of the play's unique status as the author's posthumous farewell to his community. The play forms a deliberate closure to Sophocles' career as a tragedian. In telling the story of Oedipus' final moments, Sophocles has found a means of absorbing his own persona into the artifice of the play. In effect, he "stages" himself before the citizens in the Theater of Dionysus, fashioning a dramatic character that may stand in for himself as artistic creator and defender of Athenian society. By immortalizing himself in the stage figure of Oedipus, Sophocles also seeks to give a mythic, theatrical permanence to his city's greatness, just as that greatness may well have seemed about to slip into the realm of history and myth. Sophocles understood the paradox of theatrical illusion as well as he did the paradox of tragic heroism. When Oedipus, the aged pariah, learns that his wretched body contains a beneficent power for whatever land may claim him, he asks incredulously, "When I am nothing, *then* am I a man?" (393). By transferring the image of a noble, stainless Athens into the seemingly fragile medium of a dramatic text, Sophocles bestows the gift of eternity upon his polis and himself as an artistic creator. Sophocles has learned the lessons of over sixty years in the service of Dionysus, that stage illusion may mirror spiritual truth. He knows that the craftsmen of Dionysus practice an art as magical as the deathless, self-renewing Athenian olive trees.

In the third book of the *Rhetoric*, Aristotle gives advice for oratorical disputation. "Ambiguous questions . . . that appear likely to make us contradict ourselves should be solved at once in the answer, before the adversary has time to ask the next question or draw to a conclusion." Aristotle affords an intriguing real-life example. "For instance, Sophocles, being asked by Pisander whether he, like the rest of the Committee of Ten, had approved the setting up of the Four Hundred, he admitted it. '*What then?*' asked Pisander, '*did not this appear to you to be a wicked thing?*' [τί δέ; οὐ πονηρά σοι ταῦτα ἐδόκει εἶναι;]. Sophocles admitted it. '*So then you did what was wicked?*' [οὐκοῦν σὺ ταῦτα ἔπραξας τὰ πονηρά;]. '*Yes,*' he said, '*for there was nothing better to be done*' [ναί," ἔφη· "οὐ γὰρ ἦν ἄλλα βελτίω]."[1] This Aristotelian passage affords a rare glimpse of the playwright as an old man, still actively engaged in Athenian politics.

Following the debacle of the Sicilian expedition, Sophocles was one of the ten *probouloi* selected to steer Athens through the resulting crisis. In 411 B.C., these *probouloi* voted for the short-lived oligarchy of the Four Hundred. The Four Hundred were eager to reinstate the brilliant turncoat general, Alcibiades, and take advantage of offered gold from Persia, both projects ultimately resulting in failure. The Four Hundred came to be hated for its brutal suppression of opposition and its "deceptive" (ἀπάτη) behavior.[2] In 410 B.C., full democracy was restored. Sophocles, along with the other *probouloi*, was harshly interrogated for his role in the suspension of democracy. Apparently his defense, that at the time there was no "better" solution than the "wicked" one, was successful. Aristotle affords another glimpse of old Sophocles under fire, perhaps during the same interrogation. "Sophocles said that he trembled, not, as the accuser said, *in order to appear old* [ἵνα δοκῇ γέρων], but from necessity, for it was against his wish that he was eighty years of age."[3] In 409 B.C. Sophocles was just over eighty and won first place with a trio of plays, which included *Philoctetes*. Tragedy, from its very inception, must have reflected the political and intellectual events that surrounded it. In his last plays, however, Sophocles appears to mold his mythic stories to fit the pressures of Athenian life more overtly than in his earlier work. As in Euripides' contemporary *Orestes* and the *Bacchae*, Sophocles uses theatrical character and situation as an allegory for a society in profound crisis.

For several generations, critics have searched for direct parallels between *Philoctetes* and the political events of the late 410s. Much energy has been devoted toward interpreting the principal characters as attempts to place actual contemporary personages on the tragic stage. As with another late play, *Oedipus at Colonus*, *Philoctetes* has been seen as a form of dramatized autobiography. It is reductive to suggest that Philoctetes directly represents the expatriated Alcibiades (or Sophocles as a "deceived" *proboulos*) and that the magic bow symbolizes Persian aid.[4] Nevertheless, the reported exchanges between Sophocles and his accuser Pisander touch on issues central to this play. Situations in which evil or wickedness appears to be the only solution occur frequently in both *Philoctetes* and *Electra*, a play that probably preceded *Philoctetes* by one to ten years. It is interesting that the old poet was accused of pretending to tremble in order to "seem" old, presumably to gain sympathy. Sophocles assured his accuser that the trembling was involuntary, not a result of deception or playacting. Deception or ἀπάτη was freely practiced by the despised oligarchs and demagogues who contributed to the denigration of Athenian political life in the closing years of the Peloponnesian War. In *Philoctetes*, as in *Electra*, Sophocles will place strong emphasis on the theme of deception and role-playing-within-the-role.

These two late plays, *Philoctetes* and *Electra*, show other striking similarities. Both of the respective protagonists exhibit great heroic endurance, and each tragedy ends with an apparent triumph or vindication of its hero. Both plays however raise nagging ethical questions, which on examination render their "happy endings" provisional at best. Perhaps the greatest underlying similarity is their metatheatricality. Both plays confuse "reality" and illusion and create drama within drama.

A comparison between *Philoctetes* and the much earlier *Ajax* is also informative. The characters of both Philoctetes and Ajax embody archaic, intractable heroism, which is as out of place in the post-Homeric worlds of their respective plays as in the streets of mid to late fifth-century Athens. Both plays enframe their heroes, making them the spectatorial objects for the other characters onstage and the audience in the theater. This enframement serves to heighten the two characters' sense of alienation from their environment, while it also creates a commentary on the art of tragic performance. Both heroes suffer from a sickness or νόσος that separates and, on some level, elevates them from the rest of humanity. Ajax' νόσος is his madness, the delusional condition in which he attacks the livestock. Athena, the playwright-within-the-play, imposes this madness on Ajax during the night preceding the play's action, a night that separates Ajax' compromised and debased present from his heroic past. Ajax can only free himself from Athena's dramaturgy by the deception speech and his use of Hector's sword to play a part in his ruse. He successfully rewrites his heroic position by orchestrating his suicide.

As in the opening moments of *Ajax*, Odysseus enters the prologue of *Philoctetes* intent on hunting his human prey. But in this later tragedy, Odysseus never learns any sobering lesson about human frailty that might cause him to change his bestial view of his nemesis. Instead, the Odysseus of *Philoctetes* takes on Athena's role as the internal playwright. Odysseus "hunts" his prey Philoctetes throughout the play and it is Neoptolemus, playwright Odysseus' reluctant actor, who undergoes an apparent transformation. Neoptolemus' role demonstrates the development of Sophocles' use of metatheatrical device since *Ajax*. Neoptolemus will come to sympathize with Philoctetes only after the prince's deceptive role playing has brought him into close contact with the famous archer. Neoptolemus is a surprising combination of internal actor, a character playing a "role" within his role and onstage audience to Philoctetes' suffering.

Philoctetes' νόσος is far more problematic than the sickness suffered by Ajax. The reasons for Philoctetes' wounding by the divine snake is never clearly articulated by Sophocles. Unlike Ajax' madness, Philoctetes' "sickness" is part of what gives his character its heroic status. Edmund Wilson is one of myriad critics who interpret the snake bite as a metaphor of heroism.[5] One of the play's central issues concerns Philoctetes' νόσος and whether it may be cured without compromising the wounded man's heroic standing. Sophocles resorts to the *deus ex machina* to resolve this crisis during the closing moments of the tragedy; and it will be argued here that the playwright's contrived resolution deliberately evades the issues raised by all that has gone before.

The setting of *Philoctetes* is the barren landscape of Lemnos and the primitive cave dwelling of the protagonist. Sophocles' verbal description creates a locale that complements and defines Philoctetes' character before he enters the performance area. Odysseus briefs Neoptolemus regarding Philoctetes' cave.

> Look where there is a rock with two mouths here,
> the kind where, during winter one may twice sit in the sun,
> and, in summer, a breeze blows sleep
> though the double-pierced grotto.
>
> (16–19)

The double entrances of the cave are referred to throughout the play (159, 952), raising interesting though unresolvable questions about how the skene would have been utilized or adapted by Sophocles in the Theater of Dionysus.[6] The emphatic reminders that Philoctetes' cave, the play's principal scenic element, is "double mouthed" seems a fitting metaphor for the ensuing action. Caves have long been regarded in the collective unconscious of myth as places of encounter between mortals and the divine. Antigone's entombment in a cave suggests to the Chorus of that play not only a ghastly martyrdom but a possibility, however terrible, for divinity to intersect with human life (*Antigone* 944–87).[7] The rocky, uncivilized dwelling of Philoctetes serves a similarly paradoxical function. Much of Philoctetes' *arete* or heroic integrity derives from the hardships of his existence. Philoctetes' two-mouthed cave suggests the duality of the harsh Lemnian setting, a place of simultaneous bestialization and ennoblement. The play's concern with the duality of language and role-playing-within-the-role finds a fitting resonance in the "double mouthed" skene as well.[8] Philoctetes' cave takes on a quasi-theatrical duality: it is a double-mouthed "home which is no home" (ἄοικον ἐξοίκησιν, 534).

The similarity between the prologues of *Philoctetes* and *Electra* are numerous and repay examination. As in *Electra*, the two speaking characters presented to the audience are engaged in a kind of master-pupil relationship with strong echoes of contemporary sophistic teaching. Both Odysseus and the Paedagogus are unscrupulous older men attempting to control the behavior and moral outlook of their younger "pupils" and having considerable success. Odysseus urges the young man's compliance in terms that contain theatrical resonances.

> Well I know, son, that it is not in your nature
> to speak nor contrive such evil things;
> but since the prize of victory is sweet to win,
> take courage, and at another time shall we appear honest.
> For now give yourself to me for a brief, shameless
> portion of a day and for all the rest of your life
> be called the most moral of people.
>
> (79–85)

Odysseus, like the Paedagogus, has his eye on the sweet prize of victory (κτῆμα τῆς νίκης, 81). He pleads for the young man to speak and practice evil techniques for the duration of a day, the common length of time portrayed by most fifth-century tragedy. Moral and immoral behaviors, Odysseus asserts, are like masks or theatrical roles, which may be donned for a day and then changed. In order to gain the prize (the reunion of Philoctetes and his bow with the Greek army) Odysseus and the prince must studiously separate language and deed (λόγος, ἔργον). Only *Electra*, among the surviving Sophoclean plays, focuses as strongly on the perils of separating language from its referent, behavior from inner identity. Throughout the prologue, Odysseus coaches his "actor" Neoptolemus for his upcoming "performance," the deception of Philoctetes.

ἀλλ᾽ ἤν τι καινόν, ὧν πρὶν οὐκ ἀκήκοας,
κλύῃς, ὑπουργεῖν, ὡς ὑπηρέτης πάρει.

(52–53)

If you hear something new which you have not heard
before, help it along, since you are here as a helper.

Despite Neoptolemus' collusion with Odysseus' plot, these words warn the young man that whatever he had heard before may not be true. Neoptolemus the coconspirator is put into a position akin to that of the audience in the theater. More than perhaps any other Greek tragedy, *Philoctetes* makes the audience continually unsure of its premise. There are several points in the play where Neoptolemus and even the master plotter Odysseus appear unsure about the goal of their mission on Lemnos, and the audience must interpret the "real" situation from a surprisingly nebulous and unstable expository background. "In this play," Reinhardt writes, "intrigue is not so much an isolated venture as the general state of the world."[9] Like Neoptolemus, the attentive audience member is put on the alert for shifting stories.

Odysseus outlines his plan to deceive Philoctetes. Neoptolemus must "steal the soul of Philoctetes by the words which you speak" (τὴν Φιλοκτήτου σε δεῖ / ψυχὴν ὅπως λόγοισιν ἐκκλέψεις λέγων, 54–55). The young prince is to use playacting upon the suffering cripple to gain a desired emotional response. Like the "Tragedy of Orestes" which invades the middle of *Electra*, an enacted deception, scripted by Odysseus, is inserted within the larger enactment of the play, *Philoctetes*. It is well to remember that the word διδάσκαλος (teacher) carried a theatrical meaning during the fifth century. In addition to its more common nontheatrical sense, it was one of the names for the playwright describing his function as director or "teacher" of his play to the actors and chorus. Tragic poets, as Aristophanes observes, were also considered the "teachers of adults."[10] Plato perceived poetry's and music's insidious power to mold and alter the emotions of an audience. The relation of performer and audience within the context of tragedy, with its potential for intellectual and moral surrender, is markedly similar to the teacher-pupil relationship. Plato bans the poet from the ideal state as a false teacher, a person who pretends to knowledge he does not possess and as a seductive misleader of the soul. Neoptolemus will draw a pointed analogy between the roles of teachers and politicians (and perhaps playwrights) when he asserts that "Armies, like cities are entirely / what their leaders are: disorderly people become evil / through the speeches [λόγοισι] of their teachers [διδασκάλων]" (386–88).[11]

Odysseus serves as a fine example of the playwright-within-the-play. He appears concerned that Neoptolemus might hesitate to perform his "role." The young prince is positioned in the prologue to become a complex surrogate for the audience itself.[12] As the son of Achilles, the "greatest" (4) of the Greek heroes, we look to Neoptolemus to see how he will behave in the theatricalized world in which Odysseus bustles, where "it is the tongue, and not deeds, that wins everything" (99). As an audience surrogate, Neoptolemus falls into the pattern established by Odysseus in *Ajax*, Deianeira, and King Oedipus. Neoptolemus will prove a far more ambiguous figure than those earlier characters, due to his ironic placement within the play, the convolutions of Sophocles' plot, and his character's troubling relationships with the mythic tradition.

Achilles son, best known to modern readers as the "bloody Pyrrhus" of the Player's speech in *Hamlet*, was often seen in the fifth century as perhaps the most impious and brutal Greek to take part in the sack of Troy.[13] Neoptolemus' professed role as reluctant deceiver compels the audience to look for what may be called his "subtext." The appropriation of such a Stanislavskian term applies not to the acting style used for the play but to the unique blurring of truth telling and fabrication found in Neoptolemus' character. This blurring separates the character's deeds and actions to such a degree that the audience feels compelled to delve below the surface of the spoken word and gesture to try to understand what the character "really" feels and intends. It is a fascinatingly futile exploration since the character's nature is clothed in a bewildering mask of subterfuge. There are moments of intense speech and gesture that impress as being more "real" than others, but the soul of Neoptolemus can never really be known. In hardly any other Greek tragedy can such a phenomenon be found.

The prime example of this confusion of "acting" and "reality" is manifested in the story the prince tells Philoctetes concerning the arms of Achilles. In the prologue, Odysseus rehearses the prince for his first encounter with the protagonist.

When he asks you who you are and where you are from,
say, Achilles' son: this must not be hidden.
But say you are sailing home, having left the Achaean host's
fleet, an enemy hating them greatly because
they sent for you with prayers to come from home
having this alone as their hope of capturing Ilium,
yet they did not deem you were worthy to be given
Achilles' arms when you came asking them as your right.
Rather they were handed over to Odysseus—Say what ever
you want about me—the vilest of vile evils;
for with none of this will you hurt me. But if you do not
do this, you will bring grief to all the Argives.

(56–67)

This speech creates many of the disturbing interpretive problems in
this play. Obviously, Neoptolemus is not on a voyage back to Skyros; he
is on a mission to assist both Odysseus and the Atreidae. But the "story"
Odysseus proposes about the arms may be interpreted as a "fact"
within the artifice of Attic tragedy. The audience could be expected to
know that the Achillean arms *did*, at least at first, go to Odysseus and
not to the great man's son.

Between Odysseus' directions to Neoptolemus and the prince's im-
plementation of the deception comes the entrance of their victim,
Philoctetes. Like many tragic protagonists, Philoctetes' entrance is signaled by his offstage cry. But rather than the usual exclamations of ἰώ
μοί μοι or μοι τλάμων, familiar verbal formulas of tragic grief, Philoctetes' cry is an unscripted, inarticulate howl described by the Chorus
(201–10). Philoctetes' physical and emotional pain is too great to put
into words. His entry cry is brilliant theater. Suspense has built for the
cripple with the horrifying wound to appear and interact with the
plotting visitors. Philoctetes, like Ajax, enters his tragedy as a spectatorial object both to the theater audience (as do all characters) and to
all of the characters with whom he shares the stage. His honest nature
is contrasted constantly with his visitors' deception. Philoctetes never
"acts" within his tragedy. The protagonist never says a word he does not
believe to be true, and this sincerity serves to enframe or "stage" his
character within his onstage environment. His inarticulate entry cry is
closer to nature than the speeches of the other characters, which have

been scripted in one way or another by Odysseus—and, ultimately, Sophocles himself. The scream creates a protorealistic effect, which serves to italicize the protagonist, setting him above and apart from the "actors" who surround him.

Upon meeting Philoctetes, Neoptolemus takes Odysseus' earlier hint and uses the story about Achilles' arms to deceive the crippled man and win his trust (343–90). It is the longest narrative in the play, with vivid allusions to the outrage and dishonor the prince allegedly suffered at the hands of the Greek generals. The history of the armor and what might be a prince's presumed reaction to being denied his patrimony creates a troubling background to Neoptolemus' speech of deception. Is Neoptolemus making up a credible though entirely fictitious story, or might there really have been an argument between Neoptolemus and the Atreidae?[14] Even if there were no angry confrontations between Neoptolemus and the generals, the prince's rhetoric is almost strong enough to convince us that there were. Neoptolemus' deceptive narrative of the arms is analogous to the false messenger speech in *Electra*. Both plays devote remarkable lengths of performance time to enacted falsehoods. Even with the clear demarcation between truth and fiction established in the *Electra* prologue, the false messenger's rhetorical power may momentarily sweep the audience along. In *Philoctetes*, such a clear boundary between truth and fiction is never established.

The story of Achilles' arms enjoys an ambiguous position between truth and falsehood, linked as it is with so much detail that is undeniably "true" within the artifice of the play and the mythic world out of which it is built. Sophocles focuses attention on these very anomalies when Philoctetes asks the prince how Ajax could have "endured to see" the arms go to Odysseus (411). Neoptolemus responds that Ajax is dead, otherwise the Atreidae would never have robbed the arms from Achilles' son (412–13). Neoptolemus is, of course, lying about Ajax' potential advocacy of his cause. Sophocles' *Ajax* was devoted to the story of the madness that was engendered, ironically enough, by the Atreidae's denial of the Achillean arms to that great soldier. By verbally appropriating Ajax as a potential advocate in his alleged dispute over the arms, Neoptolemus makes his story seem all the more dubious. The prince's words would unavoidably recall Ajax' downfall, and perhaps Sophocles' earlier tragedy, to the minds of the theater audience.

The spectators are consequently encouraged to contrast Ajax' comparatively "pure" archaic heroism against the machinations of Neoptolemus and Odysseus.

The prince's remarks about Ajax' potential advocacy of Neoptolemus allow the prince to subtly and opportunistically don the role of that fallen hero within his fictitious narrative. The mention of Ajax also directs Neoptolemus' "performance" before Philoctetes into a recitation of the heroes who have fallen at Troy during the decade of Philoctetes' absence (410–52), creating another strange mixture of truth and illusion. The mention of each hero's death brings forth an anguished response from Philoctetes, resulting in an interplay of Neoptolemus' deceitful enactment and Philoctetes' honest emotional response to that performance. The casualty list, with Philoctetes' angry assertion that "nothing evil has yet died" and that the Gods protect the wicked while the good perish (446–52), would have had great impact on the audience of 409 B.C.[15] By this last decade of the Peloponnesian War, it would be difficult to imagine the Athenian citizens listening to such a casualty list without thinking of their own sickening losses. The list of lost heroes before the Trojan gates would easily stand in for fallen soldiers in the "real" world surrounding the theater performance. But even if the audience is moved to empathize with Philoctetes' emotions, an astute auditor would be aware of the mixture of fact and fiction present in this seemingly objective list of the war's casualties and survivors. The epic tradition supports Neoptolemus' remarks concerning Ajax, Nestor, and Antilochus; but when he asserts that the worthless Thersites is still living (445), he seems to be telling another lie.

The epic tradition claims that Achilles slew Thersites, and it may be assumed that the audience would be aware of this. Neoptolemus' apparent lie is a deceptive strategy deployed to increase Philoctetes' vulnerability and bond him more closely to the prince. Philoctetes' aforementioned speech (446–52) indicates that Neoptolemus' mixture of fact and fiction has had its desired effect upon the onstage audience. This is a complex, layered moment of stage time, in which the theater audience may, at once, be moved by Philoctetes' words and encouraged to maintain some measure of ironic distance from Neoptolemus' deceptive "enactment." Neoptolemus' performance has utilized both falsehood and accepted "facts" from myth, as well as suggesting the grim realities that confronted the theater audience of 409 B.C.

What makes this mixture of truth and fiction so difficult to interpret is the extraordinary way Neoptolemus' supposedly fabricated story seems to be accepted as truth by the end of the play. Philoctetes uses the alleged theft of Achilles' arms as a major reason why the young prince should abandon his destiny and return Philoctetes to his home-land (1363–65). While Sophocles was certainly free to modify his mythic material, it should be borne in mind that at least some versions of the present story entail Neoptolemus receiving his father's arms from Odysseus. Neoptolemus does not take the opportunity Philocte-tes affords him to retract his story, and within forty lines he appears to acquiesce to Philoctetes (1402).

It may be argued that, during a single performance at a dramatic competition, such a curious discrepancy would pass by the audience, unnoticed. But Sophocles' use of the Achillean arms at this most unex-pected reversal, where the play seems perilously close to spinning off course, can only be a most carefully considered dramaturgical deci-sion. Perhaps Neoptolemus is at heart a callow liar and disinclined to break the truth to Philoctetes at this embarrassing moment. Sophocles is playing games with the nature of truth and fiction, within the artifice of tragic performance.[16] Lies must be accepted as truth to bring the play to its expected outcome.

The boundaries of truth and illusion in *Philoctetes* are further stretched by Sophocles' handling of the Chorus. The parodos intro-duces Neoptolemus' sailors and establishes their complicity with their master in the deception. They are ordered to "take their cues" from the prince (148–49).[17] This "perjured chorus" is unique in Greek tragedy for its use of role-playing-within-the-role for nearly half of the play's duration.[18] In other tragedies the chorus may be called on by the dramatist to take a fairly active part in the play's action. A chorus may withhold the truth or even tell a lie on occasion.[19] But no other tragic chorus practices such a long, sustained deception. In no other play is the chorus's attitude so ambiguous and disconcerting.

After Neoptolemus has completed his narrative detailing his alleged conflict with the Atreidae, the Chorus interjects a ten-line strophe in which the sailors invoke the goddess of Earth, the Asiatic "mountain mother," as witness to their master's sufferings (391–402). Using the goddess as a witness helps to make their master's indignation appear genuine. The Chorus is, in effect, singing and dancing a rather sacri-legious lie.[20] Sophocles remains acutely aware of the all-pervasive trickery of the prince and the Chorus and encourages his audience to be alert to the labyrinth of internal illusion that he has so carefully constructed. Philoctetes' reference to the Chorus's completed song (προσᾴδεθ', 405) self-consciously hints at the artificiality of the Chorus's false performance.

The illusion-within-the-illusion deepens upon the entry of the two sailors. One sailor is a mute extra and presumably dressed like a member of the Chorus ("one of them is from our crew," 540), while the other wears the costume of a "foreigner" (ὁ ἀλλόθρους, 540). As with the false messenger's arrival in *Electra*, we have been warned in the prologue by Odysseus, the internal playwright, that such an entrance may occur. The Merchant is the scout or spy (σκοπός, 125) whose mask made an appearance at the opening of the play when the role was undertaken by a mute supernumerary. Now the actor who had played Odysseus has changed into the role of the fake Merchant and, as is most fitting, the Merchant speaks literally with the same voice as Odysseus, the man who has scripted his lie. Before his exit in the prologue, Odysseus had carefully established this twist in the plot. The spy was to make an appearance in disguise if Neoptolemus is "too slow" in leading Philoctetes to the ship (126).

οὗ δῆτα, τέκνον, ποικίλως αὐδωμένου
δέχου τὰ συμφέροντα τῶν ἀεὶ λόγων.

(130–31)

and then, son, [after the spy appears] when he talks artfully
you must go along with whatever he says that helps you.

The present reconnaissance mission of the σκοπός will entail a fluid blend of rehearsed or artful speech and spontaneous improvisation with Neoptolemus. The phony Merchant begins his scene with a smooth passage of plausible but utterly false exposition. Like all good theatrical figures, he identifies himself and gives an alibi for his appearance on the scene at this particular moment (542–49). Neoptolemus engages in deceptive dialogue with the "Merchant," helping to build on the new story elements of the imaginary twin expeditions for both the prince and Philoctetes (552–71). The exchange between the Merchant and Neoptolemus is a kind of play-within-the-play or metadrama performed for Philoctetes' view, and the theater audience is absorbed in watching the effect of these new stories on the duped man. Of course, in reality Odysseus, together with Neoptolemus, has led a Greek expedition to capture Philoctetes and his bow. Now the false Merchant, played by the "Odysseus" actor and following a script of Odysseus' devising, creates an imaginary threat for the crippled man, entailing the pursuit of both Philoctetes and the prince. Perhaps it would be more accurate to say that it is simultaneously a real *and* an imaginary threat.[21] The Merchant describes himself as a "messenger" (ἄγγελος, 564) who, chancing upon Neoptolemus, relays to him news of the encroaching danger. The prince asks the Merchant why Odysseus has not already arrived to "be his own messenger" (αὐτάγγελος, 568). The Merchant responds that Odysseus is already hunting another man, Philoctetes. The use of αὐτάγγελος at 568 contains keen performative irony when it is recalled that the "Odysseus" actor *is* functioning as "his own messenger" in the person of the duplicitous Merchant. Neoptolemus and the Merchant's exchange at 572–77, which prompts Philoctetes actively to join in the conversation, marks a deepening of the inner illusion.

> *Neoptolemus*: Who was this man that Odysseus himself
>   was sailing for?
> *Merchant*: There was a man—but first tell me who
>   this man is—but whatever you say speak softly.
> *Neoptolemus*: This man before you, stranger, is the famous
>   Philoctetes.
> *Merchant*: Don't ask me any more, then, but quick as you can
>   get on a ship and get yourself away from this land!
> *Philoctetes*: What's he saying, boy? Why does the sailor
>   traffic about me in dark whispers?
>
>   (572–79)

The Merchant and Neoptolemus engage in a sotto voce exchange, which is meant to remain inaudible to Philoctetes onstage but must be intelligible to the theater audience. This early example of an "aside" is all the more remarkable for its sophisticated use within the context of the play-within-the-play. The "aside" serves as an indication of the depth of illusion that Sophocles has created.[22]

The use of the "aside" succeeds in arousing Philoctetes' suspicions. Now the false Merchant proceeds to relate information that is vital both to the plot of the metadrama being performed for Philoctetes and to the "real" plot of Sophocles' tragedy. The Merchant recounts the alleged reason for the pursuit of Philoctetes. His narrative (603–21) gives the audience the first information of the prophecy concerning Philoctetes, his bow, and the fall of Troy. According to the Merchant, the prophet Helenus predicted that the Greeks would never capture Troy "unless by persuasive words / they bring this man from the island where now he dwells" (612–13).

Many critics naturally take this report as a factual account of the prophecy. They point to the use of persuasion as the only god-sanctioned means of bringing Philoctetes back into the civilization he despises. It so happens that a form of persuasion does win out in the final moments of the play, but both Odysseus and Neoptolemus show themselves ready to use deception or violence to "steal the soul of Philoctetes" at various points in the play. Within the false merchant's report of the prophecy, Odysseus is alleged to be willing to use force against Philoctetes should persuasion fail. Is this a reflection of Odysseus' plans, despite the tenor of the prophecy? Is this a bluff that Odysseus is playing through the decoy to fluster Philoctetes? Again Sophocles has left the audience to draw its own conclusion, in effect constructing its own play. The prophecy's content seems to vary throughout the text of the play. Perhaps the apotheosis of Heracles serves as a divine clarification of that prophecy; nevertheless Sophocles has deliberately created much confusion about this issue through his use of role-playing-within-the-role. We learn of the prophecy from a trickster under Odysseus' employ, a scout or spy pretending to be a merchant, couched in artful (ποικίλως, 130) speech. The "Merchant" is an actor both within the Theater of Dionysus and within the artifice of the play. Sophocles has given the clearest report of Helenus' prophecy to the most dubious and artificial person in the play, deepening the already considerable metatheatrical paradoxes.[23]

One of the paradoxes in the Merchant scene is Odysseus' promise to the Greek host, related by the role-playing σκοπός, to "bring the man and display [δηλώσειν] him to the Achaeans" (616). After the Merchant's exit, Philoctetes recalls this visual figure of speech with tones of understandable revulsion.

> Is this not monstrous, child, that Laertes' son
> should have hoped by soft words to have
> led me from a ship to show [δεῖξαι] me amidst the Argives?
>
> (628–30)

One may appreciate the dramatic skill and verbal manipulations of the offstage playwright Sophocles (and Odysseus), which have already delivered the character of Philoctetes before the Greeks beneath the southern slope of the Acropolis.

Once the Merchant has left the stage, Philoctetes begs Neoptolemus to take him aboard the ship and to his home. The prince hesitates, claiming that the winds are not yet favorable for this voyage (639–40). Within four lines Neoptolemus relents. His acquiescence to Philoctetes is actually a triumph for the deceptive plan. The quarry is now willing and eager to put himself under the control of Neoptolemus and his sailors. It is worth examining Neoptolemus' words as he gives in to Philoctetes' request. After Philoctetes has said that no opposing wind will stop those bent on robbery, Neoptolemus replies:

ἀλλ᾽ εἰ δοκεῖ, χωρῶμεν, ἔνδοθεν λαβὼν
ὅτου σε χρεία καὶ πόθος μάλιστ᾽ ἔχει.

(645–46)

Well, let's go then, if it seems so to you, when you have
taken whatever you need and most desire from inside.

While εἰ δοκεῖ ("if it seems to you," that is, "if you like") is a common enough expression, its presence here is not entirely casual. Philoctetes is at last at the point of surrendering to Neoptolemus' power, brought there by the elaborate game of "seeming" perpetrated by Odysseus and company. Philoctetes has been tricked by false perception; and δοκεῖν, a verb of perception and seeming, delicately marks the conclusion of the artifice of the false Merchant and Neoptolemus' elaborate performances. Δοκεῖν is an apt verb to touch on the perceptual confusion of this turning point in the play's action. It serves to italicize the layers of artifice that surround and confound the protagonist.[24] As will be examined later, δοκεῖν emerges again (1402) near the end of the play at another high point of perceptual confusion.

After Philoctetes leads the prince into his cave to gather the belongings he wishes to take with him, the Chorus sings what is perhaps the most ambiguous stasimon in Greek tragedy. Alone on stage for the first and only time, the sailors of the "perjured Chorus" express their sympathy for the agonies of mind and body that Philoctetes has endured. Their apparent pity for Philoctetes' plight makes the final antistrophe of the stasimon all the more jarring. After the harrowing images of Philoctetes' very real desolation, their ode ends in what we know to be premature rejoicing and a bold-faced lie.

> But now, he shall be happy
> and great after these troubles,
> having met with the son of a good family
> who after the fullness of many months
> will bear him on his oceangoing ship
> to his father's land, haunt of
> the Malian nymphs,
> beside the banks of the Sperchius . . .
>
> (719–26)

Sophoclean choruses often sing in celebration just before devastating tragic reversals, but here the effect is even more ironic than usual. The "happy ending" of Philoctetes' troubles is not only grossly premature but a deliberate falsehood. Strangely enough, this falsehood is uttered by this dissembling Chorus when it is alone on stage and there is no apparent need to play up its master's trickery.[25] There is no removing of the troubling double perspective created by this stasimon wherein the Chorus sings with compassion for a person it is conspiring to deceive so heartlessly.[26]

Philoctetes is overcome by a seizure resulting from his wound. As he sinks into an exhausted sleep, the Chorus begins a kommos with Neoptolemus. For half a strophe (827–32) the Chorus sings a lullaby to Philoctetes. But this brief lyric is yet another deceptive performance, for the remainder of the strophe (833–38) is devoted to prodding Neoptolemus to action. The implicit suggestion seems to be that, with the bow in the prince's hand, Philoctetes may be abandoned. The caressing sounds of the "lullaby" are thrown into brutal relief as the Chorus drops its deceptive mask of compassion.[27]

Neoptolemus responds to the Chorus, explaining his inaction in heroic hexameter (839–42). Neoptolemus declares that they have "hunted in vain" if they sail without Philoctetes. "For the crown of victory is his, he is the one god told us to bring. / It would be a foul shame to boast of something incomplete and joined with lies" (841–42). Neoptolemus' words are clothed in the medium of epic heroism. The use of heroic meter serves as a reminder of another mimetic performative form. By using hexameters, Neoptolemus speaks in the "accents" of his father Achilles, suggesting a reawakened conscience and a desire for heroic integrity.[28] There is also, as Winnington-Ingram observes, a "dissonance between the Homeric meter and the unheroic enterprise in which the son of Achilles has allowed himself to be engaged."[29] This "dissonance" is made all the sharper when the Chorus sings its antistrophe, closing the stasimon with a reiteration of its treacherous sentiments.

Neoptolemus' moment of "heroic" verse indicates the prince's deepening humanity and the stirring of his Achillean nobility. But there are other implications in Sophocles' portrayal of the bow and its possessor. The bow appears to symbolize a kind of prelapsarian heroism as the former property of the semidivine Heracles. Heracles gave the bow to his mortal friend Philoctetes out of gratitude for the latter's lighting of the funeral pyre on Mount Oeta. Rather than using it as Heracles did for destroying monsters or conquering cities, the divine bow serves rather incongruously as a weapon to kill animals and ensure its current possessor's physical survival. Philoctetes needs the bow, not only to survive, but also to maintain his heroic stature, since it embodies his friendship with Heracles. While even the unscrupulous Odysseus may reluctantly concede that Troy will not fall without Philoctetes to handle the bow, it is never questioned by anyone in the play that Troy can fall without the bow, a prop that embodies a magical bygone era of heroism.

The bow hints not only at Philoctetes' strength, his heroic status built out of his friendship with Heracles, but also, paradoxically, at Philoctetes' weakness—the strangely fragmentary nature of his heroism. Without Hector's sword, Ajax would still have been a hero, bravely selecting a different means of death to reinstate his integrity after Athena's machinations had done their worst. Philoctetes' prop, on the other hand, merely reflects a glory borrowed from Heracles, who was undeniably a greater hero in the Greek imagination than Philoctetes and Neoptolemus combined. Heroic integrity has been reduced to a hand prop—something all too tangible and vulnerable to exploitation by the unscrupulous. The situation is underscored by Philoctetes' repeated quibbling on the word βίος which means "bow" as well as "livelihood" and "life" (931–33, 1282). This bow, whose very name in Greek embodies physical as well as heroic livelihood, is given an anthropomorphic dimension in one of the archer's speeches. Philoctetes imagines the bow as a kind of audience beholding his tragic situation.

Surely the bow itself, Philoctetes remarks, "if [it] has feelings" (φρένας εἴ τινας / ἔχεις, 1130–31) will "pity the sight" (ἐλεινὸν ὁρᾷς, 1130) of him and will "witness" (ὁρῶν, 1136) deceit. Just as language and meaning, words and actions are torn asunder by Odysseus' plotting, so too the bow suffers an analogous fate, as a prop whose proper use is subverted by the wounding of Philoctetes and his abandonment by his comrades. Its heroic identity will be further compromised when it is briefly stolen by Odysseus, and, at the end of the play, when a subdued Philoctetes prepares to use it against the Trojans in a struggle that compels him to work beside the very people who had so disgracefully abandoned him.

The play explores a situation of epistemological crisis, where *logos* and *ergon*, deed and action, are separated. The dichotomy between signifier and signified is embodied in the physical presence of Philoctetes within the theater, holding the prop bow. Philoctetes presents the image of a savage-tempered cripple with a repulsive wound, carrying a divine weapon that he uses for the hunting of food. The character and the bow represent heroism and its negating degradation. Greeks commonly viewed physical beauty as an indicator of moral or ethical beauty. The curing of Philoctetes, promised by Neoptolemus if he consents to go to Troy, will render Philoctetes more physically attractive to the eye. Paradoxically, this seeming assonance of his physical self and the divine bow will seriously compromise his heroic integrity. It will take the apotheosis of Heracles in the play's concluding moments to "reconcile" the cure with the bow, but the dissonance is impossible to remove. Ajax was able to out maneuver Athena and her rewriting of his integrity. Philoctetes and Neoptolemus remain pitifully incapable of breaking free of Odysseus' divinely sanctioned "play."

When Philoctetes revives from his sleep, his relationship with Neoptolemus reaches a new crisis point.

> *Neoptolemus*: Ah, me! What ever am I to do next?
> *Philoctetes*: What is it, son? Where are your words straying?
> *Neoptolemus*: I don't know where I should turn my words.
>
> (895–97)

Touching Philoctetes for the first time seems to draw Neoptolemus completely away from the deceptive role he has been playing.[30] The exchange at 895–97 reveals a separation between word and action similar to what is found in *Electra* (1174–75), when Electra's real grief draws the normally self-controlled Orestes out of the shell of his role playing. Both Neoptolemus and Orestes describe their inability to continue in a situation wherein word and deed, the basic components of dramatic action, are hopelessly separated and unresponsive to each other. From the beginning of the play, the audience has been watching Neoptolemus watch and be affected by the suffering Philoctetes. The prince admits to a "terrible pity" (οἶκτος δεινὸς, 965), which he has felt "for a long time" (966). Ironically, it has been role-playing-within-the-role that has given Neoptolemus an audience's distance and perspective on Philoctetes' suffering. Just as Neoptolemus, Odysseus' chief actor, becomes paralyzed, the master plotter himself enters the scene.

At the point of Odysseus' second entrance, the fulfillment of the myth, that Philoctetes will go to Troy, seems virtually impossible. Sophocles has created the potential for a countermyth, radically different from accepted tradition. Odysseus' offstage manipulation of the onstage action appears to have failed, and now he resorts to actual physical intervention. In his attempt to wrench the situation from the faltering Neoptolemus, Odysseus commandeers the bow and threatens to return to Troy without the intractable Philoctetes (1055). Is Odysseus unconsciously rephrasing the oracle for his own convenience, or is this whole threat a mere bluff to bring Philoctetes to relent and go to Troy?

Odysseus begins to lead Neoptolemus offstage ostensibly to prepare for their departure from the island and to give Philoctetes a final opportunity to relent. The Chorus also prepares to leave with them. Philoctetes asks the sailors, "Will you leave me too, friends, / desolate and without any pity?" (1070–71). Sophocles has created anticipatory tension by this simple gesture toward the Chorus. Not only does Philoctetes wish to avoid being left entirely alone, but the conventions of tragedy allow the Chorus to leave the orchestra only at the very end of the drama. Aeschylus' *Eumenides* and Sophocles' earlier *Ajax* are exceptions to this practice which serve to prove the general rule. When the sailors seem to prepare themselves to leave, they are threatening not only to leave Lemnos without Philoctetes, but to leave the drama unfinished. Their gesture threatens to close down the play. Odysseus' threat to leave Lemnos without Philoctetes may only be a feint on the part of a character in the play. The Chorus's threat is unquestionably a feint on the part of Sophocles.

Neoptolemus gives the men a rather weak excuse to stay on stage, if we accept that he and Odysseus really are planning to leave. At the risk of seeming softhearted, he says he will allow his sailors to remain while the ship is prepared and prayers are offered. Perhaps, he reasons, Philoctetes may yet relent (1074–80). The Chorus pleads to Philoctetes to change his mind, but the crippled man rejects its compromised self-portrayal as "a friend who approaches you with all good intentions" (1163–64). Again the sailors announce that they are about to exit (1180). This repeated device intensifies the conflict with its threat of closing the drama. Sophocles is buying time during this tense though static exchange between the Chorus and Philoctetes for Neoptolemus' change of heart.

The young man now enters to restore the bow to Philoctetes (1222). Odysseus follows, then appears to exit after a face-off with Neoptolemus at 1260. But perhaps Neoptolemus' apparent change of heart is yet another deception performed in order to gain Philoctetes' cooperation.[31] The play is disturbing, not because we *know* that Neoptolemus is deceiving Philoctetes again, but because the characters and structure of Sophocles' play leave this option as a possibility.

Neoptolemus offers the bow to Philoctetes.

Philoctetes: What are you saying? Am I being tricked a second time?
Neoptolemus: No, I swear by the pure majesty of Zeus most high.
Philoctetes: O welcome saying, if your words are true.
Neoptolemus: The deed shall prove the word. . . .

(1288–91)

While Neoptolemus' actions seem to reunite word and deed, the prince's relationship with Zeus will prove to be problematical. Odysseus has referred to Zeus as the ultimate instigator of his quasi-theatrical plotting (989–92). Just when Neoptolemus and Philoctetes are physically, if not emotionally, reunited by the return of the bow, Odysseus makes a sudden reentrance and threatens the newly won amity with a self-conscious melodramatic force (1293).[32]

Philoctetes uses his restored bow to frighten Odysseus from the stage (1304), and the character is never seen again. This clever metatheatrical strategist leaves the stage in defeat, his attempt to interpose himself directly in the play's action an apparent failure.[33] The audience is confronted again with the configuration of Philoctetes, Neoptolemus, and the Chorus for one last impassioned *agon*. The Helenus prophecy, which made up a part of the false Merchant's story, figures in the prince's attempts to persuade Philoctetes (1330–40). At first glance, this seems to affirm the "truthfulness" of the Merchant's false tale. Philoctetes reminds the prince of his alleged loss of Achilles' armor.

> It behooves you never to go to Troy again yourself,
> and to hinder me too; they outraged you,
> robbing you of your father's arms. After that will you
> fight beside them, and compel me to do the same?
>
> (1363–66)

This last example of injustice comes at the climax of a speech that begins the play's most extraordinary reversal: Neoptolemus' apparent decision to forsake the war and return Philoctetes to his homeland. Philoctetes has appropriated the central information from Neoptolemus' deceptive narrative; and the young man, rather than taking the opportunity to confess the lie, instead remarks that Philoctetes' argument is "reasonable" (εἰκότ: "like truth—likely, probable, reasonable," 1373). Sophocles has manipulated the story of Achilles' arms so that the truth is hopelessly buried in ambiguity; and what was uttered as a lie in the earlier portion of the play is seamlessly appropriated into the "truth" by the play's end. Indeed, this untruth is made a decisive point of Philoctetes' argument, which finally sways Neoptolemus.

Neoptolemus agrees to return Philoctetes to Malis in contradiction of the traditional story, the myth regarded as history by the ancient audience. At this climax of perceptual confusion, between true and false reports, between well-established myth and the shockingly unhistoric yet psychologically plausible action taking place on stage, δοκεῖν appears again in Neoptolemus' almost casual words of acquiescence: εἰ δοκεῖ, στείχωμεν ("If it seems so to you, let us depart," 1402). The repetition of δοκεῖν echoes line 645. Line 1402 serves as a kind of response to the earlier agreement to return Philoctetes, which had been a deception. Now Neoptolemus appears to be making the offer again. As at 645, his words suggest his acquiescence to the older man's perception of the reality surrounding him. At 645 there was the expression of a delicate irony, since the audience was aware of how skillfully that environment had been manipulated through playacting. Neoptolemus' words at 1402 may well make the audience all the more watchful, lest a similar deception is being practiced upon Philoctetes now.

As the two men and the Chorus prepare to leave the orchestra, Heracles appears in apotheosis above the action. This use of the *deus ex machina* to bring resolution to an action moving away from conformity with traditional myth is unexampled in the other surviving Sophoclean plays. Critics fall into two camps when examining the *deus* in *Philoctetes*. Faced with a supernatural event that is unheralded in the drama, some scholars attempt to diminish any apparent rupture in the text. Whitman tries to interpret away the embarrassing divinity who seems to threaten the autonomy of Philoctetes as an ἀρετή hero. Heracles, for Whitman, is not an intrusive *deus* or really even a *deus* at all. He is a projection of Philoctetes' inner ἀρετή.[34] Other critics find Heracles' appearance vaguely disappointing, at least to modern sensibilities. Linforth is particularly troubled by Heracles' "total disregard of all that has occurred through the course of the play." Linforth notes that no attempt is made to allay Philoctetes' hatred of the Greeks or to assuage the humiliation his journey to Troy would entail. "The tight dramatic structure of the play, upon which Sophocles has expended all the resources of his art, is thus suddenly abandoned." While it is possible that the audience would view the return to Troy as a reassuring concession to tradition, it is carried out "in defiance of the dramatic truth of all that has preceded."[35]

In the ancient theater, the protagonist and deuteragonist played only the roles of Philoctetes and Neoptolemus, respectively. It should be remembered that Heracles, the spokesman of the gods, is played by the tritagonist, who assumed the roles of Odysseus and the false Merchant. This doubling carries symbolic meaning and is dramatically apt, since the Merchant serves as Odysseus' spy and internal actor. The association of Odysseus and his spy with the demigod is a paradox that encapsulates the troubling nature of this entire play.[36] The *deus*, played by the "Odysseus" actor, allows the playwright-within-the-play to have the last word in the drama's outcome after all other performative strategies (Neoptolemus' "script," the false Merchant) have failed. At last, a "teacher" or διδάσκαλος has emerged who cannot be denied. Why would Sophocles resort to the *deus* at this point in the play? Aristophanes' parodies of Euripidean uses of the *deus* indicate that many members of an ancient audience might have had as keen an awareness of dramatic absurdity as any of their successors. One need not disbelieve in gods to disbelieve in a *deus ex machina*. Sophocles has utilized his consummate dramatic technique to bring the action to the point of negating traditional myth. He has fashioned a hero who has too much integrity (or ἀρετή, to use Whitman's formulation) to consent to helping those who so grievously harmed him in the past.

The content and style of the demigod's speech are shockingly banal and out of keeping with the rest of the tragedy.

> Not yet, indeed, son of Poeas,
> not before you have heard my *words* [μύθων].
> Take it that you are listening to
> the voice of Heracles and seeing his face.
>
> (1409–12)

The awkward periphrasis of these words points to the discrepancy of outward appearance and inner identity. Heracles refers to his divine message as μύθοι, a word with general connotations of rational discourse as well as specific implications of stories, narratives, or *myths*. Sophocles has given this demigod a singularly weak opening statement. His words encourage a listener to doubt the identity of the divine apparition by mawkishly separating the phenomenon of sight and sound.

Even the superficial sense of closure usually found in a *deus ex machina* speech is thwarted by a seemingly gratuitous reference to a disaster lying in the future. After assuring Philoctetes of his glory at Troy and likening the archer and prince to "twin lions" (1436), Heracles delivers a brief but stern warning.

> But remember this when you shall come to
> sack that land, show reverence to the gods. For everything
> else is held to be of secondary importance by father
> Zeus; for piety does not die with men;
> rather in their life and in their death it is immortal.
>
> (1440–44)

These words are ominously suggestive of the notorious sacrileges committed by Neoptolemus during the sack of Troy. Sophocles has gone out of his way (as he does with the prophetic words of Aegisthus at the end of *Electra* 1497–98) to point to events in the future that, perforce, become a part of the present drama.[37] We have just witnessed Neoptolemus' moral struggle and his apparent triumph. As the young man stands next to Philoctetes and seems to enjoy a parity with this hero, we are reminded of his incredible moral collapse in the days to come.[38]

Philoctetes articulates a crisis of language and meaning as well as a questioning of the tragic theater's ability to give new life to old myths. At first Neoptolemus will obey Odysseus' commands to create deceiving strategies and false stories in order to win Philoctetes' return to the Greek camp. But once Neoptolemus' conscience compels a full disclosure of the truth, the deceptive plan is defeated and no honest means are capable of winning Philoctetes' consent. Only a *deus ex machina* can restore the hero to the Greek camp, reconciling the stage characters to their traditional destinies. This is as powerful a dissonance as we have in ancient tragedy. If by some act of misattribution the play had been ascribed to Euripides, far more critics would be taking note of the profoundly ironic appearance of Heracles and its perverse destruction of the very closure it is ostensibly there to create.[39] Sophocles' use of the *deus* is frustrating to the audience. The conventional resolution it offers for Philoctetes' story is manifestly inappropriate for all that has been seen earlier in the tragedy. Sophocles is allowing us to see the seams of his craft. Having created characters who adamantly refuse the fates assigned them by myth, by the gods, and ultimately by the playwright himself, Sophocles resorts to the *deus* to force them arbitrarily into compliance with the preordained pattern.

The discrepancy between the *deus* and the rest of the play may be discerned easily after Heracles has given his commands. We are returned briefly but unforgettably to the soul of Philoctetes via his farewell to both his island home and, by extension, his audience. Though he will presumably be able to return to Malis once he has fought at Troy, there is no joy in his acceptance of the gods' will. Instead he says a tender farewell to the environment that has been the scene of his sufferings. This new tone of sublime sadness contrasts with the joy he had expressed when Neoptolemus consented to return him directly to Malis.[40]

By his consent to leave his isolation, Philoctetes has "died" as a tragic hero. While we may be glad that he will receive relief from his pain and recognition for his prowess as an archer, we may well mourn with him the loss of the moral purity that was his unique possession. "Healing is always payment for submission," observes Kott, who deems Philoctetes to be "the only one of Sophocles' tragic heroes who is broken."[41] Seen in this way, his "victory" carries much the same ambiguity as Electra's triumph at the end of her tragedy. Philoctetes' farewell to Lemnos (1452–68), his place of tragic isolation, is also the character's farewell to the Theater of Dionysus. His lines carry a poignancy similar to Prospero's farewell to *his* island/theater in Shakespeare's *The Tempest*.

In both *The Tempest* and *Philoctetes*, the playing space offers the audience a scene where man exists in uncivilized isolation. Both Prospero and Philoctetes have been betrayed by their respective societies—in effect, the worlds of the audiences that have come to watch their plays.[42] Both men ultimately renounce their privileged places in the performance space to resume their places in society. It is interesting to compare Prospero's sophisticated "rough magic" with the crude technologies Philoctetes has developed on his "bare island." Both men confront the duplicity of their civilizations in the persons who visit their island/theater. Their positions of physical isolation, synonymous with a performer's isolation before his audience, cannot be maintained indefinitely. Both men are compelled to renounce their places on stage and reenter a world of moral chaos. To view either denouement as a purely happy ending is extremely simplistic.

The critical assumptions surrounding Sophocles' reputation have blinded many of his readers to what he has actually created in *Philoctetes*. Here Sophocles appears to push myth to the breaking point and utilizes the devices of theater to call attention to the gulf that separates reality from art, human aspirations from fulfillment.

7 | *Electra*

Prologue

In his last play, *Oedipus at Colonus*, Sophocles would use his craft to comment subtly upon his position as a tragic dramatist and to impart a kind of immortality upon himself and his dying polis. In *Electra*, this same self-conscious craftsmanship seems to point in an opposite, negating direction. *Electra* was composed during the final decade of the Peloponnesian War, a time when social and moral standards were frequently at a point of collapse. In the second stasimon of *Oedipus Tyrannus*, probably written shortly after the outbreak of the war, the Chorus fearfully describes a world lacking moral boundaries. When pride leads human beings to touch what should be left untouched, the ordered life of the polis is gravely threatened. "If behavior like this is honored," the Chorus asks, "Why should I be in a chorus?" (*OT* 895–96). *Electra* is often compared with the earlier Oedipus play for its perfection of dramatic form and because it appears to be the next play chronologically in the surviving Sophoclean corpus. In *Electra*, Sophocles has expanded and developed this idea of a disordered, hubristic world where all boundaries are violated, where what is just unavoidably contains elements of injustice. If noble deeds and words do not exist in the real world outside of the theater, their representation can be no more than a shell, a false shape standing in for an equally false original—a prime illustration of Plato's view of poetic mimesis. Just as Orestes' urn, despite its visual appearance and its effect on Electra, remains a "prop," empty of the (imaginary) ashes that would fill it with genuine tragic substance, so Electra's status as a tragic hero is similarly compromised. Her heroic stance is a chimera of impressive words and gestures, a kind of illusion within the illusion, which the theater audience can never fully accept.

Of all the Sophoclean plays that have come down to us, *Electra* has been the most controversial and difficult to interpret. While it is universally admired for its superb dramatic structure and technical virtuosity, many scholars confess, at least informally, to finding the great play curiously unsatisfying or even repellent.[1] Perhaps no other ancient play has been subjected to more conflicting attempts at interpretation. This plurality of interpretive strategies arises from the play's extraordinary tonal ambivalence. This ambivalence is rooted in the tragedy's metatheatrical nature. *Electra* is a tragedy that is about tragedy, a play that draws the audience's attention to its own theatricality. The play's metatheatrical resonances explode conventional notions of closure and compel the audience to perceive duality almost everywhere within the dramatic action. An appreciation of duality, of one thing standing in for something else, is a phenomenon inseparable from the paradox of theatrical illusion. Sophocles' obsession with self-conscious theatricality creates a play that presents a striking revision of the Orestes myth, while deliberately reminding the audience of other, conflicting versions of the story. The play toys with theatrical convention in ways that are analogous to the sophists' intellectual projects of the 410s, when Sophocles, an aging master in his seventies, composed the *Electra*.

Criticism tends to fall into two sharply conflicting camps when dealing with this play. Each view articulates a conflicting aspect of the tragedy. These conflicts of tone will find a harmony when the *Electra's* metatheatrical nature is understood. Many scholars, beginning with Jebb, interpret the play as Sophocles' attempt to "Homericize" the story Aeschylus had told in his *Oresteia*.[2] These "Homeric" interpreters, whose ranks include Waldock and Whitman, view the play as a kind of gloss or expansion of the remarks found in the *Odyssey*, which refer to Orestes' killing of his mother and Aegisthus. Homer's references to the matricide omit all suggestion of guilt or remorse on the part of Agamemnon's avenger, and seem to extol the murders of Clytemnestra and her lover as an unambiguous act of justice. Orestes' vengeance is held out as a model to be emulated by Telemachus.[3]

While this "Homeric" line of interpretation puts admirable focus on dramatic structure, disciplining the reader to avoid automatically reading Aeschylean assumptions into the play, it does have considerable shortcomings. The "Homeric" interpreters tend to ignore, or reason away, the many sinister or ironic implications that Sophocles has embedded within the text. These implications suggest that Sophocles' view of the matricide was far more complex than a simplistic celebration of crime and punishment. The character of Electra is not even mentioned by Homer, yet Sophocles builds his tragedy around her. She is the focal point of the play, not Orestes, Clytemnestra, or Aegisthus. Why should Sophocles have chosen such a focus if he were at all concerned with reinstating the "Homeric" view of the play. The critical myth of the "Homeric influence" fades under close examination.[4]

The other interpretive camp sees the play far more ironically. These critics, led by Winnington-Ingram and Charles Segal, view the tragedy as a subtle interplay of heroism and undercutting gloom. Both the "Homeric" and "ironic" schools of interpretation were formed to deal with the troubling moral issues raised by the tragedy. The structuralist/poststructuralist emphasis placed on language has led to some useful work on the text, which focuses on linguistic structure in *Electra*. Thomas Woodard defines the central thematic tension of the play as a struggle between λόγος (word) and ἔργον (deed).[5] To Woodard, the play represents a dialectic between Electra, whose strength lies in her command of the "feminine" world of rhetoric and λόγος, and Orestes, who functions in the more "masculine" realm of deeds or ἔργα. By the end of the play, Woodard's Electra leaves the domain of words and begins to operate in the masculine sphere of deeds.

Woodard's emphasis on linguistic constructs points toward the aspect of the play that so many scholars admit to disliking, the artificial and contrived nature of Sophocles' dramaturgy. Not only does Sophocles appear to rewrite self-consciously Aeschylus' *Choephoroi*, already an established classic by the late fifth century; he also appears to recycle parts of *Antigone*, one of his most beloved plays. The relationship of Sophocles' Electra and her more timid sister, Chrysothemis, clearly recalls the conflict of Antigone and Ismene. It is as though Sophocles had imported the sisters from his earlier play and imposed their relationship on the Orestes story.[6] It is difficult to read or see *Electra* without being reminded of *Antigone*. Furthermore, both Electra and Antigone are obsessed with an absent brother. This strong reminiscence of the earlier, much loved play creates a disturbing effect when we compare the incongruity of Antigone's martyrdom in the cause of familial love with Electra's struggle and success in accomplishing her mother's murder.

Virtually all Greek tragedies were revisions of well-known myths. Many tragedies dramatized material that had been utilized by earlier playwrights. In *Electra*, however, Sophocles seems unusually concerned that the audience recognize his dramaturgical ingenuity in rehandling and juxtaposing materials from earlier tragedies. *Electra* reminds us of other plays and, in doing so, calls attention to many of the conventions of tragic drama. *Electra* is a very self-conscious tragedy. This self-conscious aspect may be identified as its metatheatrical quality. In this context it is worth recalling Bruno Gentili's definition of metatheater as *any* drama "constructed from previously existing plays."[7] Metatheatrical phenomena are effects of extraordinary contrivance on the part of a playwright; and, appropriately enough, *Electra* is often disparaged as a "contrived" play. A metatheatrical view of *Electra* articulates the play's peculiar, troubling qualities, synthesizing the seemingly conflicting views of the play examined earlier. *Electra* simultaneously presents the audience with both affirmation and disillusion, a feat made possible by the play's strikingly self-conscious ambivalence. Woodard's useful λόγος/ἔργον opposition leads to an implicit (meta)theatrical analogy: that of word and action, the building blocks of drama itself.[8] The opposition of λόγος and ἔργον in *Electra* reflects not so much a literary or philosophical conceit as an exploration on Sophocles' part of aesthetic or theatrical self-consciousness and the boundaries of mimetic representation.

The remainder of the present study will constitute a sequential examination of Sophocles' *Electra* which attempts to define the play's metatheatrical nature as it would be manifested during performance in the ancient theater. *Electra* is a play concerned with characters who play roles within their roles, and it is imperative to examine the literal role playing allotted the three actors in Sophocles' theater. As in *Oedipus Tyrannus, Antigone* (the role of Creon), and *Philoctetes,* the protagonist played only one role throughout the tragedy—the part of Electra. This helps to focus attention on Electra as the center of the action. The deuteragonist undertook the roles of both Orestes and Clytemnestra. This extraordinary act of doubling prevents the mother and the matricide from ever sharing the stage. The tritagonist doubled the Paedagogus with Aegisthus, an interesting double in that it allows the same actor to play two mature characters who are separated by a chasm of social class and political enmity. The Paedagogus has dedicated his life to training the man who will kill his other "character," Aegisthus. Both men also represent rival internal dramatists in that each character endeavors to control the stage. The Paedagogus proves the abler actor and director. Chrysothemis could be played by either the deuteragonist or the tritagonist. The deuteragonist is a tempting assignment, in that it allows Electra's three relatives to be played by the same man. The tritagonist seems the more likely candidate for the role, however, when one considers the patterning of entrances and exits; he has slightly more time to shift back and forth between his characters than the deuteragonist would.

The performative ramifications of a Paedagogus/Chrysothemis/ Aegisthus doubling lies in contrast and some surprising consonance. Chrysothemis, a young and very passive woman, marks a striking contrast from the tritagonist's other two roles of the Paedagogus and Aegisthus, two very active enemies. The Paedagogus and Chrysothemis share several unexpected elements within the play. The Paedagogus exits the prologue accompanying Orestes and the mute Pylades to leave libations on Agamemnon's tomb (82–85). Chrysothemis makes her first entrance bearing offerings for that same tomb (405–6). We next see Chrysothemis returning from the tomb after seeing the offerings left by Orestes in the Paedagogus' company (871–919). Chrysothemis, the character least capable of action, literally stands between the forces represented by the tritagonist's other two characters. Her entrance, after she sees and correctly interprets the offerings at the tomb, gains in irony and poignancy when the same actor who had delivered the devastating lie about Orestes' death now stands before Electra and declares the truth. As in all of the Sophoclean tragedies, the sharing of roles among the three actors reveals not so much a master dramatist making a virtue of necessity but a subtle craftsman who scores his play for three voices, much as a composer scores a composition with particular instrumental voices in mind. In each instance, the textual or musical material acquires nuance and meaning depending on what specific instrument is assigned to transmit it to the audience's ear.

The play begins before the palace of Mycenae. Three figures enter the stage, Orestes, his friend Pylades, and Orestes' tutor, the Paedagogus. This Paedagogus acts as a kind of playwright/director-within-the-play throughout most of the tragedy, much as Odysseus does in *Philoctetes*. It will be recalled that the playwright's official title in the records of the ancient festivals was *didaskalos*, which means "teacher" or "trainer," referring to his original function as trainer of the chorus. Sophocles' society made associations between tragic playwrights and teachers. In the *Frogs*, Aristophanes describes the tragic poet as a "teacher for adults" (διδάσκαλος . . . ἡβῶσι).[9] One scholar writes: "The instruction of young boys in traditional values through poetry . . . was the foundation of Greek political life. Poetry, politics, and *paideia* [education] could not be separated in the polis. To gain control over one it was necessary to control the others, as Plato showed so profoundly in the *Republic*."[10] It is fitting that two of Sophocles' greatest internal playwrights, the Paedagogus and Odysseus of the *Philoctetes*, are associated with the role of teacher or leader of youths. Both men create "artistic" deceptions to gain political advantage.

The Paedagogus utters the first words of the play.

Ὦ τοῦ στρατηγήσαντος ἐν Τροίᾳ ποτὲ
Ἀγαμέμνονος παῖ, νῦν ἐκεῖν᾽ ἔξεστί σοι
παρόντι λεύσσειν, ὧν πρόθυμος ἦσθ᾽ ἀεί.

(1–3)

O son of Agamemnon, once the general at Troy,
now it is possible for you to see at first hand
what you have always desired.

These words create a dichotomy between past and present, between a lost hero from times gone by (ποτὲ, 1) and his son who stands before us now (νῦν, 2). The formal, rather pompous patronymic takes a line and a half.[11] It serves the task of identifying Orestes as well as creating a historic, potentially heroic template in the figure of Agamemnon, who hovers over the play's action. The Paedagogus' opening words suggest a kind of role for the actor playing Orestes to assume, that of a legendary hero's son. The audience is compelled to judge the present actions of the son against the heroic father. They are encouraged to judge how well the present "performer" lives up to the role that has been assigned to him.

"Ancient Argos" is the scene (4). What significance might this city have for the playwright and his audience? One scholar has argued that Thebes provided Athenians with "a stageable other," a dramatic setting that could show the democratic polis its tyrannical opposite. Thebes figures as a chaotic "anti-Athens" in plays such as *Seven Against Thebes, Oedipus Tyrannus, Antigone*, and the *Bacchae*. "Argos however occupies the middle space between the two extremes that Athens and Thebes represent. . . . It's a city capable of being saved."[12] This view of Argos as representing an ambiguous halfway point between enlightened Attic democracy and ruinous despotism harmonizes with the shifting, ambiguous tone of the *Electra*.

Orestes, like the theater audience, has entered a place advantageous for seeing (λεύσσειν, 3). The word for theater, θέατρον, literally means "seeing place." The old man's first speech is concerned with seeing and setting the scene for the ensuing action. The Paedagogus proceeds to enumerate the features of the locale which may lie in part or in whole outside of the actual performance area and within the audience's space. Like the Theater of Dionysus, the action of the *Electra* is set in the very heart of civic life. The spectators were surrounded by "groves" (5) and "temples" (8) like the ones enumerated by the Paedagogus.

The Paedagogus' words serve as a kind of verbal skenographia. They paint an ambiguous, problematic space suggestive of transformation and duality. We are near a "grove" once traversed by a girl turned into a cow (Io, 5). Within sight is the "agora of the wolf-killing Lycean Apollo" (τοῦ λυκοκτόνου θεοῦ / ἀγορὰ Λύκειος, 6–7), a deeply ambivalent appellation, which suggests the god's affinity both with light and with wolves, with wolf killing and with wolflike behavior.[13] The Paedagogus goes on:

οἳ δ᾽ ἱκάνομεν,
φάσκειν Μυκήνας τὰς πολυχρύσους ὁρᾶν,
πολύφθορόν τε δῶμα Πελοπιδῶν τόδε

(8–10)

The place we have come to
you may say, is Mycenae which you *behold*, rich in gold;
and here is the house of the Pelopidae rich in murder.

Within a few lines Sophocles has created a kind of rhetorical double vision, which will permeate the texture of the play. The house of "much gold" (πολυχρύσος) is filled with "much slaughter" (πολύφθορον). Line 9 is curiously periphrastic. Rather than simply saying "behold Mycenae," a gentle dichotomy is established between what is seen within the *theatron* and what we interpret as either audience in the theater or actors within the play. Words denoting speech (φάσκειν) and sight (ὁρᾶν), the two principal elements of theater, frame line 9. What we are "seeing" is "to be called Mycenae." Attention is directed to the separation of referents from their theatrical signifiers within the performing space. We are in a place where speech and behavior bestow identity on objects and people, a place where things stand in for other things, where even the self-confident Paedagogus plants the smallest seeds of doubt whether the scene painter's "Mycenae" may be the "real" one after all.

The Paedagogus' brief description of the surrounding locale has united the stage space and its immediate environs with the fictive world of the play. The Paedagogus now directs attention overhead.

ὡς ἡμὶν ἤδη λαμπρὸν ἡλίου σέλας
ἑῷα κινεῖ φθέγματ᾽ ὀρνίθων σαφῆ
μέλαινά τ᾽ ἄστρων ἐκλέλοιπεν εὐφρόνη.

(17–19)

For us already the bright flame of the sun
stirs the clear morning voices of the birds
and has eclipsed the dark "kindly time" of stars.

In a play comparatively barren of ornate language, this sudden burst of poetic elaboration is quite striking. The appropriation by the play of the "real" world surrounding the theater assists in the wedding of the spectator with the drama. Such a merging of real and unreal is especially appropriate in this play, which will examine the interpenetration of fiction and reality. Sophocles will continue this strategy of uniting the stage action with the natural environment of the theater. Electra's opening lines later in the prologue will be a salutation to the sun (86). Even Clytemnestra, after her terrible dream, will confide in the sun, which blazes above actors and audience alike (424–25).[14] Dawn had theatrical associations since the rising sun marked the beginnings of the tragic competitions at the City Dionysia. Dawn triggers the beginning of the *Electra*'s action just as it signals the beginning of the competition in which the play competed. "The clear morning voices of the birds" is an attractive piece of nature description. It contrasts ironically with the bloody business being plotted in the prologue.[15] The image of birds residing near the action foreshadows the recurrent imagery throughout the play, which compares Electra to a bird. Perhaps too the birds are indicative of Furies lurking about the house.

The palace exterior represented by the skene becomes a place of sight and sound, where *actions* are imminent (ἔργων ἀκμή, 22). It is time "to immediately plan what must be *done*" (τί χρὴ δρᾶν ἐν τάχει βουλευτέον, 16). The Paedagogus now begins to marshal his onstage forces.

> So before anybody comes out of the house, we must
> join in words [λόγοισιν]. For it is no longer the ripe time [καιρός]
> to hesitate; rather it is high time for actions [ἔργων].
>
> (20–22)

These lines train the audience's eye expectantly toward the doors of the skene. Any character entering from the skene is potentially a victim or aggressor. The motif of expediency and timeliness (καιρός, 21) also enters the play, along with the use of words or *logoi* in an artful manner to gain a desired effect.[16]

Now it is Orestes' turn to speak.

> ὦ φίλτατ᾽ ἀνδρῶν προσπόλων, ὥς μοι σαφῆ
> σημεῖα φαίνεις ἐσθλὸς εἰς ἡμᾶς γεγώς.
>
> (23–24)

> O dearest of manservants, how *clear* the *signs* you *reveal*
> being the good fellow you are to me.

The rather pompous hyperbole of Orestes' address matches the tone of the Paedagogus' first line (1). The prince's words also stress the notions of revelation and appearance, which fit in with the "theatrical" nature of their plans. The Paedagogus has observed or read the signs (σημεῖα) for his pupil. The turning point in the tragedy will involve Electra's misreading of the deceptive σημεῖα created by the Paedagogus, a misreading that will lead from her traditionally passive role to the brink of heroic action in her proposal to single-handedly assassinate the usurpers. During the recognition scene Orestes will become a revealer and reader of signs, interpreting the situation "clearly" to his sister.

Orestes goes on to address his servant in a heroic language bordering on parody.

> For just as a well-bred horse [ἵππος εὐγενής], though he be old,
> does not lose heart amidst dangers
> but pricks up his ears, just so you
> spur us on and yourself follow in the forefront.
>
> (25–28)

By likening the slave to a ἵππος εὐγενής, not only does Orestes bestialize the man but he has called him "noble" or "well-born." Of the two speakers, it is Orestes who is truly εὐγενής in the eyes of an ancient audience. Sophocles suggests something unusual in the relationship of this master and his servant. Orestes' language implies an unnatural fluidity between social classes as well as between human being and animal, just as Apollo shifts between giving light and killing wolves. The bestialization of human beings is often associated with tyrants in tragedy. Creon in *Antigone*, Aegisthus in *Agamemnon*, and Pentheus in the *Bacchae* are three stage tyrants who use images of animal husbandry to describe their relationship with their subjects. Such a confusion of man and beast is antithetical to the civilized polis of Athens. Orestes' animal comparison is more subtle than the "yoking" images used by the tyrants mentioned above. While he is trying to compliment his servant, the metaphor of the horse's ears standing straight up takes on a slightly ridiculous quality. Orestes is straining for verbal heroics but succumbs to bathos.[17]

With his heroic father gone, Orestes' only male role model has been the Paedagogus, who has created an efficient young machine bent on the goal of vengeance and establishing control over his patrimony. Up until now, the Paedagogus has served as a kind of playwright/director, rehearsing Orestes for his role as Agamemnon's avenger. Now we watch as Orestes reverses these roles, making the Paedagogus an actor in the deceptive "play" he has "authored."[18] Enough of their former relationship survives that Orestes asks the Paedagogus to correct him, should he "make any mistake" (31) while reciting his plan of deception.

Orestes details his visit to the Pythian oracle for advice.

> For when I came to the Pythian
> oracle, in order that I might learn by what way
> I might win justice upon [father's] murderers
> Phoebus declared to me that which you shall quickly
> learn; that I myself, unfurnished with either arms or army
> *by trickery shall steal off with my righteous slaughtering hand*
> [δόλοισι κλέψαι χειρὸς ἐνδίκου σφαγάς].
> Therefore, since [ὅτε] we have heard such an oracle,
> go in . . .
>
> (32–39)

The language used at this critical moment of exposition is notable for its indeterminacy. Orestes did not ask *what* he should do but *how* he should carry out vengeance on his mother and her lover.[19] As in *Philoctetes*, an important oracle is conveyed to the audience through a character's questionable reportage. In line 37, the oracle's directives to Orestes are charged with the powerful tensions of the entire play; the "trickery" (δόλοισι) and "slaughter" (σφαγάς) syntactically enframe the "just hands" (χειρὸς ἐνδίκου). A just slaughter is to be "stolen" by trickery. *Electra* brings us to a moral and aesthetic no-man's-land where what is just and righteous becomes absorbed into and indistinguishable from its opposite, just as the play itself confuses its own purported fact with fiction.

Orestes continues:

> Therefore, since we have heard such an oracle,
> go inside the house when the opportunity
> comes to you, learn all that's happening,
> so that you may report [ἀγγείλῃς] your findings clearly to us.
>
> (38–41)

The use of ἀγγείλῃς foreshadows the Paedagogus' role in the play as a false messenger or ἄγγελος. Its recurrence will be noted throughout the play. The old servant will carry out a mission of deception and reconnaissance. As Orestes explains, the Paedagogus will not be recognized in his former home due to the changes wrought by time on his features.

> For you will surely not be recognized due both to your age and the
>   long time [you've been away]
> nor will they suspect you with your gray hair [ἠνθισμένον].
>
> (42–43)

Ἠνθισμένον is a participle meaning to dye something so as to change its color. The lexicon cites this line and glosses the word "dyed gray by age as a *disguise*." "Time" itself, which Orestes sees as an accomplice in his mission, has performed the services of a costumer for the Paedagogus, *disguising* him to make the plot a success.

> Tell them a story [λόγῳ] like this, that you are a stranger
> come from the Phocian Phanoteus.
> He happens to be the greatest of their allies.
> And adding an oath, report [ἄγγελλε] that
> Orestes has died from an unavoidable accident
> at the Pythian games, having rolled from the
> whirling chariot. *Establish the story like this* [ὧδ' ὁ μῦθος ἑστάτω].
>
> (44–50)

Like an actor playing a messenger (ἄγγελος), the Paedagogus must establish his "playwright's" *mythos* by "announcing" (ἄγγελλε, 47) a fictitious story. As in *Ajax* (719), *Trachiniae* (180–81), and *Philoctetes* (568), words relating to the messenger figure in tragedy—such as ἄγγελος (messenger) or ἀγγέλειν (to announce)—are used to call attention to theatrical convention. At this moment both Sophocles and the avengers are establishing their *mythos*, which will impose a pattern on the events on stage. The Pythian games, held in Apollo's honor, recall the god's agency in Orestes' and Sophocles' plots. Orestes' fictional or metatragic death occurred while engaged in an *agon* (competition). The "real" Orestes is also engaged in an *agon* to reclaim his patrimony, and the actor portraying this "real" Orestes is himself part of an artistic *agon* performed in honor of Apollo's brother. With the Paedagogus inside the palace, Orestes will pay a visit to Agamemnon's tomb, decking it with "libations and delicate locks shorn from the head" (52). This sets up false expectations in the imagination of the attentive spectator, who will recall how similar tomb offerings served as the tokens of the recognition scene in Aeschylus' *Choephoroi*. At the point of highest tension in Sophocles' play, Chrysothemis' discovery of these tokens seems capable of pulling the course of the action into the Aeschylean pattern. Orestes continues:

εἶτ᾽ ἄψορρον ἥξομεν πάλιν,
τύπωμα χαλκόπλευρον ἠρμένοι χεροῖν,
ὃ καὶ σύ θάμνοις οἶσθά που κεκρυμμένον

(53–55)

Then shall we come back again, having furnished
our hands with a wrought thing with ribs of bronze,
which, as you know, is hidden somewhere in bushes.

Of all Sophocles' plays, *Electra* is the most barren of imagery. In this spare, cold work, the hypertrophy of τύπωμα χαλκόπλευρον (54), seems out of place, especially coming from Orestes, who is a self-styled man of action. His other poetic images are accordingly succinct and blunt, yet τύπωμα χαλκόπλευρον takes up half a verse line. Greek has simpler ways to describe an urn. Sophocles chooses words for Orestes that seem to touch lightly the edges of the object described without handling its body. It is a wrought or fashioned thing (τύπωμα), which suggests the notion of an urn without using the word. Χαλκόπλευρον indicates its sides (literally, its ribs) are made of bronze. This phrase appropriates the word πλευρόν, often used to describe the sides of living bodies. The listener may be reminded that the urn is an empty shell. Τύπωμα reminds us that the object comes from the world of artifice. It is a piece of handicraft resulting from an artisan's mold. It will be molded yet again through deceptive word and action into the prop Orestes desires.[20] This indeterminate shell, like an actor who has yet to don his mask and costume, will assume a character and "content" in the unfolding of Orestes' vengeance plot. Like an actor, or an actor's "shell" of mask and costume, the urn must perform an act of mimesis. It must convince its intended audience (Aegisthus and Clytemnestra) that it contains Orestes' ashes.

The reference to the bushes as a hiding place contains further ambiguities. Rather than retrieving from the bushes weapons for their hands or armor for their sides to carry out an assault upon the tyrants, Orestes and his cohorts are embarked on a strategy of deception and playacting. *Their* weapons are words and quasi-theatrical props. Bushes do not represent an obvious site for heroic men to carry out manly strategy. These bushes serve as a kind of skene, masking a prop from the eyes of its intended audience until the time is ripe. Bushes are fit receptacles for an antihero's "arms," be they Orestes' or Archilochus'.

The men seek to avenge Agamemnon's murder, a crime committed through deceit and subterfuge, creating a climate of inverted nature. When Agamemnon was invited to "the unspeakable feast" (203), when the tyrants "split his head with a deadly ax / like woodsmen to an oak" (98–99), the inner sanctum of the house became converted to its opposite. The play makes frequent references to the inside of the house as a battlefield. Even women have Ares, the war god, living within them (1243–44). The tyrants rule brutally, stifling the natural expression of dissent against their unnatural crimes.

To live in the *Electra* world, one must play a role. A person's exterior can never reflect the inner self. Deception and subterfuge are necessary for survival, creating the kind of "theatrical" environment that has surrounded ancient and modern tyrants. To survive in comfort, Chrysothemis (whose name means "golden norm") has learned to play the role of the obedient daughter. Clytemnestra herself is compelled to perform hollow theatrical acts such as preparing the offerings for the grave of the man she murdered. The *Electra* world is a classical equivalent of the topsy-turvy environment created by the regicides in *Macbeth* or *Hamlet*. While it lacks the exuberance of Shakespeare's imagery, it is a theatrical world where "nothing is but what is not," where what is καλόν is also κακόν.

Orestes plans to use falsehood (δόλος) to purge the corrupted court of Argos. He seems to take a strange satisfaction in his own fictitious death and using the urn to substantiate his fabrication.

> Cheating them in word [λόγῳ] we may bring them
> a sweet rumor, that my body is destroyed,
> burnt up already and reduced to cinders.
> For how does this trouble me, when in dying by word [λόγῳ],
> by deeds [ἔργοισι] I save myself and carry off fame?
> I suppose no word is bad if it carries advantage with it.
>
> (56–61)

Orestes' ruthless pursuit of advantage (κέρδει, 61) would have found a strong resonance among the theater audience during this late stage of the Peloponnesian War. One is reminded of the ruthlessness of the

Athenian negotiation in Thucydides' portrayal of the Melian debate.[21] In lines 59–60 Orestes neatly sets λόγος and ἔργα in opposition, recalling Woodard's analysis of the play's dialectical design. But what else may Orestes' death by λόγος suggest? May Orestes be sacrificing his *arete*, his spiritual excellence, by such a deception?[22] Orestes continues:

ἤδη γὰρ εἶδον πολλάκις καὶ τοὺς σοφοὺς
λόγῳ μάτην θνήσκοντας· εἶθ᾽ ὅταν δόμους
ἔλθωσιν αὖθις, ἐκτετίμηνται πλέον·
ὡς κἄμ᾽ ἐπαυχῶ τῆσδε τῆς φήμης ἄπο
δεδορκότ᾽ ἐχθροῖς ἄστρον ὡς λάμψειν ἔτι.

(62–66)

I have often seen before clever people [σοφοὺς]
who have falsely died in word. Then, when they come back
to their homes, they are honored even more from then on.
Even so I am confident that from this rumor
I'll live, shining like a star upon my enemies.

Here is surely one of the stranger aporia in ancient drama. Who are the wise or clever people (σοφοί) who have died bogus deaths in word (λόγος) and returned home to greater honor than ever before? Kells believes this is a lost "contemporary allusion." "One thinks perhaps of soldiers (for the play was written in the depth of a long war) who are reported missing, then enjoy the fuss when they come home safe and well."[23] This passage clearly contains a reference that lies provocatively outside the text of the play. The passage may have been inspired by some lines from the intrigue scene in Euripides' *Helen*.[24] In this most whimsical of Euripidean tragicomedies, Helen masterminds a plot to fool her Egyptian captors into thinking her husband Menelaus is dead. Helen and the living Menelaus will effect their escape while performing a sham memorial ceremony for the living man at sea. The passage in question runs as follows:

Ελ. βούλει λέγεσθαι μὴ θανὼν λόγῳ θανεῖν;
Μεν. κακὸς μὲν ὄρνις· εἰ δὲ κερδανῶ λέγων,
ἕτοιμός εἰμι μὴ θανὼν λόγῳ θανεῖν.

Helen: Though alive do you consent to be spoken of *in word* as dead?
Menelaus: *Unlucky* omen. But if words *will advantage me*,
I am willing, though not dead, to be dead *in word*.

Helen may be dated to 412 B.C., close to the time when Sophocles' *Electra* was probably composed. Whether or not the metatheatrical intrigue plotting in the Euripidean *Helen* influenced Sophocles is impossible to determine. The fact that such an influence is possible, linking Sophocles' *Electra* with a drama that so notoriously plays with the boundaries of truth and fiction, is very telling. For all the differences between late Sophocles and late Euripides, here is another point of contact where we are made to recognize that these playwrights breathed the same air.

These "wise fellows" who die fatuous deaths in *logoi* seem more suited to comedy. Orestes' *sophoi* make us think anachronistically of New Comedy and the "returning soldier" motif encountered in a play like Menander's *Aspis*. By virtue of its position in the text, Orestes' first speech is vital to the audience's understanding of the plot and tone of the play. Why would Sophocles insert such a passage which suggests either a comedic plotting device or an equally "unheroic" topical allusion? The passage calls attention to the act of dramatic plotting in a strangely self-conscious way. Sophocles hints either at the world outside of his drama or at the world of drama itself. This world of drama serves as a handy repository of ready-made plots capable of fleshing out a play as occasion demands.[25]

The star to which Orestes likens himself (66) is yet another example of the ambiguity residing in virtually every important scene and speech of this play. Seale describes the effect of this rather forced striving for a heroic metaphor, which helps to close the young prince's first speech. "The self image [of the star] corresponds with the bright promise of the new dawning day, but it is undermined by the cynical and deceptive means by which it is to be realized. The enterprise is already an enigma of fact and fiction, a dilemma of real and apparent light."[26]

As the men conclude the prologue, Electra's first lines are spoken offstage. The sound of the protagonist's voice before her entrance creates a powerful effect: ἰώ μοί μοι δύστηνος (Alas for me, wretched me, 77), she cries. The slaughter-rich house of the background has acquired a voice. Electra, who compares herself to a nightingale (147–49) and is compared to the "birds on high" (1058), is first heard in a cry that, in some respects, is birdlike in effect. The rapid, liquid repetition of vowels, especially the repetition of μοί, which is not needed for sense, may call to mind the repetitive patterns of bird cries. We may think of her clear voice being moved by the new dawn to join those of the birds surrounding the palace (and the theater itself).

Electra's cry from within the skene represents a dramaturgical surprise. Three figures have been carrying the play's action for seventy-six lines of text. The audience has heard from both the Paedagogus and Orestes, but Pylades has remained silent. As it turns out, Pylades is a silent role, a "silent mask" (κῶφον πρόσωπον) in Sophocles' play, though Aeschylus and Euripides use him as a speaking character in their versions of the story. An audience might naturally assume that all three actors are presently engaged onstage as the three men plot their intrigue in the orchestra. Electra's offstage cry at 77 startles the spectators. Sophocles has kept his third actor in reserve for this unexpected delayed entrance. Pylades is now clearly revealed as a nonspeaking supernumerary, and the confrontation between brother and sister, a famous scene in Aeschylus' *Choephoroi*, seems imminent and inevitable. Sophocles will surprise his audience again in the ensuing lines. Orestes asks if they should stay and greet Electra. His old tutor replies:

> Absolutely not [ἥκιστα]! Let's attempt nothing before performing the commands
> of Loxias and making a good start of this,
> pouring libations for your father. For this brings,
> I say, both victory and mastery in our doings.
>
> (82–85)

Orestes' hesitation teases the audience with the possibility that the recognition between brother and sister may be about to take place before the entry of the Chorus. The recognition scene in Aeschylus' *Choephoroi* took place soon after Orestes' arrival and Sophocles is making another intertextual reference to that earlier play. Fraenkel detects an almost playful theatrical self-referentiality in the Paedagogus' emphatic ἥκιστα (82). "It is as though Sophocles says 'I have not forgotten the *Choephoroi*, rather I am doing something different.'"[27]

Like a god in a Euripidean prologue, Orestes leaves the stage with his friends, refusing to interact with suffering humanity. The prologue scene between the three men establishes motifs that will reverberate throughout the ensuing action. When the Chorus reminds Electra of Orestes, "a youth hidden from sorrows" (κρυπτᾷ τ' ἀχέων ἐν ἥβᾳ /

ὄλβιος, 159–60), the use of κρυπτᾷ (hidden) recalls the hidden urn (κεκρυμμένον, 55), as well as Orestes, an internal dramatist, who is indeed hidden and isolated from the sorrow surrounding Electra. When Electra complains about Orestes' delay and all "the false messages" (ἀγγελίας ἀπατώμενον, 170) reporting his return, one thinks of the false message yet to be delivered by the false messenger (ἄγγελος). The duality of language established in the opening moments of the play keeps the listener alert to these resonances in the parodos. Orestes, in Electra's imagination, is not simply to arrive on the scene but to "appear" (φανῆναι, 172). Sophocles' choice of language will make Orestes' entrance with the urn into a true "appearance," a kind of epiphany.[28]

With the exit of the three men, the protagonist finally enters the theater. She too greets the light of day, creating a dramatic rhyme with the Paedagogus' speech about the birds and Orestes' image of himself as a bright star. She too acknowledges the fresh morning light, which envelops the characters in the play and the Theater of Dionysus itself. Electra has completed another "night-long festival of lamentation" (τά . . . παννυχίδων . . . στυγεραί, 92) for her father. The audience in the Theater of Dionysus witnessing *Electra* as part of a civic religious observance savors the irony of a kind of festival being made out of lamentation.[29] Electra's strategy is to adopt a stance of mourning and a self-conscious pattern of action. Electra's "festival of lamentation" counteracts Clytemnestra's marking the anniversary of Agamemnon's murder by "establishing choruses" (χοροὺς ἵστησι) and animal sacrifices (277–81). Both mother and daughter have established performative rituals memorializing the king's "death by trickery" (279); and these rituals within the play's narrative reflect back on the civic and performative rituals of tragedy with its choruses and sacrificial offerings. Clytemnestra and Aegisthus' crime has imposed a kind of theatrical role upon Electra, and she will play it to the hilt.

μὴ οὐ τεκνολέτειρ' ὥς τις ἀηδὼν
ἐπὶ κωκυτῷ τῶνδε πατρῴων
πρὸ θυρῶν ἠχὼ πᾶσι προφωνεῖν.

(107–9)

Not unlike some nightingale that has lost its child,
with wailing before my father's doors here
I'll not fail to utter voice publicly to all.

Later, in a lyric exchange with the Chorus, Electra equates herself and her behavior to that of a bird.

ἀλλ' ἐμέ γ' ἁ στονόεσσ' ἄραρεν φρένας,
ἁ "Ἰτυν, αἰὲν "Ἰτυν ὀλοφύρεται,
ὄρνις ἀτυζομένα, Διὸς ἄγγελος.

(147–49)

No, the sad, grieving, distraught bird fits
my mind, which "Itys," always "Itys" wails,
Zeus' messenger.

Electra is persistently linked with birds. The nightingale's repeating cry of "Itys" conjures images of Procne and eternal grief. It also suggests a verbal pattern repeated to the point where words lose their meaning and only empty sound remains. An empty pattern of sounds is appropriate for a protagonist who has herself been emptied of life by the unnatural political and domestic situation in which she finds herself. Electra's name, "unbedded" or "unmarried one," is a negation, a symbol of emptiness. Ironically, she has forced herself into an abnormal, seemingly inhuman behavioral pattern in order to better confront the "theatricalized" court of Aegisthus. There is within Electra's character an unusual awareness of both her own inner nature and the alleged discrepancy between that nature and the role she feels compelled to play.

Electra has self-consciously placed herself "before the doors" (the actor's actual position in the theater), and promises to utter voice publicly to all (πρὸ θυρῶν ἠχὼ πᾶσι προφωνεῖν, 109). These lines were intended for a skilled performer standing before the skene door of the Theater of Dionysus, speaking to an audience representing the entire Athenian polis, creating the kind of "double vision" so frequently found in English medieval and Renaissance drama. The audience is self-consciously made the witness of Electra's "performance" in language that hints at this overlapping of the performative phenomenon.

In her speech, Electra presumably addresses the audience. Tragedy frequently employs such a device to introduce a character and convey exposition. Euripides makes frequent use of such speeches at the beginnings of his plays; and Sophocles may well have been influenced by his younger rival in this instance, as in the opening speech of Deianeira in *Trachiniae*. Bruce Heiden writes of the Deianeira passage:

Such a gesture [as Deianeira's address] threatens the dramatic illusion, since the character seems to address the audience and not to inhabit the universe of the drama; but by thus breaching the screen that separates the character from the audience, it exposes not merely the dialogue between the actor and the audience in the theatre, that is, the immediately performative aspect of his language as it affects his listeners, but also the theatricality of the characters represented *within* the drama, *her* need for an audience and her speech as a theatrical simulation, a calculated illusion.

Heiden suggests that Deianeira is "her own audience" within the drama.[30] This metatheatrical idea has even more resonance when applied to the *Electra*. Heiden's idea suggests the next lines of inquiry, Electra's unique modes of rhetorical/dramatic self-representation in her confrontations with her sister, her mother, and the Chorus before the Paedagogus' reappearance.

Electra and the Eccyclema of Logos

During the parodos and first episode, the audience is made aware of Electra's rhetorical style, which reflects a striking new sense of theatricality in Sophoclean tragedy. Throughout the play, Electra exhibits a talent for "staging" the situation in which she finds herself. Her speeches describing the conflict with her mother and Aegisthus show an acute concern on the character's part for dramatic storytelling. Electra is keen to detail the "scenes" within the troubled household to which she is a witness.

> But just like some unworthy alien
> I serve in the halls of my father,
> in such shameful garb as this,
> and I stand before an empty table.
> (189–92)

Electra reveals a dramatist's eye for the communicative power of costume and setting. Many of her rhetorical flourishes offer her listeners a strong visual image akin to a dramatic tableau emerging from the eccyclema of the mind.[31] Details of setting and clothing vivify the images of her world for the audience. The rag-dressed princess, standing before an empty table, is a powerful image which, in effect, positions Electra on an imaginary stage. The "empty table" may be only a figure of speech, but the reference to "such shameful garb as this" clearly indicates the costume actually worn by the actor playing Electra. This has the effect of moving the "empty table" closer to actuality.

A little later, in referring to Aegisthus, she creates an image of the murdering usurper sitting on his victim's throne and dressed in the victim's actual clothing.

> . . . I see Aegistus sitting upon the throne
> of father, and I behold him wearing those clothes
> of [father's], and at the hearth
> pouring libations where he killed him.
>
> (267–70)

Electra goes on to offer another "revealed scene," placing the criminals within the victim's bed.

> I see the ultimate hubris of all,
> our family murderer in father's bed
> with my wretched mother . . .
>
> (271–73)

Leon Reissman portrays Electra's mission or function throughout the play as an attempt "to keep the horror [of the tyrants' injustice] alive, to hear the murdering ax still ringing against the oak boards, to give meaning to the passage of time" until Orestes can return.[32] The text affords many examples of her "staging" her enemies and their crimes, keeping Agamemnon's murder ever present in our consciousness through the recreative power of word and gesture.[33] This play of so many verbal tableaux will end with a ghastly and very "real" tableau of Clytemnestra's shrouded corpse exposed to the audience.

In addition to her more "directoral" or "dramaturgical" skills of staging "revealed" scenes through words, Electra also exhibits an unusually effective gift for mimicry. In reference to her mother, she says,

> For the woman noble [γενναία] in words [λόγοισι]
> loudly casts foul reproaches such as these:
> "You god-hated, awful thing: are you the only girl
> whose father has died? The only person mourning?
> May you have a bad end, and may the gods below
> never get rid of your present groans."

She insults me like this—except when she hears
from someone that Orestes has come. Then, frantic,
she comes to me crying: "Aren't you responsible for this?
Aren't you the one who did this, since you stole Orestes
from my hands, smuggling him away?
Be assured that you shall pay for this!"
So she howls, and near by her, egging her on in this,
her famous bridegroom is present . . .
                                    (287–300)

The tremendous rhetorical force of Electra's speech is immediately apparent. Karl Reinhardt has written of this rhetorical power as "an outpouring which invades and overwhelms the mind of the listeners."[34] It
is a new aspect of Sophocles' style, not found in the four surviving plays
(*Ajax*, *Antigone*, *Trachiniae*, and *Oedipus Tyrannus*) that precede *Electra* chronologically.

The language in *Electra* is "imitative," Reinhardt writes. In examining Electra's passionate descriptions of her situation to the Chorus in
the parodos and the first episode, Reinhardt observes: "So important is
it that the listeners should understand exactly how the speaker feels
that the language becomes imitative—in an unprecedented fashion;
not merely in the sense that every speech in a theatre is imitative, but
imitative in a way that stems from the inner movement of the words: to
make it known what she has suffered, Electra must start to imitate the
voice she hates (287ff.)."[35] In other words, Electra "stages" her mother
in speech for the benefit of both the Chorus and the theater audience.
Electra's habit of imitating the words of her opponents leads Clytemnestra to exclaim, "You shameless brat! Truly my words / and my deeds
make too much matter for you to talk about" (622–23). Clytemnestra is,
in effect, objecting to being turned into a quasi-theatrical figure by her
daughter's shrewd mimetic talents.[36]

As so often in this play, when a character is being disparaged, they
are accused of a kind of theatricality. Electra's speech at 287–300
portrays a Clytemnestra who is noble in words (λόγοι), but something
quite different in actions (ἔργα) and in private speech to her daughter.
Electra's exasperation with her brother is expressed by noting the disparity between his words of promise and the deeds yet undone (169–
72). Argos is a place where word and action are separate entities. Not

even Electra herself is immune to such an accusation, as will be seen later when she confronts Chrysothemis (328–31, 995–98). The distance between words and their referents is an obsessive motif throughout the play. This is only fitting in a tragedy that is so acutely aware of the art of tragedy.

Bruce Heiden writes: "One might conclude that the characters of Sophocles, not just apparent sophists like the Odysseus of *Philoctetes*, but all of them, have dramatic or rhetorical techniques of their own." Heiden suggests that the poet, in addition to creating characters who display rhetorical or dramatic self-consciousness, assumed that his audience would be capable of appreciating such nuances in performance.

> The rhetorically self-conscious spectator . . . suspends disbelief in the play's representation, but he also suspends belief: he simultaneously watches the author, the characters and the actors. And when, in watching the characters, he observes them making representations in *their* speeches and gestures, he similarly suspends both disbelief and belief, contemplating *what* the characters represent, the *effects* such representations may have on the characters portrayed in the play, and the material elements of the characters' representational performances. In short, he sees the represented world as a stage, the characters as players, the drama as an illusion of an illusion.[37]

Electra (and Orestes) have learned from the "theater" of court life in Mycenae. Several times throughout this play, Electra will acknowledge the baseness or unpleasantness of her own conduct, which she attributes to the necessity of meeting evil with evil. Electra tells the Chorus

ἐν δεινοῖς δεῖν' ἠναγκάσθην·
ἔξοιδ', οὐ λάθει μ' ὀργά.
ἀλλ' ἐν γὰρ δεινοῖς οὐ σχήσω
ταύτας ἄτας,
ὄφρα με βίος ἔχῃ.

(221–25)

Terrible things compel me to be terrible.
I know my temperament well, it hasn't escaped me.
But since terrible things surround me, I shall not

repress these ruinous ways,
so long as life is in me.

Electra sees herself as wrenched from her expected passive, feminine role by the outrageous conduct of the usurpers.

I am ashamed, o women, if I seem
to you to be grieving excessively with many laments.
But since violent compulsion forces me to do this,
forgive me.

(254–57)

A little later, Electra reiterates the idea expressed in 221–25 and 254–57.

ἀλλ' ἐν τοῖς κακοῖς
πολλή 'στ' ἀνάγκη κἀπιτηδεύειν κακά.

(308–9)

Among evils
it is necessary to make a practice of evils.

All of Sophocles' protagonists behave in a headstrong and self-righteous manner. Only Electra behaves in this way while at the same time apologizing for her actions as the reluctant yet necessary assumption of a kind of attitude. Her paradoxical stance of strength and apology is indicative of the separation of the inner nature of her character from the "role" she plays in the drama. "Acting" consequently becomes a major subject of the *Electra*.

The kind of alienation expressed by Electra has been elucidated by Judd D. Hubert in his definition of a play.

"Playing" makes its presence felt not only in "interplay," but also, by etymology (*ludere*, in "illusion" and "elusion"). . . . Elusion designates such negative or unraveling aspects of dramatic unfolding as a character's explicit or implicit reluctance to perform the part assigned by the author. Without elusion, *Hamlet, Prince of Denmark* might hardly have outlasted the first act; and Racine's *Phaedra* might never have reached the stage if we take into account Hippolyte's intent to leave Troezene and the name character's unwillingness to enter the scene. . . . The built-in tension between the author, who enforces casting, and his characters, who must willy-nilly accept his dictates, could scarcely go much further.[38]

Electra offers a fine example of a consummate playwright exploring the extremes of "elusion" and "illusion," to use Hubert's construct. In *Electra*, "illusion" becomes clearly personified in the metatheatrical elements of props, set speeches, and discovered scenes that serve to confuse the boundaries of "truth" and "illusion." Electra is not the only character to attempt to distance her "real" nature from the "role" she plays in society. Both Chrysothemis and Clytemnestra will protest that they are compelled to behave in ways contrary to their own better natures (332–34, 523–24). The play inhabits an environment where characters claim, with varying degrees of plausibility, not to be represented by what they do and say onstage, making the audience entertain images of characters who are doubly masked, from each other and even from themselves.

In addition to her concern for justice, Electra cites her social rank as a factor compelling her present behavior.

> For how could any well-born [εὐγενὴς] woman
> who has seen her father's sufferings not act like this.
> (257–58)

Electra's insistence on her social rank as setting the prerogatives for her and her mother's behavior (287) is very telling. Grote recounts the fact that, as the aristocratic class began to lose power during the late fifth century, its sense of identity was enhanced by a kind of "role playing." "The aristocratic classes reacted to their changing social and military realities by emphasizing the external trappings of their past greatness, and sought their exclusive culture in what may be called 'manners,' civilized charm and courtly grace."[39] Both class consciousness and ritual reveal a potential to distort human behavior into a "theatrical" or "performative" stance.

At one point Electra asks the Chorus to imagine the kind of day she passes within the house of her father's killers. Electra describes her mother laughing at her crimes.

> But as it is, she laughs at what she's done.
> Finding that day of the calendar when
> my father was killed by deceit [ἐκ δόλου],
> that day she establishes dances [χοροὺς] and offers sheep
> in monthly sacrifice to the savior gods.
> And I, miserable one, seeing it [ὁρῶσα], cry in the house;

I pine, and I lament
for the miserable feast named for father,
all by myself.

(277–85)

Electra's description of the perverted ritual is reinforced by the visual imagery (ὁρῶσα, I watching it). Her vivid language seems to create an almost cinematic effect as she directs the imagination of her listeners from the horrible ritual celebrating a murder to "reveal" Electra herself, the pitiful witness, *watching* it all as a helpless audience. Electra's vivid portrayal of Clytemnestra's perverted ritual, complete with "feasts" and "choruses," sends reverberations throughout the play itself, designed as it is to be a performative act at one of the most important of Athenian civic religious rituals. Electra and Clytemnestra have established "festivals" that offer differing interpretations of Agamemnon's death through the medium of word and gesture.[40]

Electra's chronic mourning is an outgrowth of the violence inflicted upon the normal cycles of death and mourning by the assassination of Agamemnon.[41] The perverse ritual observances of Agamemnon's death are reflected in the play itself, which becomes a kind of "perverted ritual." In *Electra* metatheater is created where drama becomes not a mimesis of an action but a mimesis of a mimesis. Agamemnon's death was brought about by deceit (ἐκ δόλου, 279), and this crime is enshrined in an unwholesome kind of ritual performance by his wife. Orestes will use deceit (δόλοισι, 37) to achieve vengeance, creating comparable scenes of cruel, perverted ritual in the mourning over an empty urn and the burial ritual that Orestes interrupts in order to slay his mother. The deceit or δόλος of the tyrants is to be pitted against that of Orestes. This "theatrical" δόλος comes near to destroying Electra as well as the traditional resolution of the story. In the end, the superior rhetorical/theatrical power wins; and its victory manifests itself in a deadly earnest "staging" of the defeated rival power when Clytemnestra's body is revealed to Aegisthus and the audience.

Chrysothemis and Clytemnestra

Electra's interactions with her sister and mother contain important similarities and need to be examined apart from the rest of the play. All three characters claim to be enacting roles they do not wish to play.

The parodos and the opening of the first episode have established the Chorus as Electra's confidante. The audience learns that Aegisthus' temporary absence has allowed Electra to escape from the house/ skene and permitted the Chorus to drop its submissive mask (310–15). The Chorus announces the arrival of Chrysothemis "carrying in her hands grave offerings from the house, / such offerings as are established for the dead" (326–27). The things Chrysothemis carries will be revealed as fitting offerings to emerge from such a house, representing as they do another hollow prop and theatrical gesture.

Chrysothemis' first words are to criticize Electra, and she does this by challenging her for the theatricality of her actions. Electra is uttering words "outside at the doorway" (πρὸς θυρῶνος ἐξόδοις, 328) "frivolously [literally, emptily] indulging an idle passion" (θυμῷ ματαίῳ . . . χαρίζεσθαι κενά, 331). Chrysothemis is just as aware of the present painful circumstances as her sister is, but she refuses "to seem [δοκεῖν] to do something and not do hurt" (336). Chrysothemis' taunt presents Electra herself as a being whose words are disconnected from any reality. Furthermore, Electra indulges in this empty rhetoric from her position at the door of the palace/skene, the gateway to the imaginary offstage world through which protagonists traditionally make their entrance. Aegisthus' threatened punishment promises to remove Electra from her theater: she will be taken from the skene door where she "laments" (γόων, 379) as a good tragic character should and be buried alive in a dungeon, away from the light of the sun (ἔνθα μή ποθ' ἡλίου / φέγγος, 380–81), the light the actors share with the audience.

In closing, Chrysothemis enunciates the trite maxim that "in all things the ones in power must be hearkened to" (340). The *peripateia* of this play will come when Electra appropriates this adage and, with self-conscious irony, turns it on its head (1464–65). Electra's response to her sister is almost predictable. She accuses Chrysothemis of being a theatrical character. Electra asserts that Chrysothemis has no will of her own, but is controlled by her mother, much as a dramatic character is controlled by a playwright.

ἅπαντα γάρ σοι τἀμὰ νουθετήματα
κείνης διδακτά, κοὐδὲν ἐκ σαυτῆς λέγεις.

(343–44)

For all the warnings given to me by you
were learned from her, and nothing you speak is from you.

Electra accuses her sister of having learned (διδακτά) her speech from their mother, a playwright-within-the-play, who instructs her "actor" Chrysothemis in all that she says. Electra rhetorically offers to replace Clytemnestra as Chrysothemis' "playwright." Electra even offers to learn speech from Chrysothemis herself if there is indeed any advantage to her giving up her present behavior. "Teach me then, or rather you learn from me / what advantage there would be for me if I gave up these lamentations" (ἐπεὶ δίδαξον, ἢ μάθ' ἐξ ἐμοῦ, τί μοι / κέρδος γένοιτ' ἄν τῶνδε ληξάσῃ γόων, 352–53). The metatheatrical word/deed dichotomy is thrown back at Chrysothemis who "hates in words, while in deeds [she] sides with her father's murderers" (ἡ μισοῦσα μισεῖς μὲν λόγῳ, / ἔργῳ δὲ τοῖς φονεῦσι τοῦ πατρὸς ξύνει, 357–58). Electra creates another of her brief verbal tableaux to combat her sister. "For you be laid the rich table and an abundant life" (361–62). The image of her sister before the groaning table contrasts with the bare table we have "seen" Electra stand beside (192). Electra's words may be empty of deeds but she has an infallible ability to "stage" her opponents in verbal pictures. Her speech reveals a theatricalizing power, which strongly compels her listeners to see the world through her eyes.

Chrysothemis has called Electra's speech the "empty [κενά] indulgence of an idle passion [θυμῷ ματαίῳ]" (331). Her words are "empty" in the sense that tragedy itself is empty, an enactment imitating reality. Electra, like tragedy itself, seems by mimetic words to *do* something, but in reality does no hurt at all. The play has a rhetorical obsession with the dichotomy of word and deed, appearance and reality, inner need and outer compulsion.

Chrysothemis reports the queen's nightmare vision (ὄψιν, 413) in visual language which, like Electra's "stagings" of her enemies, gives the listener indelible visual images. The description of Clytemnestra's dream has much the same effect as a dumb show "discovered" in the inner-below of a Shakespearean playhouse. The dream figures move from place to place and assume poses that have the abstract power of pantomime.

The story [λόγος] is that she saw herself together
with father, yours and mine I mean,
after he had returned to the light . . .

(417–19)

The imagery seems to place the resurrected man in the royal bedroom with his murderess. Then the scene shifts quickly with the newly arisen Agamemnon commandeering a "prop" and "setting" already filled with associations from Electra's previous "stagings."

> Then he took the scepter, the one that he himself
> once carried, but is now born by Aegisthus,
> and placed it at the hearth. And up from
> this grew a blooming young branch, by which all
> the land of Mycenae was overshadowed.
>
> (419–23)

Chrysothemis has heard the "story" from "one who was there" when Clytemnestra "revealed her dream to Helios" (424–25). As mentioned earlier, the detail of the queen declaring her dream to the sun unites the as yet unseen character of Clytemnestra with Electra and the men in the prologue who have all greeted the sun, that most prominent and brilliant feature of the open-air Mediterranean theater (17–19, 86–91).

Terrified by the dream, Clytemnestra has sent Chrysothemis to Agamemnon's tomb with offerings to appease his spirit. Electra's response is swift and pointed. These impious offerings should be either thrown to the winds or hidden (κρύψον, 436) in dust (κόνει, 435) where they will serve as burial offerings for Clytemnestra when she dies. The notion of hiding the rich offerings in the dust unites these highly ambiguous objects with the hidden urn of Orestes. Clytemnestra's grave offerings find a macabre dramatic rhyme with Orestes' empty urn (55). Both objects are "props" inside the fictive world of the tragedy. Within the play, the queen's offerings have a real form and tangible content. But for all their solid and costly materiality, they are spiritually empty. Conversely Orestes' urn is empty, but the deadly mimesis it helps to illustrate brings death to the king and queen. The urn is empty of ashes, yet full of destructive power. Clytemnestra's hypocritical grave offerings will only find spiritual meaning if they are saved to adorn her own grave. Paradoxically, Clytemnestra will be killed by her son while in the act of adorning his empty urn (1400–1401).

Electra demolishes Clytemnestra's conciliatory stance toward her victim with another of her visual stagings, this time of her father's murder.

Does it seems likely to you that the buried dead
will receive honors from her with friendly feelings;
she, who shamefully killed him like an enemy,
dismembering him, and for absolution wiped
the blood stains off on his beard.

(442–46)

In place of Clytemnestra's lustrous but empty offerings, Electra presents her own gifts to the grave. The lock of hair ("it's little but all I have,"
450–51) and the girdle ("unadorned with ornaments," 452) are poor but
heartfelt substitutes for Clytemnestra's insincere offerings. Electra's
offerings are "little" (σμικρὰ, 450) and "unadorned" (ἠσκημένον, 452),
qualities that set her apart from the rich and treacherous court—as well
as her brother's artful schemes. She will be deceived by the urn, which
is "falsely adorned by words" (λόγῳ . . . ἠσηκημένον, 1217). Electra's
offerings also recall the grave offerings that became recognition tokens
for Orestes and his sister in Aeschylus' *Choephoroi*. In Sophocles' play,
with Agamemnon's tomb located out of the audience's sight, these potential recognition tokens serve as self-conscious dramaturgical devices, building suspense for the inevitable recognition. Gellie wryly
comments that "Sophocles is preparing for his recognition scene with
something like the Aeschylean props."[42] In retelling a story that had already received so masterful and famous a treatment, Sophocles would
have been aware that his *Electra* would be read and seen against the
background of the earlier text. His version of the story points away from
itself toward other plays, deliberately toying with the devices of plotting
and tragic tradition.[43]

The story of Clytemnestra's dream emboldens the women of the
Chorus, who sing their first stasimon expressing hope that "a many-
footed, many-handed, / brazen-footed Erinys who hides / in terrible
ambush will come" (ἥξει καὶ πολύπους καὶ πολύχειρ ἁ / δεινοῖς
κρυπτομένα λόχοις / χαλκόπους Ἐρινύς, 487–91) and bring justice to
the Mycenaean court. Their language compels the audience to view
the human characters as agents of the Erinys' will, actors performing a
divinely sanctioned action. The "brazen foot" of the Erinys recalls the
brazen prop urn of Orestes (54). All brazen things are not on the side of
the avengers, however, as we learn that the double-edged ax that slew
Agamemnon was made of bronze as well (484–85). The brazen nature
of ax, urn, and Erinys' foot binds the Clytemnestrian and Orestian

parties together in a field of moral ambivalence. The stasimon's final strophe brings the story of Myrtilus into the mythic background. Myrtilus' "ancient horsemanship [ἱππεία], full of trouble for the house of Pelops" (504–5) prefigures the Paedagogus' "horsemanship" of *logoi* and suggests that Orestes' fictional horsemanship at Delphi represents but another stage of an ongoing curse, which has its roots in quasi-theatrical trickery.

Electra has already established the idea of Clytemnestra as the playwright and director of Chrysothemis' hollow actions and words. The entire play represents a metatheatrical conflict between the rivals for the Mycenaean throne and their various partisans. Both the Orestian and Clytemnestrian camps are masters at creating *logoi* and putting those *logoi* into the mouths of those who serve them. The metatheatrical ironies inherent in the conflict between rival internal dramatists insures that Clytemnestra's presumptive evil and Electra's presumptive virtue are presented in an ambiguous and troubling light.

Upon entering, Clytemnestra criticizes her daughter for being "an out-of-doors woman" (θυραίαν . . . οὖσαν, 518). One is reminded of the extreme constraint put upon upper-class women in fifth-century Athens, when such an epithet would be regarded as an insult.[44] But Clytemnestra's taunt to Electra that she is "out of doors" and consequently a "shame to [her] family" (518) also serves to attack Electra's very presence before the skene in the theater. Electra's physical position before the skene, declaring criticism of her mother both to the Chorus and the city of Argos/Athens, possesses the same tone of metatheatrical awareness noted earlier at lines 328 and 331. Clytemnestra's words allow for another perceptual "bleed through" between the Athenian audience and the equally silent "Other," the citizens of Argos.

There have already been many accusations of "theatrical" behavior laid against several characters in the play. Clytemnestra enters this discourse of theatrical hypocrisy with her self-defense before her daughter, the Chorus, and the audience in the theater.

ἐγὼ δ' ὕβριν μὲν οὐκ ἔχω, κακῶς δέ σε
λέγω κακῶς κλύουσα πρὸς σέθεν θαμά.

(523–24)

While I don't have hubris myself, I speak foully
because I hear plenty of foul things from you.

In other words, if she *seems* to possess the hubris of which she is accused, it is because of the bad *logoi* she speaks in response to Electra's bad *logoi*. The mother's claim is that her surroundings (in this case, Electra's constant baiting) compel her to use similar words, which create an unfavorable and false impression of her inner nature. In at least one point during the *Electra*, each of the three female characters pleads "I am not what I seem." Circumstances beyond their control compel them to project an unpleasant and unwanted persona. Clytemnestra's plea that she is not really what she seems binds her to her daughters by her use of a similar argument and hints at a "family resemblance" between the three women.

Clytemnestra rejects Electra's insistence on absolute right and wrong. Electra's stance is due not to a superior moral position but, in the queen's words, to a "differing opinion" (δίχα γνώμης, 547) of the same facts. The queen accuses Electra of rhetorical duplicity, of constantly using the murder of Agamemnon as a pretext (πρόσχημ᾽, 525) to criticize everything about Clytemnestra. This word, πρόσχημα, will surface again when the Paedagogus reenters, pretending to be a messenger from Phocis. By line 525 the word already carries suggestions of deception, of a separation of word from intention, which embodies the play's metatheatrical atmosphere.

Electra responds to Clytemnestra's attempt to make right and wrong a matter of *logoi* alone.

> You say you killed father.
> What word [λόγος] could be more shameful than this,
> whether you did it justly or not?
>
> (558–60)

Even if Agamemnon's motive in sacrificing Iphigenia had been base, as Clytemnestra has suggested, the king's murder was unjustified.

> If, however, for I'll give your argument too, [father]
> performed this [sacrifice] to help [Menelaus], did this
> mean he had to die at your hands? By what law?
> Watch that in establishing this law for people
> you aren't setting up pain and repentance for yourself.
> For if we are to kill in retribution, be assured, you
> would be the first to die, if you should meet with justice.
>
> (577–83)

It is symptomatic of this play's ambiguity that Electra's ringing condemnation of her mother will condemn the avengers of Agamemnon as well. In closing, Electra delivers yet another self-justifying attack on her mother. She reiterates the idea that if she is behaving badly it is due to the moral atmosphere surrounding her.

> Be well assured, I feel shame at these my deeds,
> even if I don't seem so to you. I know I do things
> that are unreasonable and unseemly for me.
> But it is your hostility and your deeds
> that compel me to do these things by grim necessity.
> *For evil deeds are taught by evil deeds* [αἰσχροῖς γὰρ αἰσχρὰ
> πράγματ' ἐκδιδάσκεται].
>
> (616–21)

Evil deeds externally shape Electra's behavior just as the playwright (*didaskalos*) creates the words and actions of his actors. If we believe Electra's version of the "truth" rather than her mother's, it is because of her vastly superior rhetorical skill. Like a well-graced actor, Electra charms her hearers with words and persuades them to her will. Clytemnestra is reduced to impotent name-calling. But Electra's eloquently articulated moral stance concerning her sister Iphigenia's death affords the attentive listener no finality. Her defense of her father's actions at Aulis is based solely on hearsay:

> Ask the hound-leading Artemis what transgression
> she punished by holding the ships without wind at Aulis.
> No, I'll tell you. For it's not lawful to learn directly from her.
> Once my father, so I hear [ὡς ἐγὼ κλύω], sporting himself in
> a grove of the goddess, roused by footfall from its lair
> a dappled, horned stag; he killed it and
> happened to let fall a boast about his catch.
> And enraged at this, Leto's daughter
> detained the Achaeans, so that father, in compensation for
> the animal, should sacrifice his own daughter.
> That's how she was sacrificed. For there was no
> other release for the army either to go home or to go to Ilium.
>
> (563–74)

This is the version of events which Electra chooses to believe and many critics and audience members are swept away with her strong talent for persuasion. The high moral ground she takes, however, is founded upon the shifting sands of hearsay: "so I hear" (ὡς ἐγὼ κλύω, 566).[45] In Sophocles' play, *logos* and appearance seem to carry more significance than truth, and truth itself seems virtually impossible to determine, as may be seen with the problem of what "really" happened at Aulis. Electra's attempt to engage in a rational debate with her mother flounders and, as Winnington-Ingram observes, by the end of her speech at 609: "we are back to the tone and circumstances of 516ff., and it is as though the whole intervening argument had never been. Sophocles was the supreme ironist, and perhaps we can now see that he was making ironical use of the form of a sophistic (or forensic) debate, the entire rational aspect of which turns out to be a sham."[46] Electra lives in a world of semiotic chaos where her aristocratic-moral compulsion to be noble (κάλος) makes her behave in a shameful (αἰσχρῶς) manner. This situation, where a word becomes or partakes of its opposite, where signifiers are hopelessly separated from the signified, calls to mind Thucydides' description of the perversion of language wrought by the Peloponnesian War.[47]

Electra's rhetorical powers are theatrical powers. At first Clytemnestra challenged her daughter's right to stand before the doors of the skene. After Electra's vigorous speechmaking, Clytemnestra is reduced to politely asking her daughter to be allowed to use the same stage.

> *Clytemnestra*: Won't you at least quiet your clamor and
>   allow me to sacrifice since I've allowed you to say everything?
> *Electra*: I allow you, I beseech you, sacrifice, and don't blame
>   my mouth for I shall speak no more.
>
> (630–33)

Electra is "allowing" her mother to pray on what has proved to be Electra's stage.[48] Clytemnestra asks Apollo to understand her hidden words (κεκρυμμένην ... βάξιν, 638). In the *Electra* world, hiding and concealment are as much a fact of life as they are in the world of theater. The concealed urn and concealing speech are about to work Clytemnestra's downfall. With Electra onstage, Clytemnestra may not unfold "everything to the light," lest Electra "with her malice and loud cry / sow a mad rumor through the town" (639–40, 641–42). Ironically, the "whole town" (πᾶσαν πόλιν, 642) *is* present in the form of the audience watching the play. Clytemnestra's self-consciousness makes her prayer as inhibited and cryptic as it would be if she were compelled to address Apollo in front of all her assembled subjects.

The audience is encouraged to listen to the queen with Electra's ears. A private message must be delivered in the most public environment possible. Electra's inhibiting presence theatricalizes Clytemnestra's prayer. The audience has been conditioned, by earlier remarks made by Electra, to stand for "the whole town" much as happens to spectators of medieval or English Renaissance drama. Electra has superimposed her stance within the world of the play upon her positioning in the theater itself (that is, she stands before the door talking to all). The audience feels itself made not only a surrogate for the citizens of Argos, but, for a brief moment, it shares an exciting parity with Apollo himself. At this moment, only the god and the audience may fully comprehend the situation. The wretched woman prays for succor from the very god who has orchestrated her impending destruction.[49]

Clytemnestra's "ambiguous dreams" (δισσῶν ὀνείρων, 645) have made her fear "lest someone hurl her by deceitful plots from [her] present riches" (μή με πλούτου τοῦ παρόντος εἴ τινες / δόλοισι βουλεύουσιν ἐκβαλεῖν, 648–49). This turn of phrase reenacts the first stasimon's description of Myrtilus' fall from "the golden chariot" (παγχρύσων δίφρων, 502–15). She twice uses the "Lycean" appellation of Apollo with its shifting, ambiguous suggestions of the god's nature, both "wolfish" and "wolf-killer." Seale writes that the prayer "produces the classic Sophoclean situation in which various levels of knowledge are brought into play. Electra is aware of the reasons for Clytemnestra's prayer; Clytemnestra does not know of her awareness; both are ignorant of Orestes' arrival. The situation of awareness is underlined by the visual language of Clytemnestra's prayer which suggests a dilemma of perception."[50] Clytemnestra is isolated from both the stage world around her and the audience watching her. There is no privacy in the *Electra* world. Even in prayer, Clytemnestra must "put on a show" and express her desires through subterfuge. The speech is an embodiment of a Sophoclean paradox—an aside that is not an aside. It partakes in the duality that surrounds the entire play.

Lying Words

The Paedagogus' entrance, disguised as a Phocian messenger bearing the tidings of Orestes' alleged death, stands at the apex of the *Electra*'s metatheatrical structure. That the playwright lavished over eighty lines on this section and assigned it to the exact center of the play suggests its importance in *Electra*. The whole play has proved itself to be obsessed with playacting. The house of Atreus is presented as a family decimated morally and spiritually by deception and violence. No character presents a real face to the world. Clytemnestra and her two daughters argue that their outward behavior constitutes an undesirable mask, which necessity forces them to wear. Consequently, they function like actors in a theater, performing words and actions that are imposed upon them. Aegisthus and his queen are on the verge of stopping one form of "performance"—Electra's constant mourning before the doors of the skene and beneath the brilliant sun (379–82). Behind the scenes, the family's male heir has been plotting a ruse involving playacting, scripted dialogue, and props. This quasi-theatrical presentation will lead Orestes closer to his goal but nearly rupture the traditional outcome of the myth and the bonds of the play that enframe it.

The false-messenger speech is a tragedy-within-a-tragedy. It represents a fictional story that effects an emotional response in its audience onstage and an ambiguous shift of perspective for the audience sitting in the theater. The speech constitutes the longest messenger report in Sophocles. Both Aeschylus' and Euripides' avengers use deception to assassinate the usurpers, but their use of subterfuge comes nowhere near equaling Sophocles' extraordinary elaboration. This rhetorical outpouring inhabits the central part of a play in which hollow speech and posturing have been a recurring motif. The Paedagogus' long speech will give significance to the empty urn within the sinister play he is staging with Orestes and Pylades. The speech and the urn, which will enter the action at 1098, serve as more than mere plotting devices in the play. They constitute a strange paradigm for the art of tragedy. Words, gestures, and an appropriate prop create a fictional story that threatens to destroy every character within the already doubly theatricalized court of Mycenae. The onstage audience members of Orestes' play-within-the-play react in ways analogous to an ideal audience in the theater: they are either filled with exaltation or emotionally devastated by what they see and hear. Clytemnestra believes that tragedy has befallen Orestes and feels enormous relief to be spared death at her child's hand. Electra, while undergoing shattering grief and pity for her dead brother, is stimulated by the illusion she has witnessed to emulate heroic behavior: she resolves to assume her fallen brother's role of avenger. The effect of the Paedagogus' speech on the theater audience is equally complex and ambiguous. The Paedagogus' imitation of a tragic messenger represents the most fully developed instance of the play-within-a-play in Greek tragedy, and its meta-theatrical resonance constitutes Sophocles' most personal contribution to his handling of the Orestes' myth.

Sophocles times the Paedagogus' entry with consummate mastery. Clytemnestra is completing her ironic prayer to Apollo, the god who the theater audience knows is working her downfall. Her prayer closes with a reference to the Lycean lord, "one of Zeus' children who can *see* all things" (τοὺς ἐκ Διὸς γὰρ εἰκός ἐστι πάνθ᾽ ὁρᾶν, 659). With the word ὁρᾶν (to see) as a cue, the disguised Paedagogus enters the scene to deliver his "news" for the audiences onstage and in the theater. Theater was, above all, a visual medium for the Greeks, as may be witnessed by their word θέατρον meaning "seeing place." Along with words (*logoi*) and actions (*erga*), the visual element was the most important aspect of drama; and the metatheatrical messenger's entrance and the closure of his speech will be italicized by words denoting "seeing" or "witnessing" (659, 761–64). These words of seeing, with their attendant notions of perception and knowledge, suggest that the play is entering a new and even more troubling area, where vision, gesture, and word are more ambiguous than ever.

The Paedagogus' role playing, despite its obvious fiction, allows for several moments when the theater audience appreciates an ironic reality to which the onstage audience, and perhaps even the Paedagogus himself, is oblivious. The old man announces that "I have come bearing you pleasurable / words [λόγους ἡδεῖς] from a man who is a friend [φίλου] to Aegisthus and you" (666–67). Of course, Clytemnestra will interpret the "friend" (φίλος) to be Phanoteus of Phocis; but the "pleasurable words" come directly from another kind of φίλος— Orestes, a blood relative of Aegisthus as well as Clytemnestra's son. The Paedagogus' words are ἡδεῖς (pleasurable) in several senses. They will (erroneously) free Clytemnestra from fear. They are also crafted so that, like all good tragic poetry, they create a pleasurable sensation on the theater audience, even though the beautiful words describe horrible situations, which most people would gladly avoid witnessing in real life.

The sinister irony lurking within φίλος (friend/relative) is carried further when the old man identifies himself as a messenger from Phan-

oteus. The Paedagogus' speech and bearing utterly convince Clytemnestra, who demands the old man give his report.

εἰπέ. παρὰ φίλου γὰρ ὢν
ἀνδρός, σάφ' οἶδα, προσφιλεῖς λέξεις λόγους.

(671–72)

Speak! For I clearly know you've come from a man
who is a friend [φίλου], and the words you speak will be friendly.

The Paedagogus announces that Orestes is dead. Electra exclaims in
shock: "Ah, wretched me! I am destroyed this day!" (οἲ 'γὼ τάλαιν',
ὄλωλα τῇδ' ἐν ἡμέρᾳ, 674). Both the Aeschylean and Euripidean
Electras are made privy to Orestes' plots from early in each play's
action; but Sophocles boldly delays her inclusion in the deceptive plot
until the last conceivable moment before Orestes begins the killings.
He manipulates the mythic events to place focus on Electra. By delay-
ing her discovery of Orestes' return and allowing her to be deceived
along with Clytemnestra, Sophocles not only heightens the pathos of
Electra's sufferings to a baroque extreme, but also begins to forge the
character into an unprecedented heroic pattern. The news of Orestes'
death will lead Electra to plan a suicidal attack upon the tyrants. The
false news of Orestes death does indeed "destroy" the traditional Electra character on this particular day (τῇδ' ἐν ἡμέρᾳ) in the Theater of
Dionysus. She is both destroyed and recreated, just as the tragic playwright attempts to replace, if only for a few hours of performance, the
memory of earlier presentations of a particular myth.

Clytemnestra is as shocked as her daughter to learn of her son's
death. The two women vie with each other in short, startled interjections (674, 675, 677, 678–79), allowing the theater audience to hear
and watch the Paedagogus' most important onstage audience members react to his news. The queen composes herself enough to demand
the truth (τἀληθὲς, 679). The old man replies: "I was sent for that very
end and I shall tell all" (680). This response teases with the bounds of
theatrical convention. Of course, we know the Paedagogus *has* been
sent by an internal dramatist, Orestes. But he has been sent to create a
deceitful theatrical illusion, not to relate the "truth." His line at 680
brings sharp focus upon his duty as a messenger and upon the convention of *all* messengers in Greek tragedy who are "sent" to bear their

"pleasurable words" and attendant fictive pain into the Theater of Dionysus.[51]

The story of Orestes' heroic death depicts the demise of a hero we never see, the doppelgänger to the clever, deceiving namesake we meet in the prologue. The narrative creates a colorful, heroic world for this fictional Orestes to strive and die in, as well as reflecting on the surrounding play's thematic concerns and creating an autonomous tragedy-within-a-tragedy. Orestes' metatragedy invades the reality of the *Electra* world and alters the course of the play that contains it, much as the strolling players, through their artifice, provide Hamlet with a new strategy and help bring Shakespeare's play to its climax. One scholar observes that the false story "makes Orestes, to each of the chief listeners, something more than he has ever been before. To Electra, he is no longer simply the child she saved, and the vague deliverer for whose coming she has hoped against despair. He is a splendid heir of a royal father, worth all the longing and the love, deserving none of the reproaches which his delay had suggested, a hero, hailed by all Greece as a hero, and then, in the moment when he adds glory to Agamemnon and to Argos, is suddenly dead."[52] In the Paedagogus' speech, Orestes is allowed to act out the heroic role he is unsuited for in real life.

The Paedagogus introduces the audiences onstage and in the theater to an Orestes who "came to Hellas' famous showpiece [πρόσχ-ημ'] of a contest [ἀγῶνος], the Delphian games" (681–82). The curious use of πρόσχημα hints both at the Paedagogus' and Sophocles' game. Πρόσχημα means something roughly equivalent to the modern concept of "showcase" or "showpiece"—something put forward as an eye-catching enticement—and this is how the Paedagogus intends the word to be interpreted by his onstage auditors. But the theater audience may recall its more pejorative sense. In this usage, πρόσχημα means a pretext or deception, a red herring used by a cunning orator to hoodwink an unwary listener. Clytemnestra has used the word in this sense against Electra, when at 525 she accused her daughter of using Agamemnon's murder as a πρόσχημα or "pretext" to abuse her mother. The theater audience is made aware that the Paedagogus' performance is itself a πρόσχημα, an elaborate "showpiece," which will serve as a "pretext" for allowing the old man's entrance into the palace and the avenger's infiltration of the enemy camp.[53] The old man's report serves as prologue to the true "contest" (ἀγών) between Orestes, Clytemnestra, and Aegisthus. Πρόσχημα hints at the artifice not only of the Paedagogus' metatragic speech but of the artifice of the "real" play that surrounds it, a competition piece enacted in another of Hellas' famous showplaces of prowess, the City Dionysia.[54]

Just as the real Orestes in the prologue desired to "shine upon [his] enemies like a star" (ἐχθροῖς ἄστρον ὡς λάμψειν, 66), so his fictional double is allowed to enter the first race at Delphi, "shining [λαμπρός], admired by everyone there" (685). The false Orestes, like the real one, longs for and, at least in fantasy, receives acclaim from his audiences. "He made the outcome of the [first] race equal with his nature [φύσει] / and carried away the all-honored prize of victory" (686–87). In the Paedagogus' scripted performance, the fictional Orestes is free of the spiritual malaise that plagues so many of the characters in *Electra*. His nature (φύσις) corresponds to the actions he performs, giving the audience the play's only instance of coherence between a character's inner self and outward nature. It is no small irony that this wholesome integration occurs within the Paedagogus' false-messenger speech, a fiction within the fiction of Sophocles' tragedy.

In telescoping the young man's Delphic triumphs, the Paedagogus remarks:

χὥπως μὲν ἐν παύροισι πολλά σοι λέγω,
οὐκ οἶδα τοιοῦδ᾽ ἀνδρὸς ἔργα καὶ κράτη.
(688–89)

To put much in little, I say to you I do not
know of a man of similar deeds and triumphs.

The idea of "putting much in little" recurs pointedly in future passages where the urn is mentioned as the supposed carrier of Orestes' ashes (757–58, 1113–14, 1130, 1198). The turn of phrase not only expresses the fictitious reduction of Orestes' large (μέγιστον) body to paltry (δειλαίας, 758) ashes, but also points to the tragic art itself where great things are distilled into small though powerful essences. The Paedagogus compresses events to tighten the narrative and further impress his hearers with Orestes' heroics. "But you may know one thing: he carried off all the prizes in every contest proclaimed by the judges, / and men called him fortunate" (690, 692–93). The young hero of Delphi was:

proclaimed an Argive,
his name, Orestes, son of Agamemnon who once
gathered the famous army of Hellas.
So much for that; for when a god
sets out to cause hurt not even a strong man can escape.

(693–97)

The proclamation of Orestes' paternity (694–95) recalls the stilted
heroics of the Paedagogus' first words at the start of the prologue. Now
Sophocles has given us a fictional Orestes truly worthy of the Paedagogus' florid rhetoric. The conventional remark about a god's implacable destructive impulse bringing down a strong man closely parodies
tragic gnomic utterance. The passage recalls Athena's similar moralizing during her play-within-a-play at the closure of the *Ajax* prologue
(*Ajax* 127–33).

The Paedagogus continues:

For on another day [γὰρ ἄλλης ἡμέρας] when at sunrise [ἦν
 ἡλίου]
there was the swift-footed competition [ἀγών] of the chariots,
he entered it along with many charioteers.

(698–700)

The sunrise signals the beginning of the final *agon* just as its progress
marks out the day of competition in the Theater of Dionysus. The old
man enunciates the ten rival charioteers, describing their places of origin. One of the phantom riders hails from Athens the "god built" (707).
The Athenian charioteer's behavior will be interesting to follow as the
race progresses. The mention of Athens would certainly have startled
and delighted the ancient audience, reminding them of their identity
as an Athenian audience in the great Athenian theater. A similar effect
occurs in *Ajax* when the title character and the Salaminian sailors
speak of Athens (*Ajax* 861, 1221–22), developing and deepening a bond
between that play's world and the festival where the play is performed.

The chariots take their places where the judges have assigned them
by lot (709–10), a detail recalling the adjudication process of the tragic
competition. The brazen trumpet (χαλκῆς . . . σάλπιγγος, 711) sounds
and the race begins. The detail of the brazen trumpet signaling the
start of the fatal race recalls the other brazen objects that adorn the
Electra world: the ax that slew Agamemnon, the fantastical feet of

the avenging Erinys, and the hidden urn. The imaginary trumpet call at Delphi that begins Orestes' ultimate *agon* serves to unite all of these metaphoric elements.

The Paedagogus had promised "pleasing words" and he does not disappoint.

οἱ δ' ἅμα
ἵπποις ὁμοκλήσαντες ἡνίας χεροῖν
ἔσεισαν· ἐν δὲ πᾶς ἐμεστώθη δρόμος
κτύπου κροτητῶν ἁρμάτων· κόνις δ' ἄνω
φορεῖθ'· ὁμοῦ δὲ πάντες ἀναμεμειγμένοι
φείδοντο κέντρων οὐδέν, ὡς ὑπερβάλοι
χνόας τις αὐτῶν καὶ φρυάγμαθ' ἱππικά.
ὁμοῦ γὰρ ἀμφὶ νῶτα καὶ τροχῶν βάσεις
ἤφριζον, εἰσέβαλλον ἱππικαὶ πνοαί.

(711–19)

And together they
shouted at their horses, shaking their reins in their
hands. And the whole racetrack was filled up
with the crash of rattling chariots. And the dust
flew up. And all close together,
they did not spare their goads, in order to overtake
the wheels and snorting horses of the others—
for about their backs and their wheels below,
the horses' breath touched them with its foam.

Lines 711–19 have great alliterative power and make the auditor visualize the contrapuntal activity of the race's outset with the visceral image of the horses' foam figuratively binding wheels and riders in the trajectory of its spray. This wealth of specific detail allows the audience to "see" the fictional event. The Paedagogus' speech thrills the listener with its vivid, "pleasurable words" and yet serves as a reflexive reminder of the artificiality of *all* dramatic performance.[55]

Orestes' fictional disaster comes during the last lap of the race. Before then, he had come close to grazing the turning post with his axle as he rounded the course. But Orestes masterfully steered his chariot away from disaster in the nick of time. As this doubly fictional *agon* is described, the theater audience realizes that Orestes is indeed at the turning post in his life's race to achieve his father's throne.[56] Any misjudgment now might lead to his undoing within the fictive *agon* of the speech and the real *agon* between the avengers and the usurpers. Just as the real world of the play features a house turned into a battlefield ("Ares" walks within the palace and inhabits women's bodies as well as men's, 1243–44, 1384–85), the normally benign space for sporting events has become a scene of untoward carnage where the "whole plane of Crisa / was filled with the wreckage of chariots" (729–30).

Seeing disaster swamping the majority of his rivals, "the clever one from Athens" (οὑξ Ἀθηνῶν δεινὸς, 731) pulls his chariot away from the course and pauses, avoiding the disaster. The Athenian driver proves a double or stand-in for the Athenian theater audience. Clever and resourceful, as the Athenians liked to view themselves, he pulls himself from danger. Sophocles places him on the imaginary scene to ensure the theater audience's engagement with the long narrative. He witnesses—for his countrymen in the Theater of Dionysus—the final moments of Orestes' life, survives the final contest, and presumably wins the race. All that is known of him is that he is δεινός, that richly ambivalent word denoting clever or precocious people as well as wonderful and sometimes terrible things. This shadowy Athenian's self-protective stratagems preserve him in a world that destroys old-fashioned heroes like the fictional Orestes. Ironically, the real Orestes is the true δεινός figure to reckon with. The unknown Athenian driver, in addition to being an audience projection, serves as a subtle doppelgänger for the real Orestes, the playwright-within-the-play who has scripted the Paedagogus' performance. The downfall of Orestes, the Delphian athlete, comes replete with the banal moralizing typical of many tragic messenger speeches and sanctimonious choral utterances. Orestes' prowess and "shining" good looks can not stave off disaster. He even possesses a spark of hubristic overconfidence before the final laps of the race (735). His overconfidence allows him to relax his rein, allowing his chariot to strike the turning post, resulting in the destruction of his car and his mutilation by his own horses' hooves.

And when the crowd [στρατὸς] saw his fall from
the chariot, it cried out in pity [ἀνωτότυξε] for the boy,
seeing what evils [κακά] had befallen such deeds [ἔργα].

(749–51)

The Delphian sporting audience reacts much like an Athenian tragic audience, crying out in pity at the disaster before them, stimulated to compassion by the painful irony of all tragic suffering, whether in the theater or in life: the discrepancy between human intentions and an unintended, miserable result.[57] The mangled Orestes is cut free from the reins, but "none of his friends / could recognize him by looking at his poor body" (μηδένα / γνῶναι φίλων ἰδόντ' ἂν ἄθλιον δέμας, 755–56). The Paedagogus' story has fulfilled Orestes' plans better than the plotters themselves could have imagined. Their metatheatrical trickery has indeed rendered Orestes unrecognizable so that none of his friends or family (μηδένα φίλων), in this case both Clytemnestra and Electra, may recognize him. Of all the characters at court, only Electra remains an unambiguous φίλος to Orestes, a family member but also a true loved one. The performative fiction is now already exceeding its bounds as Orestes' loyal sister is taken in by her brother's play-within-the-play. The Paedagogus' speech is a bold-faced lie, which has been expected for the better part of an hour's playing time. But like so much in the play, the lying speech is shrouded with ambiguity. There is metaphoric truth amid its well-orchestrated falsehoods. Orestes' mimetic death represents the spiritual demise the young man has already suffered in his ruthless pursuit of vengeance and the family fortune.

The Paedagogus describes the disposal of the hero's body, setting up expectation of the prop's entrance in the minds of the onstage audience.

καί νιν πυρᾷ κέαντες εὐθὺς ἐν βραχεῖ
χαλκῷ μέγιστον σῶμα δειλαίας σποδοῦ
φέρουσιν ἄνδρες Φωκέων τεταγμένοι,
ὅπως πατρῴας τύμβον ἐκλάχῃ χθονός.

(757–60)

And straightaway they burned him on a pyre and, in a little
bronze jar containing what was once the mightiest body, now
paltry ashes, they bear it, the Phocian men appointed to the job,
so that he might obtain a tomb in the land of his fathers.

The Paedagogus' words, like tragic art itself, distill the great "forms" of heroes into small space. The brazen nature of the urn is recalled, a bronze object working in unison with the brazen-footed Furies, seeking vengeance on the brazen-armed murderers of Agamemnon. The old man closes his performance with three lines that unleash a barrage of metatheatrical language.

τοιαῦτά σοι ταῦτ’ ἐστίν, ὡς μὲν ἐν λόγοις
ἀλγεινά, τοῖς δ’ ἰδοῦσιν, οἵπερ εἴδομεν,
μέγιστα πάντων ὧν ὄπωπ’ ἐγὼ κακῶν.

(761–63)

That is the way these things were, not only terrible
in *words*, but for those who *saw* them, as we *saw* them,
the worst of all evils which I have *witnessed*.

The lines insistently refer to language and sight, the building blocks of
tragic performance. The old man's story was terrible, not only "in
words" (ἐν λόγοις), but in its horrible visual aspects; and lest that visual
horror be ignored, he uses three visual words in as many lines (ἰδοῦσιν, εἴδομεν, ὄπωπ’). His *logoi* make Orestes' metatragic death tangible for both his on- and offstage audiences in the "Seeing Place"
(θέατρον) of Dionysus. These metatheatrical words denoting sight
and language help to ironize the preceding speech, bringing closure to
the old man's fiction and gently returning the theater audience to the
reality of the onstage action. The reiteration of words of sight remind
the theater audience that the events described were never actually
"seen" by the old man.[58] The stunned chorus responds:

φεῦ φεῦ· τὸ πᾶν δὴ δεσπόταισι τοῖς πάλαι
πρόρριζον, ὡς ἔοικεν, ἔφθαρται γένος.

(764–65)

Alas, alas! Then it is now all destroyed, so it seems,
root and branch, the race of ancient kings.

The conditional phrase, "so it seems" (ὡς ἔοικεν), would be out of
place in a normal scene of tragic mourning. Sophocles inserted this
delicate reminder of appearance and illusion to help further in re-
establishing the theater audience's ironic distance from the stirring
messenger speech they have just heard. Lines 764–65 recall that
Orestes' heroic death has only been an illusion of words and sight
created by the old man's performance.[59]

Lines 761–65, with their ironic insistence on vision-related words
and "seeming," indicate that Sophocles expects at least some of his
theater audience members to lose their ironic distance under the force
of the Paedagogus' acting. These lines redress any rupture in the
framework of the play proper. One critic of Sophocles has observed

that, "To the extent that a spectator compares his own knowledge with that of a dramatic character, he succumbs to the illusion that the character is a real person like himself. Thus the spectator partakes of the delusion represented on stage precisely when he perceives himself as most remote from it. This is irony indeed."[60]

Words and gestures have the power to deceive an audience that was thoroughly prepared to see through such artifice. With all the accusations and countercharges concerning playacting in this work, even the theater audience, which during Clytemnestra's prayer enjoyed a moment of omniscient perception, needs to recapture its ironic distance. We have seen the power of *logoi* used to manipulate reality. The false-messenger speech has created a displacement of normal audience perception, which is never fully stabilized as the avengers move closer to action.[61]

Undanceable Shames: Electra Rewrites Her Play

The sequence from line 764 to 1097 reveals Electra as a protagonist engaged in a remarkable reversal of strategy. The Paedagogus' meta-theatrical performance threatens to shatter Electra's traditional role, allowing her comparatively passive character to shift into a sphere of active heroism. This sequence climaxes with a stasimon by the Chorus, wherein the Mycenaean women praise Electra and remark on Orestes' supposed catastrophe. This sequence derives its effectiveness through its self-conscious toying with audience expectation, an expectation based on earlier versions of the Electra-Orestes story and the dramaturgical devices and strategies of Sophocles' earlier tragedies.

There have been four auditors to the Paedagogus' deceptive performance: the Chorus, Electra, Clytemnestra, and the theater audience. The theater audience eagerly examines the physical reactions of the onstage characters to the metadrama, and they wait impatiently for the characters' verbal responses. First the Chorus makes its tentative (ὡς ἔοικεν, 765) remarks. Its words ease the audience back into the "reality" of the situation onstage. Next comes Clytemnestra's outburst.

ὦ Ζεῦ, τί ταῦτα, πότερον εὐτυχῆ λέγω,
ἢ δεινὰ μέν, κέρδη δέ; λυπηρῶς δ' ἔχει,
εἰ τοῖς ἐμαυτῆς τὸν βίον σῴζω κακοῖς.
(766–68)

Oh Zeus, what shall I call this, either "fortunate,"
or "terrible, but advantageous"? Things are painful
if I save my life through my own misfortunes [literally, "my own
    evils"].

The "double perception" of the metatragedy finds an analogous doubleness in the response of the queen. Despite her mortal fear of her son, the power of *logoi* have had a wondrous though momentary effect on Clytemnestra. Her shock at Orestes' death, made real by the messenger's false words, causes her to drop her public stance and enter a process of self-reflection. The words she utters reverberate throughout the play. "Things are painful indeed when one must save one's life through one's own misfortunes." Her words could stand as a motto for the entire tragedy. They articulate a moral dilemma which would have been familiar to the audience in the latter years of the Peloponnesian War. Saving oneself through one's own misfortune suggests the cannibalistic condition of Greeks fighting Greeks.

The Paedagogus is surprised at Clytemnestra's reaction. "But why are you so disheartened, lady, at the news? [τῷ νῦν λόγῳ; literally, "at this present *logos*"] (769). Clytemnestra responds:

Motherhood is a strange thing [δεινόν]. Not even when one
has been wronged does one hate a child.

$$(770-71)$$

Δεινόν is a word suffused with Sophoclean ambiguity and double perception. The word has already been used to describe the Athenian competitor at Delphi, Orestes' shadowy rival (731). One thinks of the famous "Ode to Man" in *Antigone* where humanity is δεινός— something clever, wonderful, and horrible all in one. The Paedagogus' speech has exhibited a power analogous to that of tragedy itself. Clytemnestra has momentarily relinquished her aggressive, self-protective stance. She has been transformed, for a brief moment, by the pity and fear generated by the old man's speech. Tragedy reinforces the civic and humane values that allow people to live in communities. Like art in general, tragedy can bind human beings together with its sense of shared values and a deepened awareness of mortality and the vulnerability of the human condition. The Paedagogus' tragedy-within-a-tragedy serves to problematize the host play in several respects, not least of which is the brief moment of reflection it draws from Clytemnestra. The Paedagogus' "pleasing words" describing (fictitious) death induces introspection from the most unreflective of characters. Clytemnestra's reaction serves not only to reveal the unsuspected depths of her own character but as a convoluted reflection by Sophocles on the humanizing power of tragic performance.

The Paedagogus seems mildly surprised at the queen's words. "We have come in vain then, it seems" (μάτην ἄρ' ἡμεῖς, ὡς ἔοικεν, ἥκομεν, 772). His expression of surprise at Clytemnestra's unexpected outburst of maternal feelings, is couched in words suggestive of artifice and deception. Μάτην refers to that which is vain, false, or trivial. ἔοικεν, "it seems," recalls the Chorus's remarkable use of the same verb only seven lines earlier. Immediately, Clytemnestra snaps back into her former performative stance.

> Never in vain [μάτην]! For how could what you say be in vain
> [μάτην],
> if you have come bearing certain proof
> of the death of one, who was sprung from my life,
> but rejected my mothering and my nurture, becoming an exile?
>
> (773–77)

She resumes her verbal attack on her daughter, whose use of *logoi* makes her the "most painful thing" to her mother (784). Clytemnestra's only wish now is that the friendly old man could have stopped Electra from her loud cries (εἰ τήνδ' ἔπαυσας τῆς πολυγλώσσου βοῆς, 798), her endless repetition of wailing song. Ironically, the Paedagogus' performance *will* serve to move Electra from cries (βοῆς, 798) to contemplated action (συνδράσουσα, 1025) and ultimate complicity in the revenge plot.

"Can this be right?" (ἆρ' ἔχει καλῶς; 790), Electra asks rhetorically, referring to her mother's words of relief at Orestes' death.[62] "Not so for you," Clytemnestra responds, "but he [the dead Orestes] is right as he is" (κεῖνος δ' ὡς ἔχει καλῶς ἔχει, 791). Electra replies, "Listen, Nemesis of the man who just died!" (792). The theatrical situation that Sophocles has contrived will allow Orestes to serve as Nemesis. Clytemnestra remarks, "She [Nemesis] has heard what she ought to hear and she has ratified things well [καλῶς]" (793). Of course, things are καλῶς for Electra and Orestes and unfortunate for the exulting Clytemnestra. Orestes' metatragedy has increased the instability of *logoi*.

His mission accomplished, the old man feigns a willingness to retire.

"Should I leave then, if everything is well in order?" (799). The newly heartened queen takes command.

> Certainly not [ἥκιστ᾿]! For that would not be worthy
> treatment of the foreign friend [ξένου] who sent you.
> Rather come inside. And let her cry outdoors [ἔκτοθεν]
> over her and her friend's [φίλων] misfortunes.
>
> (800–803)

These four lines serve to move Clytemnestra and the Paedagogus into the skene. The lines also contain several layers of striking performative irony. Clytemnestra, mistaking the old man's acting for reality, confidently consigns Electra to her supposedly ineffectual quasi-theatrical state. Electra now has royal permission to remain outdoors, vainly weeping before the skene door. Of course, the metatragic fiction that makes Clytemnestra drop her guard will prove to have "destroyed" (673, 808) the Electra we know. Her cries are about to turn to cunning stratagems and anticipated violence. Clytemnestra is also misapprehending the nature of the ξένος who has sent the old man. The stranger/friend is not Phanoteus but her estranged son who fled from her as an exile (775–77). The ξένος who sent the Paedagogus is acting through the agency of Apollo, the god to whom Clytemnestra had been praying before the old man's entrance. This Apollonian connection points to a dramatic rhyme between this and an earlier passage in the play. As the three men stood furtively before the skene during the prologue, the offstage voice of Electra startled Orestes. The young man proposed that he and his companions investigate the sound. "Certainly not [ἥκιστα]!" the Paedagogus responded.

> Let us attempt nothing before performing the commands
> of Loxias and making a good start of this,
> pouring libations for your father. For this brings,
> I say, both victory and mastery in our doings [τῶν δρωμένων].
>
> (82–85)

By line 800, these "doings" are moving forward steadily. Lines 800–803 represent the subtlest of *peripateia*. The striking use of ἥκιστα, a strong word for a servant to use to his master, has already been noted in its earlier appearance in line 82. Now, at 800, the "Orestes" actor, in the guise of Orestes' maternal nemesis, delivers the word back to the Paedagogus. The peremptory word is again at the beginning of a four-line speech which ushers the same two actors offstage and begins the next phase of the revenge plot. The move of ἥκιστα from the Paedagogus to the deuteragonist, who plays both Orestes and Clytemnestra, marks the avengers' infiltration of the palace. The Paedagogus and Orestes' play-within-the-play allows Clytemnestra to believe she controls a situation that in fact controls her. The commanding tone of 82–85 was addressed to Orestes. Now that same "Orestes" actor, in the guise of Clytemnestra, delivers them back to the Paedagogus and, in so doing, seals Clytemnestra's doom. Lines 82–85 resonate in 800–803 in a way comparable with compositional technique in chamber music, where melodic or motivic material is passed from one instrument to another. The material gains structural or spiritual meaning from its architectural placement within a composition and from the contrasting sonorities of the different instruments employed.

Clytemnestra exits grandly into the palace with the false messenger while consigning her daughter to what she now believes to be an utterly fruitless ritual of lamentation outside (ἔκτοθεν) the skene. Clytemnestra believes Electra's moans have been rendered into hollow gestures, forever empty of any power to hurt her. Electra asks the Chorus and, by extension, the theater audience as well:

> Does it not seem to you that she was really suffering and
> feeling pain, poor wretch, weeping and lamenting terribly
> for the son who perished in this way?
> Rather she leapt with a laugh. Ah, wretched me!
>
> (804–7)

Electra criticizes her mother's performative behavior in response to the messenger's report. Rather than "acting" like a mother and visibly grieving for a lost son, Electra claims that her mother has perversely left the scene "with a laugh" (ἐγγελῶσα, 807). The audience's eyes and ears were witness to Clytemnestra's disturbed initial response (766–69, 770–72) to the false report. Her emotional reaction to the Paedagogus' speech seemed to have momentarily surprised even that ruthless and well-rehearsed old man (772). Clytemnestra has recovered her former hauteur but not before the lying *logoi* of the Paedagogus have allowed us to see the remaining glimmers of humanity within the woman.

The whole incident of Clytemnestra's response to the messenger's speech and her recovery reveals the discrepancies in the queen's inner life: what she projects outwardly, and what Electra in turn projects upon that. The audience at last has the opportunity to check one of Electra's "enactments" or "directoral interpretations" against its own sensibilities. A thoughtful member of the audience may well question the accuracy of all of Electra's verbal tableaux from here on.

Electra begins her lamentation for her brother. "Dearest Orestes, how you've destroyed me by dying!" (808). This line recalls Electra's first response to the news of Orestes' death at 674, "Ah wretched me, I am destroyed on this day!" These are both unexceptional figures of speech for a grieving character in tragedy, but the messenger speech puts these turns of phrase into a new perspective. Soon she will begin a plan of action and leave her passive stance. This potentially active Electra is a newly created character, contrasting with the Electra presented by Aeschylus' Oresteia. We have observed already how the "heroic" Orestes has died in the Paedagogus' speech. Perhaps Electra suffers a similar spiritual death the closer she comes to exacting vengeance on her mother. The metatragedy of Orestes fills a line like 808 with a double perspective.

The Chorus women begin their exchange with the protagonist in the ensuing kommos (823–70). They ask where are Zeus' thunderbolts or the rays of Helios "if beholding these things / they hide them unconcerned?" (824–25). Κρύπτουσιν (825), the verb of hiding, hints at the "burial" of Orestes.[63] But the notion of concealment expressed by adjectives derived from κρύπτειν (to hide) also calls to mind the "hidden" (κεκρυμμένον, 55) hand-crafted object that will soon make its appearance, as well as the world of metadramatic subterfuge, which Orestes and the Paedagogus have injected into the court of Mycenae. The theme of hiding is further developed by the Chorus's use of Amphiaraus as a paradigm for the story of Orestes' death. "He was buried" (κρυφθέντα, 838), the Chorus relates, "by reason of a woman's gold-entwined snare" (836–38). Again, suggestions of hiding and deception are reiterated by κρυφθέντα. One thinks of Orestes' false death, which results in a false burial in words, a burial that is a deception and concealment. The "woman's gold-entwined snare" may hint at Agamemnon's death in Clytemnestra's net, so memorably handled in Aeschylus' Agamemnon. This female snare also foreshadows the net of logoi that Electra will use to draw Aegisthus in for the kill later in the play (1440). Ideas of concealment and deception bear heavily on this kommos, gaining impetus from the deceptive tragedy-within-a-tragedy that the false Messenger has performed.

At this moment in the play, the audience may well expect the entrance of Orestes (with his prop urn) and the recognition scene between siblings, which is an integral part of the myth. Instead of Orestes, Chrysothemis reenters. The Paedagogus' elaborate speech has made this scene possible; and, like that previous elaboration, the sisters' present encounter hints of the unique tone and technique of the play. It is a scene where the perceptual schism of metatragedy creates a situation both of stirring heroism and troubling emptiness.

Chrysothemis excitedly tells her grieving sister:

πάρεστ' Ὀρέστης ἡμίν, ἴσθι τοῦτ ἐμοῦ
κλύουσ', ἐναργῶς, ὥσπερ εἰσορᾷς ἐμέ.

(877–78)

Orestes is with us, know this hearing it
from me, manifestly, just as you see me.

These lines contain a reiteration of words of seeing like ἐναργῶς and εἰσορᾷς, which intensify the themes of perception.[64]

Electra recoils at her sister's "false" hope.

Ηλ. οἴμοι τάλαινα· καὶ τίνος βροτῶν λόγον
τόνδ' εἰσακούσασ' ὧδε πιστεύεις ἄγαν;
Χρ. ἐγὼ μὲν ἐξ ἐμοῦ τε κοὐκ ἄλλου σαφῆ
σημεῖ' ἰδοῦσα τῷδε πιστεύω λόγῳ.

(883–86)

Electra: Ah, wretched me! And from whom have you heard this story [λόγον] you believe so overmuch?
Chrysothemis: I believe the story [λόγῳ] from my own account and not from someone else, having seen clear proofs.

As one critic observes: "Electra disillusions, or rather illusions" Chrysothemis about the offerings at the tomb.[65] Electra "pities" (ἐποικτίρω) her sister for her optimism (920). Under the spell cast by the Paedagogus, Electra feels the emotion appropriate for a theater audience when she watches her sister's apparent misapprehension of "reality." After convincing her sister that Orestes is dead, Electra proposes that they themselves carry out vengeance on the usurpers. Electra projects her vision of the future with all the extraordinary talent for scene building that has marked many of her earlier speeches. The two female characters (portrayed by male actors in female costumes and masks) will "in festivals and in any gathering of the city's people / be honored by all on account of their manlike actions [οὕνεκ᾿ ἀνδρείας χρεών]" (982–83). This passage is similar in effect to Cassius' lines in Shakespeare's theater when, kneeling over the fallen Caesar, he asks "How many ages hence / Shall this our lofty scene be acted over / In states unborn and accents yet unknown!"[66] In both the Shakespearean and Sophoclean theater the audience enjoys a double perspective; the past and present live within the same moment of self-conscious stage time.[67]

Electra's vision of their future glory is a fantasy so powerfully stated that Chrysothemis' vivid description of the evidence at the tomb is eclipsed. Electra's proposal of a last ditch, suicidal attack on the tyrants is a high point in the play. Sophocles' manipulations of the story have built toward this moment. For Whitman, Electra's new plan of desperate action represents her brightest moment of heroism.[68] One thinks of Patroclus' brief moment of glory and excellence before his death after donning the armor of Achilles.[69]

Whitman, among others, has noted the similarity between *Electra* and *Antigone* in that both plays feature female protagonists committed to a suicidal heroic posture.[70] Both Electra and Antigone are complemented by their more "normal" sisters, Ismene and Chrysothemis. Antigone's stance comes from her commitment to familial love: "It is not in my nature to join in hatred; rather to join in loving" (οὕτοι συνέχθειν, ἀλλὰ συμφιλεῖν ἔφυν, *Antigone* 523). Electra's heroic commitment is to familial hatred and murder. For all the horrors of the Mycenaean court under Aegisthus, nothing can give Electra's desire to kill her mother and her lover the positive moral force of Antigone's heroism. Antigone's heroism seems to rise naturally out of the story. Electra's character has had to undergo the virtuosic manipulations of a master dramatist in order to attain her highest expression of *arete* in her second encounter with Chrysothemis. Antigone dies for her defiant actions, setting a glorious seal to her character and moral integrity.

Electra does not die for her convictions, rather she stands ready to do so. For all the moving grandeur of her rhetoric, Electra's heroism remains in the optative. *If* Orestes had not returned, she *would* have struck out against the tyrants. In moving from *Antigone* to *Electra*, we leave a world of comparatively unambiguous "selfmanship" for a far less stable world where heroic affirmation dwells uneasily beside doubt and disillusion. Sophocles has built an entire play in order to create a heroic stance that we know from the outset is unnecessary. Again, Reinhardt's observations are insightful. The play presents

> the display of a suffering whose cause is wholly imaginary and un-founded, the violence of which greatly overshadows the true fear-someness of the revenge and the deed to be avenged. Thus this "tragedy" differs in two ways from the original form of the story: in taking lightly what should be taken seriously, and in taking seriously what should be taken lightly. It is similar to many of Shakespeare's late plays where the sense of the framework no longer coincides with the sense of the actual play.[71]

Electra's new heroic resolve to carry out vengeance is paradoxically affirming and negating at the same time. Her rhetoric is as stirring as that of other Sophoclean protagonists like Antigone, Ajax, or Oedipus. We may be sure that Electra believes the heroic words she utters. We may well be moved by such high-minded bloody-mindedness. The moment stands like a jewel in a dark and negating context that alien-ates her *arete* from its surroundings. Electra's new plan is of a piece with the empty urn, a rich gesture devoid of an organic context. It is an unnecessary stance. Orestes is waiting to carry out his vengeance while Electra's heroic posture proves itself a grand chimera. The elabo-rate messenger speech sets the stage for her active assumption of hero-ism. Her noble stance is sadly unnecessary in the "real" world of the play.[72]

As the sisters argue, the familiar paradoxes of seeming and being, of word and action, reemerge in their language. Chrysothemis accuses Electra of attempting to perform a role she is unsuited for by nature.

> Don't you see? You were born a woman and not a man
> and are less in strength of hand than your adversaries.
>
> (997–98)

Chrysothemis in effect rejects the dramatic scene her sister has pro-posed. Electra's "play" involving her sister will remain unperformed.

> Restrain your anger! And for your sake
> I will keep secret and undone what has been said.

And you learn the prudence, at long last,
being weak to yield to the stronger.

(1011–14)

Electra counters that she is not surprised at her sister's refusal and vows
to act alone. "For I shall not leave [the plan] empty [κενόν]" (1020).
Electra dismisses her sister, vowing never to call for her help again.
Chrysothemis' speech indicates to Electra that she will not "share in
the action" (συνδράσουσα, 1025). Electra has determined that it is
"very foolish to keep hunting after empty [κενά] things" (1054). The
word κενός (empty) has occurred twice in this scene. By using it,
Electra is rejecting her former stance of womanly inaction. She will
abandon her "empty" role of mourning to assume the active role of an
avenger. This promise of a new, active Electra proves in the end to be
even more "empty" than her previous stance when Orestes arrives,
empty urn in hand, to carry out the vengeance in the traditional way.[73]

The play has reached its highest point of crisis as the sisters angrily
accuse each other.

Electra: It is terrible when one who speaks well goes astray.
Chrysothemis: You describe your own fault perfectly.

(1039–40)

Word and action, inner and outer nature, seem as separate as ever.
When Chrysothemis exits, the Chorus sings an ode praising Electra's
heroism, comparing her filial duty to that of "the most prudent of birds
on high" (1058–59). Comparing Electra's behavior to that of birds may
not be an unambiguous rhetorical gesture. While embodying familial
relationships in an uncorrupted state of nature, the birds can also
allude to omen and prophecy. Perhaps birds lurk in the rafters of the
palace like waiting Furies. The birds are praised for nurturing their
parents (1058–62), but Electra, by avenging her father, is planning the
murder of her mother.

After extolling the heroine, the Chorus next turns its attention to the
"dead" Agamemnon and Orestes.

ὦ χθονία βροτοῖσι φάμα,
κατά μοι βόασον οἰκτρὰν
ὄπα τοῖς ἔνερθ᾿ Ἀτρείδαις,
ἀχόρευτα φέρουσ᾿ ὀνείδη·

(1066–69)

O divine voice speaking for mortals
in the underworld, I pray you cry down
the piteous word to the Atreidae there,
bearing the news of the shames not to be danced about.

Here is one of the most explicit metatheatrical references in Greek drama, which has gone surprisingly unnoticed in the secondary literature. The Chorus sings and dances about "shames" and misfortunes that it claims may not be sung or danced about. These misfortunes are ἀχόρευτα (undanceable) according to the Χορός, yet it is dancing (χορέσθαι) as it alludes to them. Ἀχόρευτα is an alpha-privative adjective derived from the verb χορεύω, meaning "to dance a round of a choral dance, or to take part in the chorus as a religious duty." Liddell and Scott attribute this meaning to Sophocles and give an additional Aristophanic usage of χορεύω, "to be one of the Chorus." Ἀχόρευτα could be crudely though accurately translated as referring to something "un-chorus-able."

These undanceable "shames" stem, of course, from the situation created by the Paedagogus' false speech, which has sent a still-living man into the realm of Hades, in the imagination of the Chorus and Electra, who believe there is no male left in the royal family to carry out retribution for Agamemnon's assassination and the usurpation of Aegisthus. An untenable situation has been created, seeming to demand an untenable remedy. With Orestes' return seemingly impossible, the action is veering off-course. Sophocles toys with the audience's perception of dramatic reality and its preconceptions of the Electra myth. As with the analogous choral passage in Oedipus Tyrannus (τί δεῖ με χορεύειν; "Why should I dance?," 896), Sophocles forces his audience to acknowledge the process of dramatic performance itself.

Ἀχόρευτα at Electra 1069 is even more significant when placed within the context of the play and analogous situations in earlier Sophoclean tragedies. Choral self-referentiality has already been explored in regard to Ajax, Trachiniae, Antigone, and Oedipus Tyrannus. In these earlier tragedies, the Chorus exhibits misplaced optimism, prematurely celebrating the good fortune of the respective protagonists. This plotting device of a "false reversal" is a discernible Sophoclean mannerism. The Salaminian sailors are gulled by Ajax' deception speech and ecstatically dance and sing while telling the theater audience that they are dancing and singing (Ajax 693–705). The Trachinian women prematurely celebrate Heracles' homecoming with self-conscious choric language (*Trachiniae* 216–21 and later at 640–43). The chorus of Theban elders in *Antigone* actually envisions Dionysus himself, the ultimate dance master of the universe, resolving Creon's dilemma as the king rushes to bury Polyneices and free his niece (*Antigone* 1146–52). The chorus members of *Oedipus Tyrannus* happily daydream about their king's mysterious paternity, just as Oedipus stands poised to learn the ultimate horrors about his past (*OT* 1086–1109).

All of these passages represent a dramaturgical feint, hinting toward a happy resolution shortly before destruction visits the protagonists. "False reversals" are intensely ironic, reminding the spectators that they have privileged knowledge, which separates them from the drama's onstage participants. These false reversals are all marked by metatheatrical or self-referential vocabulary: the choruses sing about singing, dancing, and various states of performative ecstasy, of leaping and crying, of Dionysian revelry. Sophocles consistently calls attention to overtly Dionysian behavior, reminding the audience that Bacchus is a god of reversals and duality, a divinity concerning himself with the schism between appearance and reality. The theater audience is reminded that it is watching a performance and that the disastrous outcome promised by the myth being enacted *will* occur, just as surely as the chorus members are performers performing before it. These false reversals are acutely self-conscious, underscoring the "unreal" nature of the choral celebration. Their performance-related words remind the audience that their celebrations are premature, are contrary to fact, are doubly theatrical. These false reversals, in their imitative behavior, are doubly unreal—both within the Theater of Dionysus and within the fictive worlds of their respective tragedies.

Turning back to *Electra* line 1069, we come to an analogous position within the latter play's structure. As in the earlier tragedies, the Chorus has come to believe a condition contrary to fact. But rather than feeling a false optimism, as in the earlier plays, the *Electra* Chorus has been deluded into feeling grief. *Electra* 1069 is a reversal of a false reversal. Rather than singing and dancing with self-referential language, as the earlier choruses have done, the *Electra* Chorus sings and dances with antichoric or antiperformative language. The (false) death of Orestes is "un-chorusable"—a statement made when the Chorus *is* functioning as a chorus. Of course, the situation is false: Orestes lives and will carry out the vengeance prescribed by tradition. The situation is, in fact, eminently danceable, as the Chorus's behavior in the orchestra bears out. Sophocles is turning dramatic convention on its head; and, by so doing, allows the audience to view the tragedy on several levels of perception at once.

The Mycenaean women of the *Electra* go on to compare the heroine to a specific bird, "the all-lamenting nightingale."

οὔτε τι τοῦ θανεῖν προμηθὴς
τό τε μὴ βλέπειν ἑτοίμα,
διδύμαν ἑλοῦσ' Ἐρινύν.

(1078–80)

Not at all cautious about her death
but ready to die, if she can
capture the double Furies.

To assert, as some critics do, that Sophocles has created a play without "the sign or hint of a Fury" is patently incorrect, as this passage shows.[74] Sophocles' language compels the audience to view his human characters as embodiments or enactments of the Furies, which are so intimately linked to the myth. The "double Fury" (διδύμαν Ἐρινύν) suggests both Aegisthus and Clytemnestra. Through the power of language, the two criminals have "become" the physically loathsome agents of retribution for the regicide. The idea of doubleness is also at home with the doubleness of perception in the theater experience, where one object or person stands in for another. The Chorus's words equate the "double Furies" with the Furies' victims.[75] By the same token, Electra, in killing the victims, attains a parity with the Furies. This epistemological confusion fits perfectly into the fabric of this play. Critical response to *Electra* is as divided as it is because the play itself creates such a distinct double image. The tragedy manages to be both a hymn to Electra's endurance and a grim exploration of the self-destructive hatred that negates her heroic qualities. The text seems to move and shift its meanings when seen from different vantage points. In this way, it resembles those children's toys that create completely different, often ironically contradictory images depending on the angle from which they are viewed. Paradoxically, the Furies of Electra are unseen yet omnipresent. They are referred to as "double" (διδύμαν, 1080). They personify the "two" plays that Sophocles has created in a single tragedy, the "double" tragedy of heroic affirmation and bitter negation. Sophocles never overplays his hand; his irony is seldom blatant. The delicate balance he creates between these "two" plays is what makes discussion of the tragedy so divisive. Sophocles has made his heroine's self-vindicating triumph seem both an exhilarating and a disturbingly provisional ending for the tragedy.

Small Dust in a Little Urn: Nothing into Nothing

Now follows Electra's encounter with the empty urn and her induction into Orestes' metatheatrical plot. The prince reenters the play at 1097, bearing the urn and accompanied by the mute Pylades. Like the Paedagogus, they are disguised as strangers from Phocis. The audience's knowledge of Orestes' deceit makes his highly conventional exchanges of information with the Chorus very pointed.

> *Orestes*: Ladies, have we heard correctly
>   and are we on the right path to where we need to go?
> *Chorus*: But what are you looking for? What brings you here?
> *Orestes*: I have been inquiring where Aegisthus makes his home.
> *Chorus*: You have arrived well and whoever told you cannot be
>   faulted.

(1098–1102)

Such generic lines could come from virtually any fifth-century tragedy. Their tone and content evoke the familiar pattern of a messenger's entrance. The placement of these lines, however, creates a situation akin to the Paedagogus' introduction to Clytemnestra (660–70). Orestes is acting as another pseudomessenger and is appropriating language and behavior for this role from the tragic tradition. To some degree *all* messenger scenes partake of this metatheatrical effect. The device of the messenger relies on a known and accepted convention, a kind of contract between audience, playwright, and actors. At the start of the play, the theater audience saw and heard the Paedagogus introducing the Mycenaean setting to Orestes. Now Orestes reenacts his earlier "role" as uninitiated visitor.[76] The audience's awareness of the metatheatrical role playing of Orestes and the Paedagogus makes these exchanges between Orestes and the Chorus doubly artificial.

Orestes unknowingly addresses his sister.

Go, lady, and having arrived inside the house reveal [δήλωσον]
that some men of Phocis are seeking Aegisthus.

(1106–7)

Electra becomes apprehensive that this strange man brings manifest
(ἐμφανῆ, 1109) proof of the rumor (τεκμήρια, 1109) she has heard.
Orestes responds:

I do not know about your tidings [κληδόν']. However old Strophius
has enjoined me to report [ἀγγεῖλαι] about Orestes.

(1110–11)

Words like δήλωσον and ἐμφανῆ with their connotations of revelation
and vision are theatrically charged. Ἀγγεῖλαι, from the verb ἀγγέλλω
meaning "to announce" or "to be a messenger," acquires a special
resonance, being used as it is by a character pretending to be a messenger or ἄγγελος. These subtle linguistic hints foreground Orestes'
role as pseudomessenger much as the Paedagogus' prefatory remarks
did for his metatragic enactment. The Paedagogus had claimed to be
a messenger from Phanoteus, a king sympathetic to Clytemnestra
(670). Phanoteus was a φίλος to Clytemnestra and undoubtedly his
name would help to put the queen at ease. Orestes now claims to be
carrying the urn from another Phocian, Strophius, a person sympathetic to Orestes' cause and a more suitable source for the urn and its
imaginary contents.[77] Both Phocian names derive from the mythic
tradition, but the metatheatrical context created here gives their names
added resonance. Phanoteus (Φανοτεύς) recalls words deriving from
the root φαν- denoting revelation and visual effect. Strophius
(Στροφίος) recalls words deriving from the root στροφ-, suggesting
turning, dodging, and trickery. Phanoteus, the "Revealer," was credited with sending the vivid story of Orestes' death. Strophius, the
"Changeable" or "Wily One," has allegedly told (εφεῖτ') Orestes, in his
role of Phocian emissary, to announce (ἀγγεῖλαι) the arrival of the urn
(1110–11).

OP. φέροντες αὐτοῦ σμικρὰ λείψαν' ἐν βραχεῖ
    τεύχει θανόντος, ὡς ὁρᾷς, κομίζομεν.
ΗΛ. οἲ 'γὼ τάλαινα, τοῦτ' ἐκεῖν', ἤδη σαφές·
    πρόχειρον ἄχθος, ὡς ἔοικε, δέρκομαι.

(1113–16)

Orestes: Carrying the scanty remains of the dead man in a
    small urn, we tend it as you see.
Electra: O wretched me, this is it, then clearly,
    I see the burden is near at hand, it seems.

Orestes' words suggest the sad dichotomy between the large, living body and its paltry remains compacted into a little urn. The compression of the body into the confines of the urn is all the more pointed by the fact that the audience views the living Orestes and the supposed receptacle of his ashes. From its earliest scenes, *Electra* has explored the various gradations of the artificial, of the empty (κενός) stance or gesture. We know the urn contains nothing, but it is about to become the focal point of Electra's "real" grief. Taplin writes, "In a society which is bound by roles and ceremonies, like that of the Greeks, symbols of status, gifts, keepsakes, heirlooms, works of art have an especially prominent place as miniature repositories of huge associations."[78] The urn compacts the fictitious corpse into a little room, much as the art of tragedy compacts into a small performable space the crises of existence.

Electra sees the empty vessel and, like a skilled actor, begins to fill it with meaning. She gives the empty container its weight or burden (ἄχθος). Her words underscore the motifs of perception. Electra's words "so it seems" (ὡς ἔοικε, 1116) would seem redundant and out of place in a "real" tragic situation. The phrase occurred before in the Chorus's two-line response to the Paedagogus' speech (764–65). Here as before, the use of words relating to sight or perception gently betray the lie of the metatheatrical situation. Rather than downplaying Orestes' ruse and focusing entirely on Electra's grief, Sophocles has drawn attention to the artifice lest the audience lose its awareness of the extraordinary illusion-within-an-illusion that has been created.

Electra asks to hold the urn and lament for her brother and lost family. Orestes, unaware of her identity, orders the prop handed to her. Electra, the arch mourner of Greek tragedy, now performs her most famous aria of grief. She laments the reduction of his "radiant" form to dust (1130).

σμικρὸς προσήκεις ὄγκος ἐν σμικρῷ κύτει.

(1142)

So you have come here, a little weight in a little urn.

The moment Electra had heard of Orestes' death she said that she had been destroyed (674). Now, as she cradles the urn, she reiterates this idea and the figure of speech seems all the closer to being realized. Recalling the child she rescued so many years before, she remarks that:

> All this has vanished in one day [ἐν ἡμέρᾳ μιᾷ]
> with your death. For everything has been taken away,
> as if by a storm, it's gone. Father's departed,
> I'm dead because of you. You are dead and gone.
>
> (1149–52)

This "one day" (1149) in the Theater of Dionysus has already proved full of reversals. Later she remarks:

> Alas for me, most terrible
> the path you have gone on, dearest; how you have destroyed me,
> truly destroyed me, o dearest brother!
>
> (1162–64)

Orestes' metatheatrical lie and its physical manifestation in the urn have destroyed not only the former, more passive Electra but, at least for the moment, the revenge play Electra had scripted for Chryso-themis a few minutes earlier. "Therefore receive me," Electra begs the urn, "into this house of yours, / nothing into nothing [τὴν μηδὲν ἐς τὸ μηδέν], so that I may / live forever with you down below" (1165–67). The object that contains nothing reduces Electra to nothing. Her heroic self-construct of 947–89 has vanished. For a moment the entire play grinds to a halt as the heroine contemplates annihilation, the urn as a symbol of "nothingness inside of nothingness," the prop that imi-tates a prop in the play-within-the-play.

Charles Segal observes:

> The urn . . . functions as a symbol of the deception of the theatrical situation per se. In this respect it is, like the severed head/mask of Pentheus in *The Bacchae*, metatragic, a symbol of tragedy calling attention to its own medium as a literary function and as a set of conventions of language, action, music, and dance. The urn em-bodies the paradoxical status of truth in a dramatic fiction. It is a work of elaborate artifice (cf. *typoma chalkopleuron*, 54) which gathers around itself the power of language to deceive or to establish

truth. It functions, then, as a symbol of the play itself, a work whose falsehood (fiction) embodies truth.[79]

During Electra's long lament, Sophocles presents the audience with a trio of "actors." First there is Electra, whose long life of incessant mourning represents a kind of living death, a mockery of life. She holds an empty urn, a "prop" in both the fictive world of the story and in the performing environment of the play. This funereal shell carries out the task of concealment and deception akin to the concealment of the tragic masks and costumes worn by the actors. The performers' costumes and masks serve as a kind of shell giving tragic significance to the actors contained in them. The urn has much the function of "a third actor" sharing the stage with Electra and Orestes.[80] The difference of course is that the urn consists solely of this shell signifying tragedy and death, while "Electra" and "Orestes" are living actors encased in the artificial covering of tragic performance. As an "empty" vessel, it also symbolizes the phenomenon of metaphor itself. It serves as a metaphor of metaphor.[81]

Sophocles has fashioned a richly molded thing that signifies death but in fact contains no real death. Such "deaths" as occur in tragedy are empty artifice; a messenger relates a story of death which took place offstage, or an actor "dies" within the shell of a mask and costume. In *Electra*, a false story of death is brought into the tragedy to reverse the pattern of tragedy. This false "tragedy" of Orestes' death enables the antagonists to be destroyed and the protagonists to live. One may well ask if Electra's life after helping to orchestrate her mother's death will be a life worth living.

Electra's display of sorrow over her brother's supposed remains has made this scene a favorite set piece for actors since antiquity. As was discussed earlier, the actor Polus' reliance on real ashes to stimulate his performance suggests a sensitivity to the paradox of the scene. Polus seems to have realized that the more genuine his grief appeared to his audience, the greater would be the metatheatrical effect of the scene. As Gellie notes, "In the *Electra* we are asked to listen to the accents of despair in the full knowledge that all is well. It is hard to keep our minds on the discipline of tragedy."[82] Sophocles conceived this scene and the whole play for an audience whose mental elasticity could appreciate his richly contrived metatheatrical perspective while "keeping its mind on the discipline of tragedy." Sophocles allows heartbreaking sentiment to coexist with powerful irony, creating a work of elaborate tonal complexity. This tonal complexity is so at odds with the conventional critical view of the stoic, even-tempered Sophocles that it often results in the play being considered a failure.

By the end of Electra's lament, Orestes is clearly shaken.

> *Orestes*: Alas, alas, what can I say? What words shall I use?
> I am speechless. I can't hold back my tongue.
> *Electra*: But what pain [ἄλγος] do you feel? Why did you say this?
>
> (1174–76)

At some point during Electra's lament, Orestes has realized who the woman is who clutches the urn. The discovery of Electra's identity has jarred him out of the set pattern of speeches he has devised to maintain his "character." "Unable to hold back [his] tongue" (1175), he can no longer maintain his role in the metatragedy of Orestes. His startling, uncontrolled words break through the metatheatrical illusion and lead to the recognition between brother and sister.[83] Orestes' words partake of a knowledge shared not with Electra or the Chorus but with the theater audience. His words seem directed out to the auditorium despite the fact that they are overheard by Electra.

The lines of stichomythia in the recognition scene allude to the dichotomy of inner and outer worlds, of being and performance. Orestes asks the rather labored question, "Is yours here the famous form of Electra?" (1177). "The famous form" (τὸ κλεινὸν εἶδος Ἠλέκτρας) recalls the deceptive shells of the urn, mask, and costume, which this play examines so intently.

> *Orestes*: It seems that I knew nothing of my own grief!
> *Electra*: How did you realize this by what has been said?
> *Orestes*: Seeing you in such obvious sufferings [ἄλγεσιν].
>
> (1185–87)

The outward shell of Electra now becomes the signifier of Orestes' own inner sufferings (ἄλγεσιν). Orestes has been jarred from his temporarily passive position as onstage audience by his sister's words. Like an ideal audience in the theater, Orestes is made to empathize with the "actor" performing before him, relating that "actor"'s (fictitious) experience and suffering to his own. Electra puts the blame for her misfortunes on their mother. "Mother she's called, but she doesn't act at all like a mother" (μήτηρ καλεῖται· μητρὶ δ' οὐδὲν ἐξισοῖ, 1194). Again the discrepancy between a person's "role" and their inner nature is manifested. Orestes asks Electra if there is anyone willing to be her advocate. She responds in a line that unconsciously hints at the fictitious presentation confronting her. "There is no one at all. For he who was my defender *you have placed before me as dust* [προὔθηκας σποδόν]" (1198).

Once he is assured of the Chorus's loyalty, Orestes begins to reveal his identity. He insists that Electra give back the urn before he reveals the truth.

> *Orestes*: Give up this urn now, so you may know everything.
> *Electra*: By the gods, please don't do this to me!
>
> (1205–6)

The recognition scene's formality depicts a move from artifice to reality, from the empty urn to the living presence of Orestes.

> *Orestes*: It is not seemly for you to address your speech to it.
> *Electra*: Am I so dishonored of the dead?
> *Orestes*: You are dishonored by no one. But this is not for you.
> *Electra*: Yes it is, if this is really Orestes' body I hold.
> *Orestes*: But it's not Orestes' body, except as it is adorned
>   by words alone [πλὴν λόγῳ γ' ἠσκημένον].
>
> (1213–17)

False words, like the hollow impressions on the urn's brazen sides (τύπωμα καλκόπλευρον, 54) have "decked out" the empty object with false significance.

Aeschylus' recognition tokens had consisted of a lock of hair, footprints, and a piece of clothing; Euripides' *Electra* utilized a childhood scar as the crucial sign uniting brother with sister.[84] Sophocles' playwright/actor-within-the play resorts to a very different prop to prove his identity.

> *Electra*: Then the man is alive?
> *Orestes*:   If there is life in me.
> *Electra*: Are you he?
> *Orestes*:   Look closely at this signet ring [σφραγῖδα]
>   of my father's; make sure if I speak clear.
>
> (1221–23)

The signet (σφραγίς) is an object used to seal letters, authenticating documents. It gives impressions upon malleable wax just as the hot bronze took the impression that molded it into the urn at the bronze worker's forge. The signet is the reason Orestes must make Electra give up the urn before he reveals his identity. The false, impressed object must be relinquished before she may take her real brother in her arms, the brother who is the source of the urn and the "ornamental" (ἠσκημένον) words that have given it such dreadful meaning. The urn has been "impressed" by the *logoi* of Orestes and his actor, the Paedagogus, and now, Electra must yield the urn to Orestes, the master artificer.[85]

> *Electra*: O dearest light!
> *Orestes*:　　　　　The dearest! I join you in witnessing it.
> *Electra*: O voice, have you arrived?
> *Orestes*:　　　　　Let the answer come from no one else.
> *Electra*: I have you in my arms?
> *Orestes*:　　　　　As you shall hold me always, forever.
>
> 　　　　　　　　　　　　　　　　(1224–26)

With the urn out of Electra's hands, she praises first "the dearest light" (ὦ φίλτατον φῶς, 1224), the sun whose beams unite players and spectators in the *theatron* or "seeing place." Orestes finishes her verse line by offering himself as a fellow witness to the "dearest light," continuing the mood of an almost ceremonial ecstasy (φίλτατον, συμμαρτυρῶ, 1224). "O voice, have you arrived?" (ὦ φθέγμ', ἀφίκου; 1225), Electra asks. Jebb calls ὦ φθέγμ' "a beautifully natural expression of her new joy in his living presence."[86] With all due respect to Jebb, it is the very *unnatural* quality of this line which strikes the reader. Certainly Electra is welcoming the sound of her lost brother's voice. Her line has a peculiar alienating effect, however, in the way it seems to divorce the voice from the body. Vision and voice, the principal elements of the theater, have been manipulated by Orestes' playacting to the point of fragmentation. Electra, still reeling from the perceptual chaos, calls on these two elements of theatrical perception in two fragmentary verse lines. Orestes steps in to complete her broken lines. A kind of order has been reestablished. Electra and the Chorus may now see through the metatheatrical illusion, while Aegisthus and Clytemnestra remain to be deceived and killed. Overjoyed, Electra turns to the Chorus and audience in the Theater of Dionysus.

ὦ φίλταται γυναῖκες, ὦ πολίτιδες,
ὁρᾶτ' Ὀρέστην τόνδε, μηχαναῖσι μὲν
θανόντα, νῦν δὲ μηχαναῖς σεσωμένον.

(1227–29)

O dearest ladies, citizens,
see Orestes here, dead by
machinations, but now, by machinations, saved.

The presence of the Chorus, the free women (πολίτιδες) of Mycenae,
allows Sophocles to bring the audience of the Athenian polis into the
stage action as witness to the ritual of reunion. Orestes died by machinations (literally, "machines" or "contrivances") and is saved by them
as well. Kells notes the repetition in lines 1228–29 and the shades
of meaning in the text. "Superficially, μηχαναῖς σεσωμένον means
that Orestes is back to Argos safely by stratagem. But the repetition
μηχαναῖσι . . . μηχαναῖς strikes that sinister note which appears at
intervals throughout the play." The word μηχανή, Kells points out, had
a "dubious moral significance."[87]

But along with the word's hint of skullduggery, μηχανή has an ines-
capable association for theater historians. The θεὸς ἀπὸ μηχανῆς, or
deus ex machina, was already proverbial from its employment in the
later plays of Euripides and others. Electra's word choice uses the
common meaning of μηχανή as a "stratagem," but in the metatheatrical environment Sophocles has created, it reminds the listener of a
prominent part of the ancient theater, the device for creating staged
epiphanies. Orestes' stratagems have been theatrical devices, and
Electra's language appropriates language of the theater to describe
them.[88] The lines 1228–29 also yield a metaphor for the experience of
tragedy itself, where one may die and experience rebirth via the miraculous devices of theater.

The ecstatic emotions stirred in Electra find release in song (1232–
87). To protect his plot from discovery, Orestes wants to impose a kind
of scripted behavior on the newly liberated Electra. Like a nervous
theater director instructing an actor, Orestes tells her "Don't desire to
speak at length when it is unseasonable" (1259).[89] The natural tide of
Electra's emotion must be harnessed into the pattern of Orestes' elaborate δόλος. He takes the upper hand when the dialogue resumes again.
Orestes admonishes Electra to "leave off superfluous words" (περ-
ισσεύοντα τῶν λόγων, 1288). After the elaborate syntax and lyric struc-

ture of the "song by the actors" (1232–87), the dramatist is acknowledging through one of his characters the heightened artificiality of the preceding section. Orestes begins to teach Electra to become a theatrical figure in his μηχανή of revenge. She must learn to live in the now (νῦν, 1293), not in the timeless stasis of grief to which she is accustomed.

Orestes instructs her not to waste time recounting the evils of Clytemnestra and Aegisthus but rather to tell him "where showing ourselves or hiding [ὅπου φανέντες ἢ κεκρυμμένοι] / we may put an end to our exulting enemies through the present enterprise" (1294–95). Revelation and hiding (φανέντες, κεκρυμμένοι, 1294) are primary devices used by all dramatists. Both Sophocles and his internal playwright Orestes are ready to use these stratagems to achieve their ultimate goals, the fulfillment (τελεωθέν, 1510) of the coup and of the tragedy that contains it.

> τούτῳ δ' ὅπως μήτηρ σε μὴ 'πιγνώσεται
> φαιδρῷ προσώπῳ νῷν ἐπελθόντοιν δόμους·
> ἀλλ' ὡς ἐπ' ἄτῃ τῇ μάτην λελεγμένῃ
> στέναξ'· ὅταν γὰρ εὐτυχήσωμεν, τότε
> χαίρειν παρέσται καὶ γελᾶν ἐλευθέρως.
>
> (1296–1300)

Behave so that mother doesn't detect
by reason of your beaming face, that we two have come
against the house. Rather make moan, as from the falsely
described disaster. For when we are successful, then
it will be possible to rejoice and smile in freedom.

Electra reassures her brother:

> . . . ἢν σὺ μὴ δείσῃς ποθ' ὡς
> γέλωτι τοὐμὸν φαιδρὸν ὄψεται κάρα.
> μῖσός τε γ ἀρ παλαιὸν ἐντέτηκέ μοι,
> κἀπεί σ' ἐσεῖδον, οὔ ποτ' ἐκλήξω χαρᾷ
> δακρυρροοῦσα. . .
>
> (1309–13)

Don't worry that
she will ever see my face beaming with a smile.
For an old hatred has melded into me,

and since I saw you, I shall never completely
cease from crying for joy.

This exchange has an intriguing metatheatrical element. Orestes
warns Electra not to let her bright face (προσώπῳ, which is also the
word for a theatrical mask) betray her joy to her mother.[90] Orestes is
teaching her to act. She must make of her πρόσωπον a πρόσωπον,
using the Paedagogus' false tragedy as an emotional spur for her performance. Sophocles is calling attention to the masking conventions of
his theater and the fact that the actor playing Electra will not be
changing his "facial expression" even after bad fortune has changed for
the better. Sophocles will use this convention to further explain the
paradoxes of Electra's inner and outer self. Electra tells Orestes that
her features are frozen, her outer appearance no longer corresponds to
what she is inside. Her mask is thus a "mask" in both the play's world
and the world of the audience. As with the urn, there is a conflict
between appearances (here, the costumed and masked figure of the
actor playing Electra) and what a character or object contains.

But while the signified seems to diverge from the signifier, they may
still be one and the same. Electra's hatred has "eaten [her] life away"
(1311) so that her facial expression may not be changed. This explains
the masking convention in a rationalistic manner of which Euripides
himself might have approved. It also suggests the troubling notion that
grief is the only emotion Electra is capable of feeling. The grave,
reserved tragic mask is both an inappropriate and a fitting reflection of
Electra's character, at the moment of her greatest triumph.[91]

From all available evidence, fifth-century tragic masks were re-
strained and chaste in their portrayal of facial expression. Exaggerated
grimaces and contortions of feature did not creep into mask design
until the Hellenistic era. Anyone who has witnessed actors working
with masks can attest to the illusion frequently created that a mask's
facial expression is somehow changing during the course of a performance. The actor's altering body language, the shifting effects of light
and shadow across a mask's features, coupled with the spectator's sympathetic imagination, all play a part in the phenomenon. The masks of
Sophocles' theater, like those still used in the Japanese Noh drama,
probably were designed with such expressive flexibility that the actors
wearing them could smoothly chart a course from happiness to despair
and back without anyone in the audience feeling a need for a change

of πρόσωπον. In this context, lines 1309–13 appear all the more self-conscious.[92] Electra has become the mask of the sorrow that her mother's crimes have impressed upon her features. Her torments have rendered joy indistinguishable from pain. Electra is trapped in a mask, like the corrupt regime she has opposed for so long.

Electra speaks repeatedly of Orestes' journey (ὁδός), referring not only to his return to his homeland but to his metaphysical journey from life to death and back again. It has been a journey from fiction to reality.

> For how could I stop [crying for joy],
> I who saw you on this one journey both dead
> and alive? You've done unfathomable things [ἄσκοπα] to me:
> so that if father should come alive to me, I'd no longer
> consider it a terrible sight but I should believe I saw him.
> Since you have arrived before me after such a journey,
> rule me yourself as your temperament will.
>
> (1313–19)

Orestes' μηχανή has brought her from extreme sorrow to extreme joy. His quasi-theatrical chicanery has stimulated the raw emotions of the tragic art. His fictitious "journey" from victory to defeat and back again describes the possible patterns of a tragic hero's journey. Aristotle's *Poetics* lists such reversals as the materials of tragic plotting. In *Electra*, the metatheatrical dimension has allowed for an unprecedented combination of story patterns. These extremes of experience have done "unfathomable things" (ἄσκοπα) to Electra and to the artifice of the play. Electra says she is now prepared to believe that the dead can walk again.[93] Orestes' guileful "art" has worked on her much as the tragic dramatist's skills work on a theater audience, rendering impossibilities possible. Where else but in the theater may we suspend disbelief and imagine that the dead walk before us?[94]

Electra closes her response to Orestes' admonitions with a glancing reference to her heroic resolution of the preceding episode.

> For left alone
> I would have achieved one of two things. Either I'd have
> nobly saved myself, or nobly perished.
>
> (1319–21)

This line serves as the epitaph for her heroic, suicidal plan to carry out revenge herself. It may be questioned whether Orestes or even Electra will be capable of unambiguously noble action in the final stages of the revenge plot. Since her outburst of glowing heroism was a product of metatheatrical illusion, one can wonder if such nobility can exist in the harsh reality of the play's final scenes.

Orestes warns her that someone is about to emerge from the doors of the palace. In an instant, Electra smoothly enters Orestes' world of deception. She even finishes her brother's verse line for him, much as Orestes had done for her before the full impact of his deception had worn off (1224–26).

> *Orestes*: Be quiet, I tell you. Since I hear someone within
>   about to come out.
> *Electra*:   Go in, strangers,
>   seeing that you are carrying such things as no one
>   would thrust away, nor rejoice in receiving.
>
> (1322–25)

A new tone of grim, savage irony has entered the play, which will intensify as the murders are committed under the deceptive blanket of props and role playing. Electra's alacrity in assimilating her brother's technique is startling in its suddenness.[95] The passage resembles the familiar dramaturgical device found in New Comedy in which entering characters complete offstage conversations with unseen partners or in which characters change the subject of conversation to protect or promote an intrigue.[96] The dramatic technique Sophocles displays here must have seemed quite new and especially gripping for its first audiences, considering how it prefigures aspects of a genre that would not flourish for another generation.

The Paedagogus enters from the palace, ordering brother and sister to silence and telling them "now is the time to act" (1368). Had the old servant not been guarding the door "you would have had our doings / in the house before your bodies" (ἦν ἂν ἡμῖν ἐν δόμοις / τὰ δρώμεν' ὑμῶν πρόσθεν ἢ τὰ σώματα, 1332–33). This line presents a figure of speech that touches on the play's fascination with dualities and the disconcerting separation of body and action, of inner and outer life. Orestes asks the old man if the false report has been believed by those inside the house. The Paedagogus responds cryptically: "Understand that here you are one of the men of Hades" (1342). The urn's symbolic power is transferred to Orestes. Orestes is in a strange "double focus," as living and dead, representing both son and murdered father. Line

1342 also suggests disaster. Though Orestes and his friends ostensibly triumph in this play, it is a Pyrrhic victory. However justified the vengeance may be, the victory of the play's last moments is brought about by a son murdering his mother. One may well conclude that Orestes "died" as a heroic figure with his fictional namesake in the Paedagogus' false report. Orestes asks his mentor how the news of his death has been received. The Paedagogus promises to tell all once the bloody task is completed. Suffice it to say, "as it is now, / everything is fine with them, even the things that aren't fine" (1344–45). As always in *Electra*, virtually everything comprises its opposite. The play gives expression to a frightening separation of representation and essence.

When the old man's identity is revealed to Electra, she greets the Paedagogus in quasi-religious language, echoing her earlier address to her brother.

> O dearest light [φῶς]! O sole savior of the house
> of Agamemnon, how did you come? . . .
> O dearest hands, with the sweetest service
> of feet, how could you be
> with me so long undetected?
>
> (1354–55, 1357–59)

There is a touch of the grotesque in Electra's rapturous greeting of the old man.[97] Her separate addresses to his hands and feet create a verbal separation between the man and his limbs similar to Electra's line addressed to Orestes' voice (1225). She goes on to reiterate the effect his powerful *logoi* have had on her.

> You destroyed me with
> words [λόγοις ἀπώλλυς], having in hand deeds [ἔργ'] that are
> sweetest to me.
> Greetings, father: for I think I see a father in you.
> Greetings. And know how I hated you the most
> and loved you the most of men both in one day.
>
> (1359–63)

The machinations of *logoi* have forced Electra to experience the wide range of tragic emotions from elation to desolation all within a "single day." As so often in this play, the cyclical passage of the sun above the theater is evoked as the demarcation of the tragic experience. Electra's reference to the Paedagogus as "Light" (φῶς) partakes of this phenomenon as well. The old man responds to Electra, reminding her of the "many circling nights and days to match / which shall reveal" all the details to Electra (1365–66). Sophocles encourages the audience to ponder the future of his characters in this play in a way unusual for fifth-century tragedy.

The Paedagogus' words compel Electra, Orestes, and the audience to imagine a future time after the murders have been committed. His words are not very different from Prospero's promise to recount all "the particular accidents gone by" for his island guests once they have retired within the Shakespearean playhouse. The promise to fill in the details at a "more convenient" time seems to belong more to the world of comedy than tragedy. In *Electra*, however, the imperative action that postpones such an accounting is not a marriage or celebratory dance but a matricide. What will be the nature of such an accounting, which lies outside the bounds of the play?

Sophocles is pushing further at the limits of tragedy, giving an open-ended quality to what is traditionally given reassuring closure. One may argue that matters lying outside the perimeters of the play itself are illegitimate critical game, indistinguishable from pondering the number of Lady Macbeth's offspring. Considering the enormous importance the Athenians gave to the myth of the fleeing, contaminated Orestes seeking justice on the Areopagus, it would be incredible for an ancient audience *not* to look beyond the bounds of the play. The spectators' attention would be all the keener to see how Sophocles would deal with this most famous part of the Orestes myth.

The long third episode closes with Electra's prayer to Lycean Apollo. This invocation reflects back to Clytemnestra's ironically futile prayers and to the double nature of the god himself—both wolflike and wolf-killing. This mixture of qualities marks a combination of the noble and the base, the illuminative and the destructive. Electra asks the god to "reveal [δεῖξον] to mankind what kind of wages / the gods give for ungodliness" (1382–83). In the approaching exodos, the god's answer will be at least partially revealed through the machinery of the theater.

The Unshakable Hounds

The closing scenes of *Electra* represent a last metatheatrical tour de force of language and stagecraft. As the men exit into the house to kill Clytemnestra, the Chorus sings its final ode describing "the unshakable hounds" (ἄφυκτοι κύνες, 1388) who enter the house tracking down villainy. After exiting into the skene with the men during the third stasimon, Electra reemerges to engage in a kommos with the Chorus. The Chorus becomes an extension of the theater audience in its breathless anticipation of the events behind the skene. This is the moment Electra has been waiting for, and she rises terrifyingly to the occasion. She commands the expectant Chorus to remain silent (ἀλλὰ σῖγα πρόσμενε) while the men accomplish the deed (τοὖργον) within the house (1398–99). The Chorus, like the theater audience, must remain silent so as to witness the action. Electra's call for silence demonstrates her intensified control of the stage action.[98] The Chorus ask for details of the situation inside. Electra replies "She's decking the urn / for the grave, and they are both standing near" (1400–1401). Electra gives the audience and Chorus her final verbal tableau. It serves as one last, "revealed" scene for the theater of the mind, wherein the urn has attained its ultimate goal. The unknowing victim is decking an empty urn, which could easily become her own tomb.

Now Clytemnestra screams from behind the skene "Ai, ai! Ah, house / barren [ἐρῆμοι] of friends, but full of murderers" (1404–5). Death is outside, not within the empty urn. Electra's response is chilling. "Someone is shouting inside, don't you hear, friends?" (1406). This exchange instigates a brief passage wherein Clytemnestra's offstage cries are responded to by Electra onstage, creating the macabre effect of question and answer between mother and daughter.

This "conversation" between Electra and her mother is all the more interesting for the fact that the roles of both Orestes and Clytemnestra would have been played by the same actor. With this detail in mind, the offstage cries of Clytemnestra and Electra's response to them gain an added strangeness. The voice so recently heard as Orestes resumes the role of Clytemnestra for these last, offstage lines. Each of Clytemnestra's three lines before she is wounded is greeted by Electra with a coy relish.

Clytemnestra: Ai, ai! Ah, house
        barren of friends, but full of murderers!
Electra: Someone is shouting inside, don't you hear, friends?
Chorus: I've heard an unbearable cry, wretched me, and so I shudder.
Clytemnestra: O wretched me! Aegisthus, where are you?

Electra: There! Yet again someone is crying.
Clytemnestra: O child, child!
            Pity the one who bore you!

                                             (1404–11)

Electra finishes Clytemnestra's verse line with blood-chilling effect:

But *he* was not pitied by *you*   ·
nor was the father that *begot* him!

                                             (1411–12)

The first blow is struck offstage.

    Clytemnestra: O, I have been struck [ὤμοι πέπληγμαι]!

                                             (1415)

Again Electra completes the verse line for her offstage mother: "Strike, if you have the strength, a second blow!" (1415). Again Clytemnestra cries out half a line of verse and again Electra seems to respond directly to the dying woman.

    Clytemnestra: Ah, again [ὤμοι μάλ᾽ αὖθις]!
    Electra: Would the cry were for Aegisthus as well!

                                             (1416)

Sophocles presents a frightening, almost surreal image. Electra, the onstage character through her voice and gestures, becomes a surrogate for her offstage brother. While obeying the apparent taboo against onstage violence, Sophocles has utilized dramatic convention to create a striking and novel effect. The exchange between Clytemnestra and her assailant becomes a conversation between mother and daughter. With mother and son played by the same actor, such a device not only sidesteps a technical problem but also makes very clear the importance of Electra's character in Sophocles' vision of the myth. Electra is seemingly carrying on a conversation with a character who in actuality cannot hear her. Electra's order that Orestes strike a second blow, if he has the strength, suggests Electra is empathizing so strongly with the act of murder that she almost believes herself to be striking the deadly blows. The actor playing Electra might well be performing a violent gesture to enact the offstage murder as a visual counterpoint to the sounds of the killing. In this way, the audience both "hears" and "sees" Electra killing her mother.

Asian theatrical conventions contain many examples of nonrealistic staging that, by their suggestiveness, can be more effective than the portrayal of graphic violence. The nonrealistic distancing or alienating effect of Electra's "conversation" with Clytemnestra and her gestures and movement while seeming to order her brother's blows presents the horrible killing in a kind of silhouette. One thinks of the chilling use made of silhouettes in 1940s film noir. Clytemnestra's death in Sophocles' *Electra* derives a similar impact from what is seen and not seen, heard and not heard. The murder becomes a frightening kind of "performance" by two actors, one seen and the other behind the skene.

Perhaps not even Euripides' *Hippolytus* presents a more disturbing view of the Greek family in ruins: a mother and son incapable of appearing onstage together and a matricide performed by the daughter in a macabre act of "remote control." Sophocles has converted physical and conventional necessity into powerful spiritual meaning. At last Electra enacts the kind of heroic action promised in her second scene with Chrysothemis. Electra's physical separation from the actual killing has the effect of making the attack seem all the more cruel and pitiless. Her gestures and words *seem* to kill her oppressor. But matricide is a dark heroic achievement and Electra's accomplishment is made paradoxically more horrible and more futile by the fact that she merely "seems" to kill her mother. Her direct agency in the death is an illusion created by her "performance" during the offstage killing. Her *arete* is manifested by a stirring but empty performance within the fictive world of the play.

Clytemnestra's offstage cries at 1415, ὤμοι πέπληγμαι, and 1416, ὤμοι μάλ' αὖθις, are markedly similar to Agamemnon's offstage shouts when he is stabbed in Aeschylus' *Agamemnon*, "Oh, I have been struck a deadly blow within!" (ὤμοι, πέπληγμαι καιρίαν πληγὴν ἔσω), and "Oh, yet again, I am struck a second time!" (ὤμοι μάλ' αὖθις, δευτέραν πεπληγμένος).[99] Whitman, who will admit "no hint of a Fury" into his view of the play, writes: "Orestes goes calmly into the palace, we hear some brief commotion, a cry for mercy, and then the two grim echoes of the dying words of Aeschylus' Agamemnon, which of course, bring the queen's original crime strongly to mind."[100] This passage in the Sophoclean play represents perhaps the only instance in surviving Greek tragedy where one dramatist quotes another play by another author and derives effect from the audience recognizing the source.

Whitman implies that a recollection of Clytemnestra's "crime" at this moment will serve to remind the audience of the necessity of her death. Undoubtedly the paraphrase of Aeschylus does recall that most famous of offstage cries. But rather than giving a sense of closure to Sophocles' play, such a reminiscence of Aeschylus, at this moment above all others, leaves the play more open and indeterminate. By recalling the *Oresteia* through the appropriation of key lines from the trilogy, Sophocles opens the possibility of further similarities between his play and Aeschylus' version of the myth.

After Clytemnestra's death, the exchanges between Electra and her allies are fraught with ambiguity. While the avengers and the Chorus all commend the matricide as necessary justice, there are strong hints in the opposite direction. Just as the offstage Orestes raises his arm to deal his mother the first blow, the Chorus declares:

> O city, o wretched family, now your
> day by day fate is dying, dying.
>
> (1413–14)

As the queen dies, it cries:

> The curses are finishing their job. They live,
>   the ones beneath the earth.
>
> (1417–18)

Both choral statements praise the killing and attempt to bring a kind of closure to the action. At the same time they leave open the possibility of the continuation of the cycle of violence. Lines 1417–18, in particular, with their mention of "the curses," hardly sound a reassuring note for anyone familiar with the myth. Orestes enters with his sword dripping with his mother's blood. Electra asks him how he fares. He answers, "Things are all right in the house, / if Apollo prophesied well" (ἐν δόμοισι μὲν / καλῶς, Ἀπόλλων εἰ καλῶς ἐθέσπισεν, 1424–25).

The construction with εἰ (if) is curious. If Sophocles wished to avoid any hint of criticism for the matricide, the delicate ambiguity of these lines, spoken amid a situation of the most appalling brutality, hardly serves his purpose. It is a line spoken at a decisive moment where *any* ambiguity affects the tone of the play. Perhaps the horror of killing his mother has made even this most unreflective of characters waver if only for a moment from his resolve. In wavering, Orestes admits further irony and contradiction into the furious momentum of the exodos.

Aegisthus' entrance will create more tensions between exterior and interior, between truth and falsehood. Aegisthus approaches "smiling" (γεγηθὼς, 1432) from his visit to the outskirts of the city. Just as Electra's mask gains significance by its stagnant form, Aegisthus' smiling mask acquires more sinister meaning as the action progresses. He is joyful to hear about Orestes' undoing and eager to see any tokens of his death. Electra of the eternal frown (1309–13) greets Aegisthus of the eternal specious grin.

As he approaches, Electra takes charge of the situation once more, ordering the "boys" (παῖδες, 1430) backstage like an efficient stage manager.[101] The Chorus is almost equally helpful to the young murderers: "Make for the vestibule, as quick as you can" (1433).[102] These lines enable Orestes and Pylades to prepare the "discovered scene" with Clytemnestra's corpse. They next advise Electra.

> It would be expedient to speak
> a few deceitfully kind words [παῦρά . . . ἠπίως ἐννέπειν]
> in his ear so that this man may rush
> eagerly toward
> the contest [ἀγῶνα] with justice.
>
> (1437–41)

"False words" will play their part in a final, deadly metatheatrical presentation, the last "contest" between Orestes and his opponent. Aegisthus enters and asks about the "strangers from Phocis" who have "announced [ἀγγεῖλαι] to us that Orestes / lost his life in the wreckage of his chariot" (1443–44). The use of ἀγγεῖλαι hints back to the Paedagogus, the false messenger (ἄγγελος). Nine lines later Aegisthus uses the verb again. "Did they actually report [ἤγγειλαν] him dead for sure?" (1452). The repetition not only suggests the character's eager expectation but strengthens the irony and self-consciousness of the poet's choice of verb. Sophocles' play owes much of its peculiar character to the employment of a false ἄγγελος. The repeated use of a verb derived from ἄγγελος recalls the messenger and his dramatic function in tragedy. It constitutes yet another instance of Sophocles using language in the metatheatrical manner of Shakespeare.

Aegisthus expresses an eagerness to be "instructed" (δίδασκε, 1450) and "to learn by revelation" (κἀμφανῆ μαθεῖν, 1454), language that hints at the didactic elements of tragedy presided over by Sophocles, the master *didaskalos*. Orestes' metatragic death and resurrection allow Electra to respond to Aegisthus with an ironic "double speak." The Chorus and audience can enjoy the irony of the "strangers" (ξένοι) who are simultaneously destructive outsiders and family members. Electra tells Aegisthus that the truth of their report has "been revealed, and not by word alone" (κἀπέδειξαν, οὐ λόγῳ μόνον, 1453) touching again upon word and revelation, the theatrical elements that can simultaneously conceal and expose truth. The "strangers," Electra informs Aegisthus, "have finished with their dear [φίλης] hostess" inside the house (1451). She warns him that the "sight" that he clamors to see is a "most unenviable one" (μάλ' ἄζηλος θέα, 1455). Aegisthus is unexpectedly pleased (χαίρειν) with what Electra says (εἶπας, 1457). The language and situation recall the paradox of tragic speech that had been hinted at earlier in the play (666–67); pleasing words describing horrible sights and experiences. In the mistaken belief that he is the master of Mycenae and the stage space before him, Aegisthus calls imperiously to his subjects:

> I command that the gates be opened and that
> all the Mycenaeans and Argives be shown the sight [ὁρᾶν],
> so if any of them are puffed up with empty
> hopes [ἐλπίσιν κεναῖς] for this man, now seeing [ὁρῶν] his corpse,
> they may accept my bridle.
>
> (1458–62)

Ostensibly speaking to the Chorus and Electra, Aegisthus' lines seem really to be directed to the theater audience. The spectators in the theater have been made into a character by the stage tyrant who views them as the oppressed citizens of Mycenae/Argos. The audience may well feel a double identity. Athens the democracy is here staging its opposite, an autocratic polis. It is a stunning moment of unity between stage and audience space. The "truth" of Aegisthus' situation is about to be revealed through the machinations of theater and illusion. It is Aegisthus' position that will soon prove "empty" (κένα). Aegisthus thinks that he has control of the stage space and can order what the audience-within-the-play and in the theater may be "shown." Instead, Orestes and his allies will prove the real showmen, the potent, internal dramatists who will bring an end to Aegisthus.

Electra now utters her last incitements to lure Aegisthus into her brother's trap. Her lines are a sophistic blend of the patently false and the deeply true.

καὶ δὴ τελεῖται τἀπ᾽ ἐμοῦ· τῷ γὰρ χρόνῳ
νοῦν ἔσχον, ὥστε συμφέρειν τοῖς κρείσσοσιν.

(1464–65)

My part is being accomplished already. For in time
I have won common sense, so as to obey the stronger.

Electra is ostensibly responding to Aegisthus' order that the gates be opened. This she tells us is being accomplished (τελεῖται) either by herself or by supernumeraries acting at her bequest. Naturally Aegisthus is deaf to the subtleties of this remark. While seeming to obey the tyrant, she is indeed accomplishing or finalizing her task of avenging her father. Her actions are also bringing the play to its end or τέλος. Within minutes the play will come to its precipitous conclusion with a word derived from τέλος, τελεωθέν (1510). The word acknowledges the very point arrived at in the drama.

Aegisthus' confidence is increased by Electra's avowal to have learned the lesson of submission to the stronger. This is, after all, the motto Chrysothemis tried so hard to instill within her sister. The Chorus and audience appreciate a rich mine of irony. By mouthing this sophistic adage Electra reminds us how far her nature is from such moral relativism. On another level, however, Electra has become something like the thing she opposes. The human symbol of eternal constancy (Electra) becomes the mouthpiece for sophistic duplicity.[103] She has learned to kill by stealth, as her mother and Aegisthus did.

Electra has learned the art of lying. Her "double speak" is sophistic *dissoi logoi* or "double words." It is interesting to compare this passage with Ajax' speech on mutability wherein he seems to accept change while in fact planning his suicide as a means of rejecting change (*Ajax* 646–92). At moments like these, theater becomes a kind of sophistic rite with doubleness at its root. Like the words under examination, theater is a manifest lie that paradoxically contains a grain of truth. The sense of doubleness has haunted *Electra* from the outset and now, in the closing moments of the play, the root of the doubleness is found to lie within the heroine herself. By upholding justice, she aids in the atrocity of matricide. By confronting the evils that surround her, she becomes like those evils. This heroic paradox of good and evil is analogous to the experience of theater, which presents untruths that may either help the audience gain a clearer perception of truth or corrupt both the audience and actors with its mimesis of shameful (αἰσχρός) behavior. Sophocles has created a dark critique of his art in this late play, which has far more in common with Plato's thoughts on the dangers of tragedy in the tenth book of the *Republic* than with Aristotle's formulas of hamartia and the median hero.

The doors of the skene are opened for the revelation of what one critic has called "the most glorious moment of pure theatre in all Greek tragedy."[104] The eccyclema wheels the very real tableau into view. Here at last is a real "discovered" scene in contrast to Electra's verbal tableaux. Aegisthus sees a vision that promises the fulfillment of his dearest hopes. A shrouded corpse is revealed surrounded by two men the king does not recognize. He mistakes the content of this "vision" or "apparition" (φάσμ', 1466) much as Electra and Clytemnestra mistook the content of the urn. This final display fills Aegisthus with a sense of awe.

> O Zeus, I behold an apparition [φάσμα] which did not befall
> without the malice of heaven. But if there is bad luck
> in saying so, I unsay it. Uncover the [corpse's] eyes [ὀφθαλμῶν]
> so that I may also mourn for my relative.
>
> (1466–69)

This scene of revelation and Aegisthus' words hint at "the things seen," the final stage of initiation in an ancient cult like the Eleusinian Mysteries. Clytemnestra's body is shrouded in such a way as to cover the features of her face/mask. Of course it is Aegisthus' "eyes" that are about to be truly uncovered when the cloth is removed from the face of the corpse. Since the same actor who played Clytemnestra played Orestes as well, the "corpse" is either a mute extra lying in the queen's mask and costume or a dummy wearing these accoutrements. Like the urn, the body is an empty shell.

The real corpse has replaced the empty urn as a prop in this final metatheatrical presentation to ensnare Aegisthus. Just as the Paedagogus utilizes the convention of the messenger speech, so too the convention of the "discovered" scene revealed from the eccyclema presents a false image, an illusion of sorts, both in the fictive world of the play and in the Theater of Dionysus. The concealment of the corpse's face and the stances of the unknown men lead the king to assume he is viewing the body of his mortal enemy, Orestes. Aeschylus' *Agamemnon* affords the most famous example of the device of "discovery" via the skene doors and the eccyclema. In that play, the visual revelation unambiguously discloses the death of Agamemnon and

Cassandra. It is typical of Sophocles' play that the skene opens at a similarly climactic moment to reveal what is (for Aegisthus at least) yet another illusion to be penetrated.

Aegisthus is advised to lift the shroud himself. He uncovers Clytemnestra's body.

> *Aegisthus*: Ah, what do I see [λεύσσω]?
> *Orestes*:   What frightens you? Do you recognize
>   [ἀγνοεῖς] someone?
>
> (1475)

Orestes, now firmly in control of the situation, finishes Aegisthus' line for him. Just as Aegisthus reiterates the visual aspect of the theatrical experience, Orestes' conclusion directly signals the moment of recognition or *anagnorisis*.

> *Aegisthus*: Who can be the men in the midst of whose toils
>   I have fallen, wretch that I am?
> *Orestes*:   Haven't you perceived
>   that you've long been addressing the living as though they were
>   dead?
> *Aegisthus*: Ah, I understand the riddle. This can be
>   none other than Orestes who speaks to me.
>
> (1476–80)

"Addressing the living as though they were dead" is reminiscent of the perversions of Creon in *Antigone* and the vindictive Atreidae in *Ajax*. In *Electra* this confusion of life and death is but one symptom of Aegisthus and Clytemnestra's usurpation and ultimately the curse on the House of Atreus. It is a world where the civilized norms of familial behavior have been destroyed, along with the boundaries between fact and fiction. It makes the noble indistinguishable from the shameful, and the killings during the exodos appear only to intensify these confusions and imbalances.

Confronted with Orestes, Aegisthus attempts to reason with his enemy but is cut off by Electra.

> Don't let him talk [λέγειν] further,
> by the gods, brother, nor prolong his words.
> For when mortals are immersed in troubles [κακοῖς]
> what benefit can he who is about to die win from time?

Rather kill him as quickly as you can, and having killed him,
throw him out to such gravediggers as are fitting he should
meet with, out of our sight. For only this could
recompense me for the evils of the past.

(1483–90)

By endeavoring to silence Aegisthus, Electra aims to destroy him both
as a human being and as a dramatic character. Electra is referring
directly to Aegisthus with "he who is about to die," but her language
suggests both the condition of the condemned villain and the pre-
carious position of the avengers.[105]

Some translators remove Sophocles' deliberate ambiguity by making "gravediggers" refer directly to "dogs." Sophocles only suggests the
exposure of Aegisthus' corpse. The Greek line maintains an elegant
indeterminacy. The lines warn of a savagery in Electra as bestial as that
of her oppressors. Like malleable bronze, her personality has taken the
impression of the harsh world that surrounds her. Her sufferings and
hatred have brought her to inverted feelings about life and death. She
has told her brother that if she saw her dead father alive and walking
she would believe it (1316–17). Now she appears to order that Aegisthus' corpse should be "punished" by exposure, much as Polyneices'
body was "punished" by Creon in *Antigone*. Electra proves herself as
guilty as Aegisthus of "addressing the living as though they were dead"
and vice versa.

Orestes commands his victim:

χωροῖς ἂν εἴσω σὺν τάχει· λόγων γὰρ οὐ
νῦν ἐστιν ἀγών, ἀλλὰ σῆς ψυχῆς πέρι.

(1491–92)

Go inside as quickly as possible. For it's no struggle
of words now, but of your life.

Indeed the contest of words (λόγων ἀγών, 1491–92) is over, to be
replaced by the "contest" between an unarmed victim and his armed
enemy, the "contest [ἀγῶνα] of justice" (1441).

Aegisthus attempts to disrupt Orestes' tidy stage-managing of the
deadly situation.

Aegisthus: Why lead me into the house? If the deed is
noble, why isn't your hand ready? What need for the dark?

Orestes: Don't you give the orders! March to where you
    killed my father, so you may die in the same place.

(1493–96)

On one level Aegisthus' objection is an understandable effort to draw
his opponent out in words and delay his execution. But in doing this,
Aegisthus points at one of the conventions of the ancient theater.
Aegisthus must be led inside the skene to die in order to avoid violating
the unspoken taboo against onstage violence. There is a rationalistic
Euripidean flavor to these lines as the wily Aegisthus assaults one of
tragedy's most important conventions.

    Aegisthus' objections force Orestes to rationalize both his plan and
theatrical convention. Aegisthus must die inside because that is where
Agamemnon died. This reminder of Agamemnon's death leads to
Aegisthus' next remark, in which he rhetorically wonders about "the
present and future evils of Pelops' race" (1498). These reminders of the
past and future refute any notion of closure in the play's final frantic
moments. Aegisthus breaks the bounds imposed on him by Orestes'
"script" for his death. The tyrant may not influence any character on
stage to look beyond the present situation to what consequences may
await the avengers for the double murders, but his words must certainly
send such messages to the theater audience. They prevent the play
from coming to a tidy closure in the exodos.[106]

    The future of Orestes and his sister lies outside of the drama.
Aegisthus' specious concern for "Pelops' race" reveals chinks in the
play's rhetorical armor and hints at darker harmonies than Orestes or
the Chorus is prepared to deal with. In this context the absence of the
Furies is as disturbing or more disturbing than their appearance might
have been.

    Orestes begins to move his victim inside, but Aegisthus has one final
ploy as he mocks Orestes' ability to "prophesy" the future by reminding
him of his father's lack of prophetic skill (1500). This marks yet another
assault on the comforting finality that Orestes would like to impose
upon the murders. Orestes says his last lines as he leads Aegisthus in
through the skene door.

Would that this penalty could come immediately to all
    who desire to act contrary to the law.
Kill them!—You would not have many criminals!

(1505–7)

Such simplistic moralizing can be comforting in a problematic world.[107] This kind of "cowboy" value system would have been a common phenomenon in Athens during the later years of the Peloponnesian War. Orestes utters this brutal platitude as he leads Aegisthus into the palace to kill him. The hollow words give no more closure to the drama than do Aegisthus' references to the continuing cycle of retribution. Aegisthus has forced us to look outside the play's action. Orestes attempts, rather mawkishly, to bring a sense of finality to the impending killing. His words are like a weak major chord incapable of wiping out the minor key darkness of Aegisthus' words.

The Chorus ends the play with a three-line tag which is almost shocking in its brevity.

O seed of Atreus, having suffered much,
so you have now come out into freedom at last,
by this onslaught brought to conclusion [τελεωθέν].

(1508–10)

This is an ending that literally *tells* the audience that it is an ending, just as Orestes had labeled the moment of climactic *anagnorisis*. Such a perfunctory tag is reminiscent of Euripides' frequent and deliberate closing banalities. The lines give an abrupt and unsatisfying end to what most, if not all audience members would have known was an ongoing story. The audience's very civic identity was rooted in the *continuation* of the story with the pursuit of Orestes to the Areopagus by the Furies. If the Furies are not to pursue Orestes, why must the play end just before the death of Aegisthus? Why could we not see a happy Orestes fresh from the double murders, preparing to enjoy his patrimony with his sister at his side?

The abrupt ending Sophocles has created seems analogous to cinematic technique wherein at the final moment the action halts in a freeze frame. What happens to the characters in such a situation is too obvious to warrant further explanation. All we need is the image of Orestes leading his victim into the darkness within the house. The illusion of closure that Sophocles has attached to this play is the work of a master craftsman. The attentive audience member or reader cannot be deceived into ignoring the glaring dissonances Sophocles has so carefully created. The close of *Electra* is as abrupt and unconvincing as the happy-go-lucky tune that bursts forth at the end of Mozart's relentlessly tragic G Minor String Quintet.

We go to the Greek tragedians to see myth artfully manipulated. Sophocles in *Electra* has not manipulated myths so much as man-handled them. *Electra* seems to spiral out of control, helped along by the poet's acute self-consciousness. The tragedy insists on an untenable closure, presenting simplistic, feeble solutions to problems that the play itself has shown to be chronic and virtually incurable. In this way *Electra* mocks the closure of art in a world where real resolution of conflict seemed a subject for fairy tale, like Aristophanes' "Cloud Cuckoo Land." *Electra* makes the viewer step outside the normal boundaries of the theater experience. The tragedy encourages the viewer to be aware of its own artificiality, to delight with the playwright in his own virtuosity. While seeming to stage the protagonists' triumph, *Electra* strongly hints toward an unresolvable tragedy too vast to be encompassed by art.[108] *Electra* is the bitterest of the seven surviving Sophoclean plays. Electra and her play exist in a world where the lessons of tragic art are unlikely to be heard or may come too late. *Electra* is a metatheatrical exploration that seems to question the survival of tragic drama and the culture that had fostered it. Perhaps this is why the play seems so barren of hope, so calculated. Perhaps this is why Electra's urn is so empty.

Notes

Chapter 1

1. Aulus Gellius, *Attic Nights* 6.5 (trans. Rolfe), 2:35–37.

2. From Talma's preface to Lekain's *Memoirs*, reprinted in Cole and Chinoy, *Actors on Acting*, p. 186.

3. *Vita* citations refer to the ancient biographical material on the playwright included in A. C. Pearson's 1924 edition of Sophocles.

4. Lesky, *Greek Tragic Poetry*, p. 117.

5. Aristotle, *Poetics* 1449a.

6. Segal, "Greek Tragedy: Writing, Truth, and the Representation of the Self," in *Interpreting Greek Tragedy*, p. 96.

7. Plutarch, *Progress in Virtue* 79b.

8. See Bowra, *Problems in Greek Poetry*, pp. 108–25, for an analysis of the Plutarch passage.

9. See also Hornby, *Drama, Metadrama, and Perception*, p. 32.

10. Schlegel, *Lectures on Dramatic Art and Literature*, lecture 5.

11. On the "three actor rule" see Bieber, *The History of the Greek and Roman Theatre*, pp. 80–81; Pickard-Cambridge, *The Dramatic Festivals of Athens*, pp. 135ff.; and Walton, *Greek Theatre Practice*, pp. 138–44. Jebb's edition of Sophocles contains a conjectural role breakdown before each play. It is only comparatively recently that the performative and interpretive aspects of the doubling has begun to be explored. See Pavlovskis, "The Voice of the Actor in Greek Tragedy" (1977); Johnston, "The Metamorphoses of Theseus in *Oedipus at Colonus*" (1989); and Damen, "Actor and Character in Greek Tragedy" (1993).

12. Aristotle, *Poetics* 1449a.

13. Abel, *Metatheatre*, p. 60.

14. The phrase "sophisticated disillusion" belongs to Herbert Weisinger in his 1961 essay "*Theatrum Mundi*: Illusion as Reality," in *The Agony and the Triumph*, p. 63.

15. Righter, *Shakespeare and the Idea of the Play*, pp. 90, 83.

16. Shearle Furnish has offered an excellent analysis of medieval theatrical self-reflexivity. Furnish takes issue with Abel's remark that "there can be no such thing as religious metatheatre." Furnish illustrates how the shepherd plays of the Wakefield Master "dramatize a world spontaneously created by human striving, human imagination, and continually improvised by men." Furnish, "Metatheatre in the First Shepherds' Play," p. 140.

17. Calderwood, *Shakespearean Metadrama*, pp. 4, 5, 11–12.

18. According to Calderwood, all that enters a play "has [a] curious ambiguity about it (what might be called, to distinguish it from ordinary ambiguities, 'duplexity')." Ibid., p. 12.

19. Ibid., pp. 12–13, 11. Important metatheatrical criticism has extended throughout the 1970s and into the 1990s with the work of Robert G. Egan, Sidney Homan, Judd D.

Hubert, and Meredith Anne Skura. Egan's and Homan's work in particular is informed by practical knowledge of the theater.

20. Hornby, *Drama, Metadrama, and Perception*, p. 17.

21. Ibid., p. 32. On the subject of role-playing-within-the-role, Hornby later writes: "Even when the role within the role is patently false, the dualistic device still sets up a feeling of ambiguity and complexity with regard to the character" (ibid., p. 67).

22. Ibid., p. 32.

23. Wilshire, *Role Playing and Identity*, p. 43. William B. Worthen has also articulated the "doubleness" of the actor who "is present as an actor, strutting his stagey stuff; but he is also absent, negated by the dramatic illusion he creates." Worthen's focus is on Renaissance, eighteenth-century, and modern drama but his observations on the metatheatrical tendencies of *Hamlet* and the Elizabethan revenge play are not out of place in an examination of Sophocles' *Electra*. "Revenge drama mediates on the meaning of moral action in a theatricalized world, where the authority of the natural order has been critically weakened." *Idea of the Actor*, pp. 3, 11.

24. Beckerman, "Theatrical Perception," pp. 168, 162, 163.

25. Taplin, *The Stagecraft of Aeschylus*, p. 1.

26. Bain, *Actors and Audience*, p. 210.

27. Walton, *The Greek Sense of Theatre* and *Greek Theatre Practice*.

28. Goldhill, *Reading Greek Tragedy*; Rehm, *Greek Tragic Theatre*.

29. See Hubbard's *The Masks of Comedy*. An entire dissertation has been devoted to the metatheatrical examination of a single Aristophanic comedy, Taaffe's "Gender, Deception, and Metatheatre in Aristophanes' *Ecclesiazusae*." Taaffe has expanded on this work in her stimulating book, *Aristophanes and Women*.

30. See in particular Goldberg, *The Making of Menandrian Comedy*, and Wiles, *The Masks of Menander*.

31. Gentili, *Theatrical Performances in the Ancient World*, p. 15.

32. Slater, *Plautus*, p. 169.

33. A point also taken by John Ferguson, who compares the Paedagogus in *Electra* to the slaves of Plautus and New Comedy as well as the servants found in Goldoni and P. G. Wodehouse (!); see *A Companion to Greek Tragedy*, p. 537.

34. Slater, *Plautus*, p. 12.

35. Zeitlin, "The Closet of Masks: Role Playing and Myth-Making in the Orestes of Euripides," pp. 69, 70.

36. Karen Lee Bassi has written a dissertation that applies a similar method to Euripides' *Alcestis* and *Helen*. Her work outlines poetic and performative self-consciousness from Hesiod to Euripides and contains much lucid insight into Euripides' aesthetics. Bassi, "Euripides and the Poetics of Deception," pp. 16–18. See also Croally's *Euripidean Polemic: The Trojan Women and the Function of Tragedy*, especially the section on self-reference, pp. 235–48.

37. Segal, "Visual Symbolism and Visual Effects in Sophocles," in *Interpreting Greek Tragedy*, p. 127.

38. Segal, *Dionysiac Poetics and Euripides' Bacchae*, pp. 215, 239, 266. See also Segal's *Euripides and the Poetics of Sorrow* for further observations on Euripidean metatheater and dramatic self-consciousness.

39. Seale, *Vision and Stagecraft*, p. 10.

40. Bruce Heiden in *Tragic Rhetoric* suggests that all Sophoclean drama should be read with a keen sense of self-conscious rhetoric. Heiden feels the audience must

distance itself from all the characters and view all information skeptically and ironically. Heiden's approach often touches upon notions of theatrical self-awareness. P. E. Easterling has taken a similar view of the closing moments of *Trachiniae, Electra*, and *Philoctetes*. Generations of scholars have tried to reason away the disturbing aporia Sophocles has created in these plays with their arbitrary closures and vague prophesy of future events. Easterling observes: "At the very end of a play Sophocles often introduces a glancing reference outside the action, suggesting, as it were, that there *is* a future . . . but this would have to be the subject of a different play. . . . The closing scene is a particularly appropriate place for this kind of device which draws attention to the play as a play; Euripides' use of the *deus* is in some respects analogous." Easterling, "The End of the Trachiniae," p. 69.

Chapter 2

1. See also Weisinger, "*Theatrum Mundi*: Illusion as Reality," in *The Agony and the Triumph*, pp. 63–64.

2. Thucydides, 3.82 (trans. Warner). John T. Hogan argues that the historian is referring not to changes of *spoken language* but to changes in the valuation of words. "They did not change the estimation of words, but in fact depended on its remaining the same. Yet they did, from Thucydides' point of view, ultimately lower this evaluative power: through frequent application to what was actually blameworthy, the praise the word formerly conveyed was worn away." "The ἀξίωσις of Words at Thucydides 3.82.4," p. 146.

3. Conner writes: "Language has now become an agent of violence, intensifying rather than alleviating the *kinesis* and the destruction." *Thucydides*, p. 101.

4. Wasserman, "Thucydides and the Disintegration of the Polis," p. 52.

5. Grote, "Sophocles' 'Electra': A Social Document of Late Fifth Century Athens," p. 278. Grote's work is particularly strong in its analysis of the war's influence upon Sophocles' tragic vision.

6. Herodotus, 1.59 (trans. Godley).

7. Herodotus, 1.60 (trans. Godley). This incident is also described by Aristotle, who offers further evidence of Pisistratus' rather theatrical strategies of deception. *Athenian Constitution*, 14 and 15.

8. Plutarch, *Solon* 29 (trans. Perrin).

9. Ibid. 30. The Homeric incident is from *Odyssey* 4.244–64.

10. Plutarch, *Solon* 29.

11. Else, *Origin and Early Form*, p. 45.

12. Plutarch, *Solon* 8. Else suggests that Solon wore a "traveler's cap." *Origin and Early Form*, pp. 40–41.

13. Else, *Origin and Early Form*, p. 41 (emphasis in original).

14. See also Arrowsmith, "The Criticism of Greek Tragedy."

15. Plutarch, *De Gloria Atheniensium* 348 (trans. Babbitt).

16. Taplin, *Greek Tragedy in Action*, p. 167.

17. See Plato's *Gorgias* 502d for tragedy's placement as a division of rhetoric.

18. *Older Sophists*, p. 42.

19. See also ibid., p. 46.

20. Verdenius, "Gorgias' Doctrine of Deception," pp. 116, 119.

21. From Gorgias' *Encomium of Helen*, in *Older Sophists*, p. 53. Gorgias here pre-

figures the Platonic (and Derridian) notion of λόγος as φαρμακός as well as pointing toward Aristotle's idea that tragedy serves as a catharsis. See also Segal, "Gorgias and the Psychology of the Logos," p. 132.

22. See also Verdenius, "Gorgias' Doctrine of Deception," p. 119.

23. *Older Sophists*, p. 52. See also Duncan, "Gorgias' Theories of Art," p. 403.

24. Verdenius, "Gorgias' Doctrine of Deception," p. 119.

25. Plato, *Protagoras* 347e. "Sophistic relativism was specifically applied to the interpretation of poetry, where it was understood that one poem might elicit a variety of interpretations and might be self-contradictory." Heiden, *Tragic Rhetoric*, p. 16.

26. *Older Sophists*, p. 63.

27. "The sophists themselves were perfectly well aware of the playful character of their art. Gorgias called his *Encomium of Helen* a game (παίγνιον) and his treatise *On Nature* has been termed a play-study in rhetoric." Johan Huizinga also notes that in sophistic literature there is no sharp distinction between play and seriousness. Huizinga, *Homo Ludens*, p. 147. One may do well to remember Derrida's frequent expression of bemused surprise that his ideas are taken so "seriously."

28. Segal, *Dionysiac Poetics and Euripides' Bacchae*, p. 269. See also Huizinga, *Homo Ludens*, p. 89.

Chapter 3

1. See also Taplin, *Greek Tragedy in Action*, pp. 40–41.

2. As noted in the preface, all textual references for Sophocles correspond to the Lloyd-Jones and Wilson 1990 edition.

3. Gellie, *Sophocles*, p. 3.

4. The staging suggested here is not the only solution, but is, perhaps, the most obvious and meaningful one. Both Jebb and Kamerbeek in their commentaries propose the placement of Athena on the theologeion. A. W. Pickard-Cambridge suggests she be placed on the ground "perhaps partly concealed in the trees of the grove which was required later in the play [i.e. to conceal Ajax' body]"; see *The Theatre of Dionysus at Athens*, p. 48. W. B. Stanford, in his edition, recommends that she stand on Odysseus' level but "away from him at the furthest side of the Orchestra, in the shadow of the scene-building" (*Ajax* 15). Stanford attributes to Kitto the idea that the goddess is portrayed by a magnified offstage voice. Hiding the goddess (who along with Heracles in *Philoctetes* represents the only *deus ex machina* in the surviving Sophoclean corpus) in a grove, in the shadows of the skene, or completely offstage seems very weak stagecraft. See William M. Calder's summary of this controversy and his argument for the use of the theologeion in "The Entrance of Athena in *Ajax*," p. 116. Mastronarde has reaffirmed Calder's suggested staging. He notes that a theologeion placement would make Athena's entrance and exit easily manageable and that her physical elevation would be "very important in a scene that plays so terribly on the theme of the limitations of human existence." Mastronarde, "Actors on High: The Skene Roof, the Crane, and the Gods in Attic Drama," p. 278.

5. John Moore, in the preface to his translation of *Ajax* for the Grene and Lattimore Complete Greek Tragedies, observes that Sophocles "contrives . . . to make us lose sight of Ajax' criminality, while making of his ignominy a capital dramatic resource." *Sophocles II*, p. 3.

6. Seale, *Vision and Stagecraft*, pp. 147, 145.

7. Seale notes Odysseus' use of the first-person plural in line 23 as an indication of

Odysseus' "identifying himself with the rest of humanity and equat[ing] his own searching with the falterings of mankind itself" (ibid., p. 145). This argument should be taken
to the next step, that Odysseus is identifying himself with the theater audience.

8. Athena's cruel delight in Ajax' downfall may seem repellent to twentieth-century
eyes, but her credo of helping her friends and harming her enemies was the common
ethical standard of the fifth century. See Blundell's *Helping Friends and Harming
Enemies*.

9. J. Michael Walton notes the unusual role Sophocles has given the goddess: "Usually in Greek drama the goddess Athena is wise and benign, a representative of Athens
itself and the Athenian people" (*Living Greek Theatre*, p. 69).

10. In the American National Theater production (1988) directed by Peter Sellars,
Ajax made his entrance in the prologue by being wheeled out in a plastic display case,
knee deep in blood. King, " 'Nailed to a Circus of Blood,' " p. 9.

11. Gellie, *Sophocles*, pp. 7, 20.

12. Poe, *Genre and Meaning*, pp. 31, 32, 35.

13. Ibid., p. 97.

14. See also Knox, "The *Ajax* of Sophocles," in *Word and Action*, p. 149.

15. *Ajax* 127 (ed. Stanford).

16. See also the Messenger's report of Ajax' fatal rebuff to the goddess (770–77).

17. See also Seale, *Vision and Stagecraft*, p. 153. This isolation of the protagonist was
given an eloquent realization in the version of the play directed by Peter Sellars. Sellars
cast a deaf-mute actor as Ajax for his modern-dress adaptation. Sellars's Ajax mimed his
speeches while the Chorus interpreted his words for the audience. King, " 'Nailed to a
Circus of Blood,' " p. 11.

18. Segal's *Tragedy and Civilization* contains a good overview of the many interpretations of this speech, pp. 432–33 n. 9.

19. Gellie, *Sophocles*, p. 13.

20. Segal, *Tragedy and Civilization*, pp. 114, 115.

21. Poe interprets the speech, too cynically I believe, as an attempt to make himself
"seem not only more innocent than he has seemed before but also greater." *Genre and
Meaning*, p. 63.

22. Reinhardt, *Sophocles*, p. 26.

23. On the subject of choral self-reference in Sophocles, see also Heikkilä, " 'Now I
Have a Mind to Dance,' " pp. 51–67, and Henrichs, "Why Should I Dance?," pp. 56–
111.

24. See also *Ajax* 719ff. (ed. Stanford).

25. Since *Ajax* may belong to the years immediately following Aeschylus' *Oresteia*
(456), Sophocles' shocking alteration of normal dramaturgical practice may have been
directly influenced by the older master.

26. Segal, *Tragedy and Civilization*, p. 142. Segal also notes: "In Ajax' violence of
suffering and action reverberate some of the major clashes of values in mid-fifth-century
Athens. The most recalcitrant and individualistic of heroes commands respect from
those who must reject his attitudes if their institutions are to survive." Arnott observes
that the Athens reference "is both a tragic hero's farewell to the living world, and an
actor's adieu to his audience" (*Public and Performance in the Greek Theatre*, p. 22). Of
course, Arnott is exaggerating slightly since the actor playing Ajax would soon reemerge
in the guise of his grieving brother Teucer.

27. O'Higgins, "The Second Best of the Achaeans," pp. 52, 48.

28. The staging of the actual suicide in the ancient theater represents a fascinating

and virtually unsolvable scholarly crux. See Gardiner's lucid summary of various conflicting theories, "The Staging of the Death of Ajax," pp. 10–14. Mills also offers a
stimulating analysis of the scene's possible staging along with observations concerning
Sophocles' exploitation and manipulation of dramatic convention throughout the play,
"The Death of Ajax," pp. 129–35.

29. Poe, *Genre and Meaning*, p. 98.

Chapter 4

1. Seale, *Vision and Stagecraft*, p. 183. I disagree with Heiden, who views Deianeira's
opening speech as a threat to the dramatic illusion "since the character seems to address
the audience and not to inhabit the universe of drama" (Heiden, *Tragic Rhetoric*, p. 21).
"Addressing the audience" only destroys dramatic illusion (i.e., their absorption with
the events on stage) in the *realistic* theater.

2. Seale, *Vision and Stagecraft*, p. 184.

3. For more on choral self-reference, see Heikkilä, " 'Now I Have a Mind to Dance,' "
and Henrichs, "Why Should I Dance?"

4. On Lichas' deceptive speech, see Davies's "Lichas' Lying Tale" and Halleran's
"Lichas' Lies and Sophoclean Innovation."

5. Gellie, *Sophocles*, p. 62.

6. The situation is analogous to a famous passage in Euripides' *Orestes* (408 B.C.).
During the chaotic moments before the entrance of Apollo from the machine, Orestes
holds Menelaus at bay by taking hostage the latter's daughter, Hermione. Orestes and
Menelaus are played by the protagonist and deuteragonist, respectively. At Orestes' side
stands his accomplice, Pylades, played by a mute extra (as is the part of Hermione). The
third actor, or tritagonist, is about to enter in the role of Apollo. Orestes tells Menelaus
that he intends to kill his daughter (1578). Menelaus turns to Pylades and asks, "And are
you too going to share in this murder, Pylades?" Orestes interjects, "His silence says it;
let me speak for him" (1591–92). This passage shows Euripides playing with the boundaries of tragic convention and, in a rather cheeky way, calling attention to the play as a
play. It is a critique on the nature of tragic performance.

7. Gellie, *Sophocles*, p. 58.

8. Whitman, *Sophocles*, p. 117.

9. The scholiast's comments on *Ajax*, line 646, appear in the scholia text edited by P.
N. Pagageorgius (Leipzig, 1888). They are reprinted in full in Hester, "Deianeira's
'Deception Speech,' " p. 1.

10. For a summary of this view in the secondary literature, see Hester, "Deianeira's
'Deception Speech,' " p. 5.

11. Reinhardt, *Sophocles*, p. 47. In a footnote, Reinhardt draws a firm distinction
between the deliberate "intrigue" of Ajax' great speech and the "pitiful delusion" he
perceives in Deianeira at this moment (p. 243 n. 11).

12. Heiden, *Tragic Rhetoric*, p. 85.

13. As discussed in Chapter 1, Euripides' *Bacchae* affords another powerful example
of doubling adding to the play's meaning in performance. This occurs when the actor
playing Pentheus leaves the stage disguised as a Maenad only to reemerge as Pentheus'
mother Agave, bearing her son's severed head. The effect of the doubling is all the more
chilling when we consider that the actor probably carries in his hands the mask of his
previous character.

14. Heracles' eagerness to make a spectacle of his sufferings is an important aspect of

his self-presentation and reveals his character's kinship to the obsessive self-revelation and exposure sought by the title character of *Oedipus Tyrannus*.

15. For giving the last lines 1275–78 to Hyllus, see Lloyd-Jones and Wilson, *Sophoclea*, pp. 177–78.

16. This practice appears alien to Euripides' dramatic technique though there are some Aeschylean examples.

17. Jebb's and Easterling's editions, 1270.

18. Gellie, *Sophocles*, p. 77.

19. Both Easterling ("The End of the Trachiniae," pp. 56–74) and Heiden have interesting interpretations of the play's final moments. Easterling believes that we are meant to notice and be troubled by the omissions at the play's close as well as to notice whenever Sophocles leaves hints to events lying outside the immediate perimeters of his dramas. Heiden goes so far as to deny the congruity between prophesy and the play's tragic outcome. Heiden draws the reader's attention to the fact that Heracles is still living at the play's close despite the Centaur's poison and that his death on the pyre on Oeta will hardly bring the prophecy to a literal fulfillment (*Tragic Rhetoric*, p. 158).

Chapter 5

1. Lesky, *Greek Tragic Poetry*, pp. 133, 152. For a more recent examination on the *Antigone* date, see the edition of Brown, p. 2.

2. Segal, *Tragedy and Civilization*, p. 444 n. 49. Both Segal and Seale have written about the play's inexorable revelation of truth. Rosevach, "The Two Worlds of the *Antigone*," pp. 16–26, is also interesting for its interpretation of the play's structure and thematics.

3. Demosthenes, "On the Embassy," 19.246.

4. Reinhardt, *Sophocles*, p. 71.

5. *Sophocles* (ed. Grene and Lattimore, 2nd ed.), 1:169.

6. See especially Niall Slater's view of the monologue from *Epidicus* (81–103), in *Plautus*, p. 21. A near contemporary parallel to Sophocles' Sentry may be found in Aristophanes' *Acharnians* when Dicaeopolis repeatedly addresses his "soul" (ὦ θυμέ, 480, 483) and his "suffering heart" (ὦ τάλινα καρδία, 485) in humorously melodramatic fashion. There is also an obvious similarity between the Sentry and a Shakespearean clown such as Lancelot Gobbo in *The Merchant of Venice*. Sophocles' bold juxtaposition of low- and high-born characters gives *Antigone* an unusually varied social view, comparable with Shakespeare's combination of Cleopatra and the asp salesman.

7. See also Brown, who cites the "out of breath messenger" motif as it appears in Euripides' *Medea* (1119–20) and Aristophanes' *Birds* (1121–22). *Antigone* 223–24 (ed. Brown).

8. See also Damen, "Actor and Character in Greek Tragedy," p. 322.

9. Seale writes of the closing moments, "All that remains is the tableau of corpses, Teiresias' prediction made good and the culmination of the whole process, concrete visualization." *Vision and Stagecraft*, pp. 108–9.

10. For the self-reflexive aspects of Dionysian allusion within this and other tragedies, see Bierl, "Was hat die Tragödie mit Dionysos zu tun? Rolle und Function des Dionysos am Beispiel der 'Antigone' des Sophokles," pp. 43–58, and *Dionysos und die griechische Tragödie: Politische und 'metatheatralische' Aspekte im Text*. On choral self-reference in Sophocles, see also Heikkilä, " 'Now I Have a Mind to Dance,' " and Henrichs, "Why Should I Dance?"

11. *Antigone* 162–210 (ed. Jebb).

12. See also Segal, "Time, Theatre, and Knowledge," p. 465.

13. Reinhardt, *Sophocles*, pp. 98, 116.

14. Seale, *Vision and Stagecraft*, p. 218.

15. A similar drawing of the theater audience into the stage action occurs on Creon's second entrance when he speaks to the members of the Chorus and, over their heads, to the theater audience (ἄνδρες πολῖται, 513). The idea of the theater audience standing in for the Theban population is further reinforced by Jocasta's first lines, warning Oedipus and Creon not to quarrel publicly before the "house" (634–38). Segal detects a theatrical self-consciousness in operation throughout the play, particularly in Sophocles' "visual" language, the way characters and situations are described as spectatorial objects—or, as in the death of Jocasta or Oedipus' blinding, objects that must not or cannot "be seen." "Time, Theatre, and Knowledge," pp. 459–89.

16. Reinhardt, *Sophocles*, p. 130.

17. The hidden similarity between Oedipus and Teiresias is the subject of an interesting article by Lattimore, "Oedipus and Teiresias," pp. 105–11. The 1984 Greek National Theatre production directed by Minos Volanakis closed the play with Oedipus' ceremonial acceptance of a walking staff similar to the one used by Teiresias, allowing the audience to "see" Oedipus "become" Teiresias. For the comparison of Oedipus to the Sphinx, see Segal, "Time, Theatre, and Knowledge," p. 466.

18. Segal, *Tragedy and Civilization*, p. 247. Taplin has analyzed the frustrating, thwarted closure of the play. He describes Oedipus' futile plea to leave Thebes and his ignominious final exit into the skene as a deliberate disappointment of audience expectation and a subtle means of making the play continue unresolved within the spectator's consciousness (Taplin, "Sophocles in His Theatre," p. 174).

19. Taplin, "Fifth-Century Tragedy and Comedy: A *Synkrisis*," p. 169.

20. Kamerbeek senses the ambiguity behind the use of χορεύειν and goes on to explicate the wider implications of these lines for the play as a whole: "The existence of the world order is bound up with the existence of tragedy; the oracles constitute the frame of this existential connection. This denial [of the validity of oracles] would imply the denial of tragedy and world order." Kamerbeek does not acknowledge, however, that tragedy asserts this order through the use of the deception and seeming of theatrical performance. "World order," in Kamerbeek's phrase, may only be as substantial as the deception and seeming that form the basis of tragic performance. Kamerbeek, "Comments on the Second Stasimon of *Oedipus Tyrannus*," pp. 89, 92.

Francis Fergusson underscores the unusual bond between the audience and its "extension," the Chorus. Jocasta's impieties threaten the "ritual expectation of Oedipus' self-revelation." The Chorus, embodying as it does Greek religious practice, sees Jocasta's irreligious attitude as a threat to their existence as a character in a drama which cannot exist without religion (Fergusson, *The Idea of a Theatre*, p. 28). Gellie takes a similar view: "In these last two lines (895–96), the Chorus has asked: 'What, if man behaves thus with impunity, is the point of my dancing?' Sophocles seems to be asking himself: 'What is the point of my writing plays?' And the audience is drawn to the consideration: 'What is the point of our turning out to see them?'" Gellie interprets the Chorus's questionings as a means of reconciling us to the seemingly gratuitous destruction of Oedipus. The stasimon tells us in effect "why we must be satisfied to see [Oedipus] destroyed" (Gellie, "The Second Stasimon of the *Oedipus Tyrannus*," p. 122).

To Segal, the questions posed by the Chorus find no comforting answers in the protagonist's downfall. The question "Why should I dance?" (896) shows the Chorus unconsciously mirroring the king's obsessive confrontation with his own negation. This confrontation of negation, Segal argues, is the essence of tragic performance. Segal views the second stasimon as a self-conscious "ritual-within-ritual," a passage that is "parallel and homologous with the larger, enframing ritual structure of the festival in which the play itself has its own ceremonial function" (Segal, *Tragedy and Civilization*, p. 235). See also Henrichs, "Why Should I Dance?," pp. 65–73.

21. Knox, *Oedipus at Thebes*, p. 47. Knox has elsewhere referred to the passage as "a sort of Sophoclean *Verfremdungseffekt*" ("Oedipus Rex," in *Essays Ancient and Modern*, p. 139).

22. Beckett, *Endgame*, p. 58.

23. For the idea of Oedipus as a character self-consciously "standing in" for others, see also Wilshire, *Role Playing and Identity*.

24. Aeschylus' *Eumenides* shifts its scene midway through its action from the temple at Delphi to the Areopagus in Athens. Euripides' *Children of Heracles* is set in Marathon, a district near to and ruled by Athens.

25. Herodotus (6.21) relates the famous anecdote concerning Aeschylus' rival, Phrynichus, who was fined a thousand drachmas for reminding his audience of the recent fall of Miletus in his tragedy, *The Capture of Miletus*. The play was banned due to its unpleasant emotional effect on its audience. Phrynichus seems to have destroyed the aesthetic distance necessary for the calamities of tragedy to bring pleasure instead of pain. Lesky, however, notes that the incident may have been a political ruse aimed at humiliating the archon, Themistocles. Lesky, *Greek Tragic Poetry*, p. 34.

26. Seale, *Vision and Stagecraft*, p. 113.

27. See also *Oedipus at Colonus* (ed. Blundell), p. 20 n. 4.

28. Birge, "The Grove of the Eumenides: Refuge and Hero Shrine in *Oedipus at Colonus*," pp. 12–13.

29. Kirkwood, "From Melos to Colonus: ΤΙΝΑΣ ΧΩΡΟΥΣ ΑΦΙΓΜΕΘ' . . . ," p. 103.

30. Johnston, "The Metamorphoses of Theseus in *Oedipus at Colonus*," pp. 280, 283. See also Edmunds, *Theatrical Space and Historical Place in Sophocles' Oedipus at Colonus*, pp. 69–70.

31. One is reminded of Bruno Gentili's definition of metatheater as any play that is "constructed from previously existing plays." *Theatrical Performances in the Ancient World*, p. 15.

32. Gellie, *Sophocles*, p. 293 n. 4.

33. Seale, *Vision and Stagecraft*, p. 113.

34. Burian, "Suppliant and Savior: Oedipus at Colonus," pp. 408–29.

35. Seale, *Vision and Stagecraft*, p. 113.

36. Reinhardt, *Sophocles*, pp. 202, 200–201.

37. Ibid., p. 204.

38. Segal, *Tragedy and Civilization*, pp. 407, 406.

39. Plutarch, *Moralia* 785. See also *Oedipus at Colonus* (ed. Jebb), p. xl.

40. See also Reinhardt, *Sophocles*, pp. 220, 222.

Chapter 6

1. Aristotle, *Rhetoric* 3.18.1419a (trans. Freese, emphasis added). As to whether Aristotle is referring to the playwright or some unknown namesake, see Webster, *An Introduction to Sophocles*, p. 13.

2. On the "deceptive" nature of the 400, see Aristotle, *Pol.* 5.3.8.1304b, and Plutarch, *Alcibiades* 26.1–2.

3. Aristotle, *Rhetoric* 3.15.1416a (trans. Freese).

4. For a lucid examination of the issue of topicality, see Jameson, "Politics and the *Philoctetes*," pp. 217–27.

5. Wilson, *The Wound and the Bow*.

6. See also Seale, *Vision and Stagecraft*, p. 27.

7. Whitman offers a particularly convincing interpretation of the *Antigone* passage. "Caves are nature's secret spots where a mortal may meet with divinity" ("Antigone and the Nature of Nature," in *The Heroic Paradox*, p. 123).

8. For a comparison between *Philoctetes'* and *Electra's* use of deceptive *logoi*, see Segal, *Tragedy and Civilization*, pp. 337–38. Michael Vickers cleverly but unconvincingly argues that the "double mouthed" cave "is probably intended to recall Alcibiades' tendency towards double-dealing and general untrustworthiness" ("Alcibiades on Stage: *Philoctetes* and *The Cyclops*," p. 176).

9. Reinhardt, *Sophocles*, p. 175.

10. Aristophanes, *Frogs* 1054.

11. I see no reason to suspect lines 385–88 deleted by Lloyd-Jones and Wilson.

12. As Seale observes, "the total picture is one which invites the audience to watch Neoptolemus' reaction, to observe him observe" (*Vision and Stagecraft*, p. 29). Greengard characterizes Odysseus not only as a playwright-within-the-play but as a director as well: "[Since playwrights were directors in the fifth century] Odysseus is in contention with Sophocles as much as with Philoctetes in the outcome of the script" (*Theatre in Crisis*, p. 25 n. 16).

13. For a brief account of Neoptolemus' poetic manifestations before Sophocles utilized him in this play, see Fuqua, "Studies in the Use of Myth in Sophocles' 'Philoctetes' and the 'Orestes' of Euripides," pp. 32–43.

14. Segal interprets the detail about the "elaborately decked out ship" (νηὶ ποικιλοσ-τόλωι, 343) that Neoptolemus says brought him to Troy as a hint that the speaker is entering the realm of fabrication and artifice (*Tragedy and Civilization*, p. 304).

15. Gellie, *Sophocles*, p. 139. Gellie suggests that Philoctetes' statement at line 452, "I find the gods evil," must have been greeted "by many nodding heads in the audience" (p. 140).

16. See also Roberts, "Different Stories: Sophoclean Narrative(s) in the *Philoctetes*," pp. 170–71. Taplin has made a similar point. "Neoptolemus allows himself to be carried by his own lie. He has to stand, so it seems, by his own words even though they were lies. . . . The falsehood becomes a part of the truth" (Taplin, "The Mapping of Sophocles' *Philoctetes*," p. 70).

17. Literally he asks them to always respond to his hand signals (πρὸς ἐμὴν αἰεί χεῖρα, 148).

18. The phrase is borrowed from Victor Bers's article of the same name in which he remarks on the "brutal" deception the sailors practice upon Philoctetes ("The Perjured Chorus in Sophocles' 'Philoctetes,'" p. 500).

19. One thinks of Aeschylus' chorus of libation bearers who briefly assist Orestes, or of the secrecy maintained under oath by the chorus of Euripides' *Hippolytus*, to name only two examples.

20. In examining the entire first meeting of Philoctetes, Neoptolemus, and the Chorus, Tycho von Wilamowitz-Moellendorff writes: "An unsophisticated spectator will take Neoptolemus' heartfelt words of farewell, the magnanimous pleas of the

Chorus and the hesitating acquiescence of their commander as seriously as he takes Philoctetes' pleas" (Ein unbefangener Zuschauer wird die herzlichen Abschiedsworte des Neoptolemos, die uneigennützige Bitte des Chores und die zögernde Einwilligung seines Herrn ebenso ernst nehmen wie Philoktets Bitten). Wilamowitz-Moellendorff, *Die dramatische Technik des Sophokles*, p. 281. But while the duplicitous role playing seriously threatens the audience's notion of an established reality, it never completely overwhelms the critical distance between the play and its auditors. Of course, the actor's use of vocal inflection and gesture could conceivably be used to clarify the difference between the "deceptive" and the "sincere" elements of Neoptolemus and the Chorus's "performance" before Philoctetes. Such distinctions, however, may only come from the subjective instincts of the performers or the director; they are not explicit in the text. See also Calder, "Sophoclean Apologia," p. 159.

21. Greengard's analysis of the metatheatrical dimension of this scene is very striking: "The stories are contradictory, but both are composed from the same or indistinguishably similar pieces of the puzzle. This is Sophoclean irony at its best and a fifth-century version of the paradoxes inherent in a play within a play." Greengard, *Theatre in Crisis*, p. 25.

22. For the "aside" in fifth-century tragedy, see Bain, *Actors and Audience*, p. 84.

23. "In lines 610–3 we are given the prophesy of Helenus, but we are given it from the mouth of a fake merchant who has just shown us what a splendid liar he is. . . . Thus we know, and we do not know, that Philoctetes must go willingly to Troy." Gellie, *Sophocles*, pp. 144–45.

24. Compare the use of εἰ δοκεῖ here with ὡς ἔοικεν ("so it seems") at *Electra* 765. In both instances the similar phrases represent signposts guiding the audience to notice the double perspective created by the playwright.

25. Jebb attempts to explain the lying strophe in terms of stage business. Jebb interprets the stasimon as being the sincere expression of the Chorus's feelings up until line 717. At 718, Jebb argues, Philoctetes and Neoptolemus have reemerged from the skene "and in the [concluding] antistrophe the Chorus once more seek to help their master's design." *Philoctetes* 676–729 (ed. Jebb). Webster rebuts Jebb's suggestion. If the Chorus members were adapting their words to Neoptolemus' plan, Webster argues, "they would then have addressed Philoctetes in the second person. They simply accept the situation as Neoptolemus has put it." *Philoctetes* 719ff. (ed. Webster). Webster's suggestion that the members of the Chorus "accept the situation" is weak considering how their character has been established in the parodos and the way they behave later when Philoctetes is unconscious.

26. See also Seale, *Vision and Stagecraft*, p. 37.

27. Winnington-Ingram notes the "harsh discord" of lines 833–38. "The sleep they pray to visit the suffering Philoctetes is something to be *used*" (*Sophocles: An Interpretation*, p. 287).

28. See Gellie, *Sophocles*, p. 149.

29. Winnington-Ingram, "Tragica," p. 49.

30. See also Taplin, *Greek Tragedy in Action*, p. 133.

31. See also Calder, "Sophoclean Apologia," p. 163.

32. Odysseus has apparently not made a full exit at 1260 but has remained somewhere within the playing area; otherwise such a sudden, unheralded reappearance from a parodos would be prohibitively difficult to manage. He must not be seen by Philoctetes, though his lurking presence, if seen by the theater audience, could considerably heighten the suspense during the sequence between Neoptolemus and Philoctetes at

1261–92. If Neoptolemus is indeed still in collusion with Odysseus as Calder asserts, the presence of Odysseus, the puppet master, would make a marvelous picturization of the situation. For Odysseus in hiding, see *Philoctetes* 1293 (ed. Webster), and Calder, "Sophoclean Apologia," p. 165.

33. See Seale, *Vision and Stagecraft*, p. 44.

34. "It is not the 'will of the gods' which operates. It is the will of Philoctetes which suddenly operates divinely." Whitman, *Sophocles*, p. 187.

35. Linforth, "Philoctetes: The Play and the Man," pp. 150, 151.

36. Richmond Lattimore has gone so far as to suggest that the deus is really Odysseus incognito—an internal playwright turned actor, to use metatheatrical terms. Lattimore cites the fact that "the actor who played the part was, in a very real sense (like the Merchant in an earlier scene) Odysseus in disguise" (*Story Patterns in Greek Tragedy*, p. 92 n. 35). The ingenious idea of Odysseus creating a phony apotheosis is echoed by Errandonea and Shucard (Errandonea, "Filoctetes. II," pp. 85–86; Shucard, "Some Developments in Sophocles' Late Plays of Deception," p. 135). The notion hardly finds real support in Sophocles' text but these three scholars have come to this delightfully whimsical idea by observing the self-conscious theatricality of the play as well as its abiding cynicism.

37. This is an effect similar to Shakespeare's operation in the epilogue of *Henry V*. There, after viewing at length Henry's triumph, the Chorus reminds the audience of the early death of Henry and England's humiliating loss of France. As soon as the Chorus has reminded the audience of these devastating losses Shakespeare attempts a kind of rhetorical damage control, asking his auditors to "accept" the sad future as well as the present happy ending with its transitory poignancy. For all of the Chorus's pleas for "acceptance," the damage has been done and the play's closure has suffered a notable and jarring rupture.

38. See also Rose, "Sophocles' *Philoctetes* and the Teachings of the Sophists," p. 102, and Taplin, "The Mapping of Sophocles' *Philoctetes*," p. 77.

39. Zimmermann compares the use of the deus in this play and in the Euripidean *Orestes*. "In the fictive context of the play [*Philoctetes*] the poet can still bring everything to a satisfactory conclusion by means of the device of the deus ex machina, as Euripides was to do in his *Orestes* one year later" (*Greek Tragedy: An Introduction*, p. 84).

40. See also Linforth, "Philoctetes: The Play and the Man," p. 156.

41. Kott, *Eating of the Gods*, pp. 169, 181.

42. Kott draws his own comparisons between these two late plays. In both plays "the audience is a sea and the stage is an island" (ibid., p. 162).

Chapter 7

1. Gilbert Murray, no great admirer of Sophocles to begin with, accused the *Electra* of "artificiality" and "a certain bluntness of moral imagination" (*The Literature of Ancient Greece*, pp. 236, 239).

2. *Electra* (ed. Jebb), p. xli.

3. The relevant Homeric passages are *Odyssey* 1.35–43; 3.193–98, 251–52, 256–75, 303–10; 4.92, 514–37; 11.428–34, 452–53; 24.97, 199–201.

4. See also Grote, "Sophocles' 'Electra': A Social Document of Late Fifth Century Athens," p. 20.

5. Woodard, "The Electra of Sophocles," pp. 125–45.

6. Eugene H. Falk writes, "Let us assume that the aging Sophocles is meditating

about some of his earlier plays. We have some justification in making this assumption when we read *Oedipus at Colonus* where he tried to answer some questions that had arisen from the writing of *Oedipus the King*. . . . I now suggest we assume that Sophocles wondered what would have happened if Creon had not rashly sent Antigone to be entombed alive, but merely kept this intention as a threat to break Antigone's courage." Antigone would presumably behave like Electra, Falk reasons. See his "Electra," in "A Symposium: Sophocles' *Electra*," p. 28.

7. Gentile, *Theatrical Performances in the Ancient World*, p. 15.

8. Leinieks has taken up and advanced the λόγος / ἔργον dichotomy with some useful qualifications and distinctions: "The contrast in the play . . . is not between *logos* and *ergon* directly, but rather between *logos* and *ergon* which correspond to each other and *logos* and *ergon* which do not correspond. For Electra, *logos* and *ergon* always correspond. For the other persons in the play this is not always so." *The Plays of Sophokles*, p. 129.

9. Aristophanes, *Frogs* 1054.

10. Ford, "The Seal of Theognis: The Politics of Authorship in Archaic Greece," p. 89.

11. Michael W. Haslam has argued that line 1 is an interpolation. The evidence, however, remains inconclusive. "The Authenticity of Euripides' *Phoenissae* 1–2 and Sophocles' *Electra* 1," pp. 149–74. Lloyd-Jones and Wilson conclude that the case of the line's spuriousness is still unproved (*Sophoclea*, p. 42).

12. Zeitlin, "Thebes: Theatre of Self and Society in Athenian Drama," p. 145.

13. Aeschylus' *Septem* 145 suggests some of the meanings inherent in Λύκειος. Λύκει' ἄναξ, λύκεοις γενοῦ στρατῷ δαΐῳ ("Lycian lord, be a very wolf to the enemy army").

14. These repeated references to sunlight may also serve to remind the attentive audience member or reader of the omnipresence of Phoebus Apollo.

15. Beare finds the bird reference a distinctly ominous device. See "Sophocles, *Electra* ll. 17–19," pp. 111–12.

16. Craig Smith has persuasively argued that καιρός carries powerfully ambiguous implications throughout this play. The word is usually translated as "opportune moment" and, as noted earlier in the section on Gorgias, it carried decidedly sophistic overtones in the late fifth century. Smith, however, reveals that καιρός still retained much of its original force in Sophocles' day, as a word denoting something that was "fit," "right," or "just." Orestes and his friends create a sardonic double perspective whenever they use the word καιρός. To Orestes, the word denotes opportunism and seizing the advantage. For at least some of the audience, the word still retains its older moral sense of "justice" which seems oddly out of place in the young man's murderous deceptive plans. See Smith, "The Meanings of Καιρός in Sophocles' *Electra*," p. 342.

17. Leinieks has beautifully characterized the Sophoclean Orestes as "the young sportsman—a cross between Pheidippides of the *Clouds* and one of Pindar's youthful athletes. His thinking revolves around horses and horse racing. The Paedagogus for his loyal performance is compared to a noble horse." Even the murders, Leinieks observes, are referred to as a kind of "athletic contest." *The Plays of Sophokles*, p. 132.

18. Batchelder has interpreted the Paedagogus as representing the tragic tradition that proceeded Sophocles' telling of the Orestes story, while Orestes himself symbolizes the younger playwright eager to make his own contribution to theatrical tradition (*The Seal of Orestes*, p. 21). The relationship between the two characters is more fluid, however. Both the Paedagogus and Orestes take turns at being dramatists and actors within their metatheatrical plot.

19. Blundell notes, "Orestes is not a heroic figure in the Iliadic mold. The wording of the oracle contrasts his use of deception to 'steal' his revenge with the use of open warfare (36 f.)." See her *Helping Friends and Harming Enemies*, p. 173. See also Sheppard, "Electra: A Defense of Sophocles," pp. 2–9.

20. See also Segal in "Visual Symbolism and Visual Effects in Sophocles," in *Interpreting Greek Tragedy*, p. 128.

21. Thucydides, 5.84–116.

22. Seale suggests that the Paedagogus' elaborate chariot speech may in effect "kill" the prince as a viable mythic hero (*Vision and Stagecraft*, p. 66).

23. *Electra* 62ff. (ed. Kells).

24. See Dale's edition of Euripides' *Helen* 1050–52.

25. See also Froma Zeitlin's analysis of the metatheatrical aspects of Euripides' *Orestes*, "The Closet of Masks: Role-Playing and Myth-Making in the *Orestes* of Euripides," pp. 51–77.

26. Seale, *Vision and Stagecraft*, p. 57.

27. "Es ist als wenn Sophokles sagte 'ich habe die Choephoren nicht vergessen, aber ich mache es anders.'" Fraenkel, *Beobachtungen zu Aristophanes*, p. 22 n. 1.

28. Electra's longing for her brother's return, an event the audience knows has already occurred, adds a fascinating, almost surreal aspect to the notion of "time" in the *Electra*. Robert Corrigan writes: "Orestes has already come. Electra's desire (in future time) is already present. It might be stated as a kind of formula: because of time past Electra looks into time future and it is already present in Orestes. In the play all is now; it has happened all at once for the audience. The audience sees Orestes and hears Electra's speech." See his essay "The *Electra* of Sophocles," in "A Symposium: Sophocles' *Electra*," p. 41.

29. See also *Electra* 86ff. (ed. Kells).

30. Heiden, *Tragic Rhetoric*, p. 21.

31. See Taplin's comments on the use of the *eccyclema* in *Greek Tragedy in Action*, p. 12.

32. Reissman, "If It Be Not Now, Yet It Will Come," in "A Symposium: Sophocles' *Electra*," p. 32.

33. Corrigan writes, "The murder [of Agamemnon] is brought closer and closer to us through repetition. Even the reason for the murder is rehearsed." "The *Electra* of Sophocles," p. 40.

34. Reinhardt, *Sophocles*, p. 141.

35. Ibid., p. 142.

36. In addition to her tendency to quote other characters' offstage speeches in an "imitative" manner, Electra also exhibits a "dominant habit of repeating her interlocutor's exact words, always with an added ironic twist." See Grote, "Electra or Chrysothemis?: The Assignment of Sophocles' *Electra* 428–30," pp. 141–42.

37. Heiden, *Tragic Rhetoric*, pp. 8, 11.

38. Hubert, *Metatheatre: The Example of Shakespeare*, p. 9.

39. Grote, "Sophocles' 'Electra': A Social Document of Late Fifth Century Athens," p. 240. I would not go so far as Grote, however, in reading Electra's horror at Agamemnon's murder as "almost as much for aesthetic reasons as for religious and moral reasons." Her repeated use of the word αἰκεῖς (unseemly) or αἰσχρός (shameful) have both moral and religious overtones.

40. See also Batchelder, *The Seal of Orestes*, pp. 55–56.

41. See Seaford, "The Destruction of Limits in Sophocles' *Elektra*," p. 323.

42. Gellie, *Sophocles*, p. 113.

43. Euripides indulges in an even more blatant bit of "intertextual" game playing with the *Choephoroi* in his *Electra* when Electra hilariously discounts the "Aeschylean" recognition tokens of hair, footprints, and cloth (Euripides, *Electra* 524–46).

44. B. X. De Wet offers a fascinating speculation on a possible topicality in Sophocles' play. "Athens at the time of the Peloponnesian War would have many a household deprived of father and brother through the ravages of war and civil strife. There would be many a household where a lone woman would be struggling to maintain the status and well-being of her household in the absence of a κύριος. Thus by focusing the attention on the dilemma of Electra, Sophocles has skillfully utilized the poignancy of a tragic reality of his time." "The *Electra* of Sophocles: A Study in Social Values," p. 36.

45. Euripides' fondness for this kind of rationalistic qualification is well known. The opening speech of Electra in Euripides' *Orestes* (408 B.C.) affords an excellent example. "Tantalus, the 'blessed one,' and I'm not mocking his misfortune [by calling him that] / was begotten by Zeus, so they say [ὡς λέγουσι]" (*Orestes* 4–5). Heiden detects a similar strain of unsettling relativism at several points in Sophocles' *Trachiniae*. See Heiden, *Tragic Rhetoric*, pp. 33, 39.

46. Winnington-Ingram, *Sophocles*, p. 222.

47. Thucydides, 3.82.

48. See also Seale, *Vision and Stagecraft*, p. 63.

49. Since the Theater of Dionysus contained an altar to its patron deity, it is possible that Dionysus' altar might have "assumed a role" at this point in the action, becoming a shrine to Apollo. Such a possibility suggests further perceptual "double images" that are at home in the *Electra*. It would be fitting that an altar to the god of drama might play a role within the fictive world of the play. See Jebb's conjectural stage business and comparison of Clytemnestra's prayer with that of Jocasta in *Oedipus Tyrannus* (911–23). *Electra* 634 (ed. Jebb).

50. Seale, *Vision and Stagecraft*, p. 63. See also Bain, *Actors and Audience*, pp. 77–78.

51. Sheppard has detected "malice in his promise 'I will tell all.'" "The Tragedy of Electra," p. 86. The passage may be instructively compared with an arch and self-aware exchange in Euripides' *Bacchae*. The First Messenger enters and addresses Pentheus:

> *Messenger*: Pentheus, ruler of this land of Thebes,
> I have come leaving Cithaeron, where never lessen
> The pure showers of white snow—
> *Pentheus*: And what mighty bit of news have you come to deliver?
> (660–63)

Pentheus' reply cuts the Messenger short and often provokes a laugh in modern performances of the play. The laugh is triggered by the collision of the Messenger's heightened poetic style of speech—just the style of speech to be expected from a character in a ceremonial role—with the deflating, sarcastic comments of Pentheus. Brian Vickers is one of the few critics to compare the tone of the Paedagogus' speech to that of Euripides. He describes the Sophoclean passage as "a unique *false* messenger-speech, which is in itself a masterpiece of *verismo*, as if challenging Euripides at his own game." *Towards Greek Tragedy*, pp. 568–69.

52. Sheppard, "The Tragedy of Electra," p. 86. See also Blundell, *Helping Friends and Harming Enemies*, pp. 173–74. "The Orestes of the speech is the hero whom Electra awaits, and who our Orestes aspires to be, but the victory he wins is not the glorious triumph of the speech" (p. 174).

53. See also Batchelder, *The Seal of Orestes*, pp. 94–95.

54. Albert Cook has compared the Athenian dramatic festival with the Delphic contests and the Pindaric odes they inspired. "At Delphi we have the first contest of the games, and then the odes of Pindar. At the Greater Dionysia, the tragedy becomes the contest, and the restricted number of entrants stand to one another as the runners of chariot races do in the Pythian games: the outcome reveals the winner, and the performance, like any contest (but not like any play in other cultures) is unique and never repeated." Cook, *Enactment*, p. 45.

55. Reinhardt views the speech as an exercise in poetic self-consciousness. "Sophocles has permitted himself in this speech of intrigue a kind of diction which as a tragic writer he had probably long abandoned for serious material. It is as though he were playing a game with his own earlier tragic style. But it is a cruel game. For to prove its power and display its beauty, it must break Electra's heart." *Sophocles*, pp. 151–52.

56. See also Musurillo, *The Light and the Darkness*, p. 98.

57. See also Batchelder, *The Seal of Orestes*, pp. 103–4. Batchelder upholds the manuscript reading of ἀνωλόλυξε against Herwerden's emendation to ἀνωτότυξε, but either word contains metatheatrical resonance within this extraordinary context.

58. See also Seale, *Vision and Stagecraft*, p. 65.

59. See also Reinhardt, *Sophocles*, p. 261. The audience of characters on stage believes the old man's performance. What of the audience in the theater? The length and detail of the speech seem capable of winning the temporary credulity of the most attentive auditor. The German scholar Georg Kaibel, who edited the play in the late nineteenth century, believed Sophocles was "giving himself the opportunity to bewitch his spectators through the art of thrilling and vivid narration, so that they accept for the truth that which they know to be a fabrication: only in this way can they follow with genuine sympathy Electra's outbursts of pain, the cause of which is unfounded in reality" (Der Dichter hat ausserdem die Möglichkeit, dem Zuschauer durch die Kunst einer packenden anschaulichen Erzählung zu bannen, also dass er für wirklich hält was er erdichtet weiss: erst so kann er den tatsächlich unbegründeten Schmerzensausbrüchen der Elektra mit wirklicher Teilname folgen). See *Elektra* (ed. Kaibel), pp. 174–75.

Kaibel was followed in this intriguing interpretation by Tycho von Wilamowitz-Moellendorff, who argued that even a modern audience would be so emotionally affected by the speech that it could lose sight of the context of subterfuge established by the prologue. That, he argues, was Sophocles' intention, "the overcoming of our better judgment" (Unseres besseren Wissens zu zwingen). See Wilamowitz-Moellendorff, *Die dramatische Technik des Sophokles*, p. 192. Opposing views may be found in Waldock (*Sophocles the Dramatist*, p. 184), Reinhardt (*Sophocles*, pp. 151–52), and Seale (*Vision and Stagecraft*, p. 65). On this controversy regarding the audience's possible belief in the Paedagogus' speech, Winnington-Ingram comes to the conclusion that the question is impossible to resolve: "Some people react one way, some another" (*Sophocles*, p. 237).

A Shakespearean analogy may be found in Edgar's "staging" of Gloucester's suicide attempt in *King Lear*, act IV, scene iv. In this scene, the blinded Gloucester is deceived through Edgar's use of playacting and "stage management" into accepting an illusory image of cosmic order. "In the context of a drama that depends almost exclusively on its own language for scene-setting, the passage is apt momentarily to convince us as it convinces Gloucester. Yet paradoxically we know that even on the play's level of reality this panorama is objectively an untruth, a purely artificial product of Edgar's imagining.

We are thus being alienated, in the Brechtian sense, from dramatic illusion and forced to confront the exercise of dramatic artifice itself: to evaluate its powers and weigh the ends toward which it is here employed" (Egan, *Drama within Drama*, p. 22).

60. Heiden, *Tragic Rhetoric*, p. 166.

61. It is interesting to note that Aristotle in the *Poetics* took exception to the Paedagogus' speech (680–763), branding it ἄλογος (irrational or illogical) and cataloging it among examples of unsuccessful "untruths" told by the poets.

> The tragic plot must not be composed of irrational [ἀλόγων] parts. Everything irrational [ἄλογον] should, if possible, be excluded; or, at all events, it should lie outside the action of the play (as, in the *Oedipus*, the hero's ignorance as to the manner of Laius' death); not within the drama,—as in the *Electra*, the messengers' account of the Pythian games [ὥσπερ ἐν Ἠλέκτρᾳ οἱ τὰ Πύθια ἀπαγγέλλοντες]; or, as in the Mysians, the man who has come from Tegea to Mysia and is still speechless. The plea that otherwise the plot would have been ruined, is ridiculous; such a plot should not in the first instance be constructed. But once the irrational has been introduced and an air of likelihood [εὐλογωτέρως] imparted to it, we must accept it in spite of the absurdity [ἄτοπον]. (*Poetics* 1460a18–20, trans. Dorsch)

Aristotle gives examples of Homer "charming away the absurdities" by "his other excellencies" in the *Odyssey*.

> Take even the irrational incidents in the *Odyssey*, where Odysseus is left upon the shore of Ithaca. How intolerable even these might have been would be apparent if an inferior poet were to treat the subject. As it is, the absurdity is veiled by the poetic charm with which the poet invests it. The diction should be elaborated in the pauses of the action, where there is no expression of character or thought. For, conversely, character and thought are merely obscured by a diction that is over brilliant. (*Poetics* 1460a35–b1–5, trans. Dorsch)

What is Aristotle's objection to the false Messenger scene in *Electra*? D. W. Lucas expounds the most common interpretation. "The objection that the games, except for the musical contests, were not founded until much later (582 B.C.) is raised in the scholia and is probably the point here. It has also been suggested that it is incredible that such news should have been brought by so lowly a character" (*Poetics* [ed. Lucas], p. 230). P. E. Easterling concurs with this view and adds that Aristotle, having researched the history of the Pythian games, would have been "particularly sensitive" to Sophocles' anachronism (Easterling, "Anachronism in Greek Tragedy," p. 8).

But does not the total context of the passage, especially Aristotle's closing remarks about the proper and improper elaboration of diction, point toward another possible explanation? Might not Aristotle be objecting to the hyperbolic description of a doubly fictitious event that sits outside the immediate action of the play, creating a strange dramaturgical mutation? The means exceed the ends of plotting, creating a virtual play-within-a-play.

Aristotle's inaccurate use of the plural for describing the messenger (ἀπαγγέλλοντες—masculine plural, not singular) betrays a faulty recollection of the text and renders even more nebulous the alternative explanation Lucas mentions, that Aristotle is objecting to the "lowliness" of the speaker. This idea makes even less sense when it is considered that most messengers, when they are characterized at all in tragedy, are depicted as slaves or servants. The "messengers of the Pythia" are set among a linguistic terrain of illogical or potentially absurd devices, dramaturgical sleights of hand that enable the plots to move forward. Anachronism is not an issue in any of the other examples of "irrationality" and such an interpretation is rather awkward when applied to the *Electra* passage.

Perhaps the scene stuck in the philosopher's mind as an instance where the device of the messenger seemed to break its normal bounds, relaying in eighty lines that which could be handled in a dozen. Such concision would have left the plot unaltered. The erroneous use of the plural may indicate how the passage grew and altered itself in Aristotle's memory, its alleged poetical excess translating into an absurd excess of personages on stage to perform a task traditionally given to a single character. It is possible that what bothered Aristotle was not anachronism but Sophocles' manipulation of the messenger convention for reasons the philosopher could not understand. Perhaps it was the metatheatrical quality of the speech that Aristotle found ἄλογος.

62. Reading ἔχει for Schmidt's conjectured ἔχω.

63. *Electra* 823ff. (ed. Kells). Kells also cites lines 838 (κρυφθέντα) and 869 (κέκευθεν) as passages containing a reminiscence of Orestes' burial.

64. See also Seale, *Vision and Stagecraft*, p. 67.

65. Ferguson, *A Companion to Greek Tragedy*, p. 542.

66. Shakespeare, *Julius Caesar* III.i.121–22.

67. Arnott reasons that the male assumption of female roles in the ancient theater affected the writing and conception of the tragic roles. He sees a "masculine" streak in characters like Clytemnestra and Electra (*Public and Performance in the Greek Theatre*, p. 87). For this topic of Greek male actors in female roles, see also Case's provocative "Classic Drag: The Greek Creation of Female Parts," pp. 317–28, and Zeitlin's "Playing the Other: Theater, Theatricality, and the Feminine in Greek Drama," pp. 63–96.

68. Whitman, *Sophocles*, p. 167. Whitman compares Electra's lines 977–85 with those of the Spartan poet Tyrtaeus wherein he "called upon the Spartan soldiers to look upon themselves in the historic light of glory (*kleos*) and drew within the scheme of the polis the ancient heroic individualism" (p. 168).

69. *Iliad* 16. Whitman has described this ultimate manifestation of Patroclus' heroism in terms that suggest an almost theatrical duality. "A kind of double image, as in surrealistic painting, is involved. Patroclus is playing the role of Achilles. For the moment, he has become Achilles, and acts more like the great hero than like himself." *Homer and the Heroic Tradition*, p. 200.

70. We may remember Falk's comments on *Electra* as being in some ways a reworking of *Antigone*. "Electra," in "A Symposium: Sophocles' *Electra*," p. 28.

71. Reinhardt, *Sophocles*, p. 137.

72. Vickers has described the frustration many critics have with the play: "By starting with the plotters, and by withholding the reunion [of brother and sister] Sophocles has in fact undercut the central situation of his play, Electra's solitude, her suffering, her doubts, her powerlessness to take revenge. We know that in fact she is no longer alone, her doubts are illusory, her revenge already under way, indeed blessed by Apollo. For this reason it is impossible for us to be really moved by her sorrow at the news of Orestes' death, for the news is false, and her sorrow comes to seem false, worked up" (*Towards Greek Tragedy*, pp. 569–70). Vickers never speculates about the playwright's possible reasons for such "worked up" contrivance and is content to follow Waldock's superficial idea (in *Sophocles the Dramatist*, pp. 169–95) that Sophocles rushes the audience past the double murders at the end of the play so that "no one has time to think" (Vickers, *Towards Greek Tragedy*, p. 571).

73. Kirkwood compares her unfulfilled plan to carry out vengeance with the earlier "empty" threat delivered by Chrysothemis that Aegisthus intends to shut Electra in a cave (379–82). "Like Electra's plans in the later scene, this threat never comes to anything, actually. But like the later incident, although in a much slighter way, it helps to place Electra in a central position in relation to the action of the play." See "Two Structural Features of Sophocles' *Electra*," p. 88.

74. Whitman, *Sophocles*, p. 152. See also Waldock, *Sophocles the Dramatist*, pp. 169–95.

75. Winnington-Ingram takes a similar view of the διδύμαν Ἐρινύν and argues for a Sophoclean *Electra* full of Furies acting through human characters (*Sophocles*, p. 232). "Electra is in fact conceived and drawn as at once the victim and the agent of the Furies" (p. 228).

76. See also Batchelder, *The Seal of Orestes*, p. 113.

77. Batchelder argues that Orestes chooses Strophius as his master in order to make his report seem more credible to Electra (*The Seal of Orestes*, p. 114). This is impossible, since Orestes is not aware of Electra's identity until she begins her speech over the urn.

78. Taplin, *Greek Tragedy in Action*, p. 77.

79. Segal, "Visual Symbolism and Visual Effect in Sophocles," in *Interpreting Greek Tragedy*, p. 128.

80. See also Woodard, "The Electra of Sophocles," p. 138.

81. The *Electra* recognition scene has several intriguing parallels with the Cadmus-Agave recognition scene in the *Bacchae*. Both scenes involve male and female family members and an object that has been misunderstood by the female character. As Segal observes, both women hold an object containing metatheatrical resonance—Electra, the "prop" urn; Agave, the "head" (i.e., mask) of "her" previous character. Seale has described the *Electra*'s recognition scene as partaking of "the elaborate process of visual substantiation. Electra hears the false and the true, then she sees the false and the true and holds them in her hands" (Seale, *Vision and Stagecraft*, p. 73).

82. Gellie, *Sophocles*, p. 121.

83. See *Electra* 1174 (ed. Jebb) and Bain, *Actors and Audience*, p. 78, for their differing views on this passage.

84. Aeschylus, *Choephori* 226, 228, 331; Euripides, *Electra* 573–74.

85. See Batchelder's excellent analysis of the σφραγίς in *The Seal of Orestes*, pp. 117–23.

86. *Electra* 1225 (ed. Jebb).

87. *Electra* 1228–29 (ed. Kells).

88. Sophocles' surviving plays make little use of the *deus ex machina* compared with the plays of Aeschylus, Euripides—or Aristophanes, for that matter. Only Athena in the prologue of *Ajax* and Heracles in the exodos of *Philoctetes* actually use the device. Whitman has written beautifully of Sophocles' sublimation of divine epiphany in *Electra*. "Orestes is, in reality, a deus ex machina, but one of the Sophoclean type. . . . The gods . . . enter not from without, but from within" (*Sophocles*, p. 169).

89. οὗ μή 'στι καιρὸς μὴ μακρὰν βούλου λέγειν. Smith's article, "The Meanings of Καιρός in Sophocles' *Electra*," pp. 341–43, was mentioned earlier (Chapter 7, n. 16). Line 1259 affords a telling example of the word's double edge. As Smith observes, καιρός still retained its older associations with "justice" and moral scruple in the late fifth century. Orestes unconsciously engages in a kind of "double speak." He intends the word to be interpreted as the line is rendered above. Nevertheless, at least some

members of the audience would appreciate the irony of the word's older meaning: "Do not desire to speak at length when it is not *morally just*." Morally upright behavior seems far from the mind of so unscrupulous an opportunist.

90. Liddell and Scott's primary definition for πρόσωπον is "face and visage." Aristotle and Demosthenes are cited for the earliest extant uses of the word to refer specifically to a "mask." Oliver Taplin in his article "Fifth-Century Tragedy and Comedy: A *Synkrisis*," pp. 163–74, argues that this linguistic fact invalidates any metatheatrical interpretation for the word when it occurs in fifth-century dramatic texts. I believe Taplin is being too literal here. The metatheatrical effect of a passage like the one under examination arises from the doubleness of the language. The fact remains that a dramatic character is referring to her face (πρόσωπον) and that face is entirely covered or constituted by a mask.

91. Sheppard, reminiscing about a production of the play at Cambridge in which he took part, writes, "We missed something of the Sophoclean reserve. We had no masks, and young men's faces are not easily schooled to hide emotion by this world's technique. It is a generous fault. Yet had the play been acted in the air of Athens behind masks, impassive, enigmatically, but with a fixed expression, be it noted, by no means of satisfaction (see *El.* 1310 ff.), the imagination might have still responded to the poet's own hints of the chaos ruling in those tragic souls." "*Electra* Again," p. 165.

92. For an excellent examination of the evidence of fifth-century tragic masks, see Johnson's "The Mask in Ancient Greek Tragedy: A Reexamination Based on the Principles and Practices of the Noh Theatre of Japan."

93. It is well to remember the effect of Shakespeare's late romances, *The Winter's Tale, Pericles, Cymbeline,* and *The Tempest,* with their miraculous resurrections and mixtures of genre. The "problem plays," *Measure for Measure* and *All's Well That Ends Well,* prefigure these staged "miracles" with their accomplishment of impossibilities through the deception and metatheatrical sleight of hand performed by the Duke and Helena.

94. Ruth Padel writes of the interaction of the living and the dead in Greek tragedy: "The dead are much with the figures of tragedy—a motive force in many plays. In real life, the spectators knew they trod ground that contained and concealed the dead. In the theatre, they saw human figures walking above a hidden unseen. Time and place that belong to the dead are alive in the tragic present in tragic space. The tragic theatre is a threshold to the underworld, paradigm of a place in which the dead impinge on the living, the past on the present." Padel, "Making Space Speak," pp. 345–46.

95. See also Seale, *Vision and Stagecraft,* p. 73.

96. See Bain, *Actors and Audience,* p. 81.

97. *Electra* 1357 (ed. Kells). Kells unconvincingly argues that Electra literally believes that the Paedagogus is her father and is consequently showing signs of "mounting madness" (1346–83).

98. See also Seale, *Vision and Stagecraft,* p. 74.

99. Aeschylus, *Agamemnon* 1343, 1345.

100. Whitman, *Sophocles,* p. 162.

101. See also Seale, *Vision and Stagecraft,* p. 75.

102. Ἀντιθύρων, the word translated as "vestibule," "seems to mean . . . a place close to the doors; probably just *inside* of them." *Electra* 1433 (ed. Jebb).

103. Leinieks's assertion that Electra is "incapable of dissembling" and is only making truthful comments that will be "ironically misunderstood by Aegisthus" (*The Plays of Sophokles,* p. 128) misses the moral complexities of this scene.

104. Walton, *The Greek Sense of Theatre*, p. 113.

105. Segal sees this passage as Electra's despairing, apocalyptic realization of the futility of all action. "Mortals mingled with suffering (or "with evils") include also Orestes and Electra." *Tragedy and Civilization*, pp. 264–65.

106. Campbell remarks, "These words of Aegisthus, when about to die, are calculated to strike awe into the spectator, who reflects with himself, 'And is this the final consummation after all, even though it appear so to the Chorus?'" *Electra* 1497–98 (ed. Campbell).

107. At the first night of Michael Cacoyannis's 1983 production of the play at Epidauros, the audience burst into applause at this sentiment.

108. It is interesting to note that much of what is concluded here about Sophocles' *Electra* could be easily applied to Euripides' radical *Orestes*, as well. Both Owen ("The Date of the *Electra* of Sophocles," pp. 145–57) and Post ("Sophocles, Strategy, and the *Electra*," pp. 150–53) have argued that this similarity between the two plays is not accidental. While it is impossible to date either the Sophoclean or Euripidean *Electra* play with certainty, Owen and Post separately argue that the Euripidean *Orestes*, in matters of plot continuity and even characterization, forms a continuation of the *Sophoclean*, not the Euripidean, version of *Electra*.

Bibliography

Primary Texts

Aeschylus. *Aeschyli Septum Quae Supersunt Tragoedias*. Edited by D. Page. Oxford: Clarendon Press, 1972.

——. *Aeschylus*. 2 vols. Loeb Classical Library. Cambridge, Mass.: Harvard University Press, 1922–26.

——. *Aeschylus*. 2 vols. The Complete Greek Tragedies. Edited by D. Grene and R. Lattimore. Chicago: University of Chicago Press, 1953–56.

Aristophanes. *Aristophanes*. 3 vols. Loeb Classical Library. Cambridge, Mass.: Harvard University Press, 1924.

——. *Aristophanes: Plays*. 2 vols. Translated by K. McLeish. Introduced by J. M. Walton. London: Methuen, 1993.

——. *Aristophanes and Menander: New Comedy*. Translated and introduced by K. McLeish and J. M. Walton. London: Methuen, 1994.

——. *Aristophanis Comoediae*. 3 vols. 2nd ed. Edited by F. W. Hall and W. M. Geldart. Oxford: Clarendon Press, 1906–7.

Aristotle. *Aristotle's The "Art" of Rhetoric*. Loeb Classical Library. Cambridge, Mass.: Harvard University Press, 1939.

——. *Aristotle's The Athenian Constitution*. Translated by P. J. Rhodes. London: Penguin Books, 1984.

——. *Aristotle's The Poetics*. Edited by D. W. Lucas. Oxford: Oxford University Press, 1968.

——. *Aristotle's Theory of Poetry and Fine Art (Poetics)*. Edited and translated by S. H. Butcher. New York: Dover Publications, 1951.

——. *Classical Literary Criticism: Aristotle, Horace, Longinus*. Translated by T. S. Dorsch. London: Penguin Books, 1965.

——. *The Poetics*. Translated by W. Hamilton Fyfe. Loeb Classical Library. Cambridge, Mass.: Harvard University Press, 1927.

Beckett, Samuel. *Endgame: A Play in One Act*. London: Faber and Faber, 1958.

The Complete Roman Drama. 2 vols. Edited and with an introduction by G. E. Duckworth. New York: Random House, 1942.

Demosthenes. *The Public Orations of Demosthenes*. 2 vols. Edited and translated by A. W. Pickard-Cambridge. Oxford: Oxford University Press, 1912.

Euripides. *Euripides*. 4 vols. Loeb Classical Library. Cambridge, Mass.: Harvard University Press, 1912.

——. *Euripides*. 5 vols. The Complete Greek Tragedies. Edited by D. Grene and R. Lattimore. Chicago: University of Chicago Press, 1955–59.

——. *Euripides' Bacchae*. Edited by E. R. Dodds. Oxford: Clarendon Press, 1960.

——. *Euripides' Helen*. Edited by A. M. Dale. Oxford: Clarendon Press, 1967.

——. *Euripides' Heracles*. Edited by G. W. Bond. Oxford: Clarendon Press, 1981.

——. *Euripidi Fabulae*. 3 vols. Edited by G. Murray. Oxford: Clarendon Press, 1902–13.

Gellius, Aulus. *The Attic Nights of Aulus Gellius.* 3 vols. Loeb Classical Library. Cambridge, Mass.: Harvard University Press, 1927.

Herodotus. *Herodotus.* 4 vols. Translated by A. D. Godley. Loeb Classical Library. Cambridge, Mass.: Harvard University Press, 1920–25.

Menander. *Menander.* Loeb Classical Library. Cambridge, Mass.: Harvard University Press, 1979.

——. *Menandri Reliquiae Selectae.* Edited by F. H. Sandbach. Oxford: Clarendon Press, 1972.

——. *The Plays of Menander.* Edited and translated by Lionel Casson. New York: New York University Press, 1971.

The Older Sophists. Edited and translated by R. K. Sprague. Columbia: University of South Carolina Press, 1972.

Plutarch. *Moralia.* 16 vols. Translated by F. C. Babbitt. Loeb Classical Library. Cambridge, Mass.: Harvard University Press, 1927–69.

——. *Plutarch's Lives.* 11 vols. Translated by Bernadette Perrin. Loeb Classical Library. Cambridge, Mass.: Harvard University Press, 1914–26.

Sophocles. *The Plays and Fragments.* 7 vols. Translated with notes and commentary by R. C. Jebb. Amsterdam: Servio, 1962–63.

——. *Scholia in Sophoclis tragoedias vetera e codice Laurentiano denuo collato.* Edited by P. N. Pagageorgius. Leipzig: Teubner, 1888.

——. *Sophocles.* 2 vols. Translated by Hugh Lloyd-Jones. Loeb Classical Library. Cambridge, Mass.: Harvard University Press, 1994.

——. *Sophocles.* 2 vols. Loeb Classical Library. Cambridge, Mass.: Harvard University Press, 1912–13.

——. *Sophocles.* 2 vols. The Complete Greek Tragedies. Edited by D. Grene and R. Lattimore. Chicago: University of Chicago Press, 1954–57; 2nd ed., 1991.

——. *Sophocles: The Plays and Fragments.* 2 vols. Edited by L. Campbell. Oxford: Clarendon Press, 1879–81.

——. *Sophocles' Ajax.* Edited by W. B. Stanford. Salem, N.H.: Ayer Company, 1985.

——. *Sophocles: Antigone.* Edited by A. Brown. London: Aris and Phillips, 1987.

——. *Sophokles. Antigone.* Edited by Gerhard Müller. Heidelberg: Winter, 1967.

——. *Sophokles Elektra.* Edited by G. Kaibel. Leipzig: B. G. Teubner, 1896.

——. *Sophocles' Electra.* Edited by J. H. Kells. Cambridge: Cambridge University Press, 1974.

——. *Sophocles' Oedipus at Colonus.* Translated by M. W. Blundell. Newburyport, Mass.: Focus Classical Library, 1990.

——. *Sophocles' Oedipus Rex.* Edited by R. D. Dawe. Cambridge: Cambridge University Press, 1982.

——. *Sophocles' Philoctetes.* Edited by T. B. L. Webster. Cambridge: Cambridge University Press, 1970.

——. *Sophocles' Trachiniae.* Edited by P. E. Easterling. Cambridge: Cambridge University Press, 1982.

——. *Sophoclis Fabulae.* Edited by H. Lloyd-Jones and N. G. Wilson. Oxford: Clarendon Press, 1990.

——. *Sophoclis Fabulae.* Edited by A. C. Pearson. Oxford: Clarendon Press, 1924.

Thucydides. *Thucydides.* 4 vols. Loeb Classical Library. Cambridge, Mass.: Harvard University Press, 1919–23.

——. *Thucydides: History of the Peloponnesian War.* Translated by R. Warner with an introduction and notes by M. I. Finley. London: Penguin Books, 1954.

Secondary Texts

Abel, Lionel. *Metatheatre: A New Vision of Dramatic Form.* New York: Hill and Wang, 1963.

Adams, Robert M. *Strains of Discord: Studies in Literary Openness.* Ithaca: Cornell University Press, 1958.

Adams, S. M. *Sophocles the Playwright.* Toronto: University of Toronto Press, 1957.

Ahl, Frederick. *Sophocles' Oedipus: Evidence and Self-Conviction.* Ithaca: Cornell University Press, 1991.

Arnott, Peter D. *Public and Performance in the Greek Theatre.* London: Routledge, 1989.

Arrowsmith, William. "The Criticism of Greek Tragedy." *Tulane Drama Review* 3.3 (1959): 31–56.

Arthur, E. P. "Sophocles' *Oedipus Tyrannos*: The Two Arrivals of the Herdsman." *Antichthon* 14 (1980): 9–17.

Bain, David. *Actors and Audience: A Study of Asides and Related Conventions in Greek Drama.* Oxford: Oxford University Press, 1977.

———. "Some Reflections on the Illusion in Greek Tragedy." *Bulletin of the Institute of Classical Studies of the University of London* 34 (1987): 1–14.

Bassi, Karen Lee. "Euripides and the Poetics of Deception." Ph.D. dissertation, Brown University, 1987.

Batchelder, Ann G. *The Seal of Orestes: Self-Reference and Authority in Sophocles' Electra.* Lanham, Md.: Rowman and Littlefield, 1995.

Beare, W. "Sophocles' *Electra* ll. 17–19." *Classical Review* 41 (1927): 111–12.

Beckerman, B. "Theatrical Perception." *Theatre Research International* 4.3 (1979): 157–71.

Beer, D. G. "The Riddle of the Sphinx and the Staging of *Oedipus Rex*." *Essays in Theatre* 8 (1990): 105–20.

Bernidaki-Aldous, Eleftheria A. *Blindness in a Culture of Light, Especially the Case of Oedipus at Colonus of Sophocles.* New York: Peter Lange, 1990.

Bers, Victor. "The Perjured Chorus in Sophocles' 'Philoctetes.'" *Hermes* 109 (1981): 500–504.

Bieber, Margaret. *The History of the Greek and Roman Theatre.* Princeton: Princeton University Press, 1961.

Bierl, A. F. *Dionysos und die griechische Tragödie: Politische und "metatheatralische" Aspekte im Text.* Classica Monacensia 1. Tübingen, 1991.

———. "Was hat die Tragödie mit Dionysos zu tun? Rolle und Function des Dionysos am Beispiel der 'Antigone' des Sophokles." *Würtzburger Jahrbücher für die Altertumswissenschaft* 15 (1989): 43–58.

Birge, Darice. "The Grove of the Eumenides: Refuge and Hero Shrine in *Oedipus at Colonus*." *Classical Journal* 80 (1985): 11–17.

Blundell, Mary Whitlock. *Helping Friends and Harming Enemies: A Study in Sophocles and Greek Ethics.* Cambridge: Cambridge University Press, 1989.

Bowra, C. M. *Problems in Greek Poetry.* Oxford: Oxford University Press, 1953.

———. *Sophoclean Tragedy.* Oxford: Clarendon Press, 1944.

Bradshaw, A. T. von S. "The Watchman Scenes in the *Antigone*." *Classical Quarterly* 12 (1962): 200–211.

Büdel, Oscar. "Contemporary Theatre and Aesthetic Distance." *Publications of the Modern Language Association of America* 76.3 (1961): 277–91.

Burian, Peter. "Suppliant and Savior: Oedipus at Colonus." *Phoenix* 28 (1974): 408–29.

Burton, R. W. B. *The Chorus in Sophocles' Tragedies*. Oxford: Oxford University Press, 1980.

Calame, Claude. "Facing Otherness: The Tragic Mask in Ancient Greece." *History of Religions* 26 (1986): 125–42.

Calder, William M. "The End of Sophocles' *Electra*." *Greek, Roman and Byzantine Studies* 4 (1963): 213–16.

——. "The Entrance of Athena in *Ajax*." *Classical Philology* 60 (1965): 114–16.

——. "Sophoclean Apologia: *Philoctetes*." *Greek, Roman and Byzantine Studies* 12 (1971): 153–74.

——. "The Staging of the Prologue of *Oedipus Tyrannus*." *Phoenix* 13.3 (1959): 121–29.

Calderwood, James L. *If It Were Done: Macbeth and Tragic Action*. Amherst: University of Massachusetts Press, 1986.

——. *Metadrama in Shakespeare's Henriad: Richard II to Henry V*. Berkeley: University of California Press, 1979.

——. *Shakespearean Metadrama: The Idea of the Play in Titus Andronicus, Love's Labor's Lost, Romeo and Juliet, A Midsummer Night's Dream and Richard II*. Minneapolis: University of Minnesota Press, 1971.

——. *To Be and Not to Be: Negation and Metadrama in Hamlet*. New York: Columbia University Press, 1983.

Case, Sue-Ellen. "Classic Drag: The Greek Creation of Female Parts." *Theatre Journal* 37 (1985): 317–28.

Chaim, Daphna Ben. *Distance in the Theatre: The Aesthetics of Audience Response*. Ann Arbor, Mich.: UMI Research Press, 1984.

Cole, Toby, and Helen Krich Chinoy, eds. *Actors on Acting*. New York: Crown Publishers, 1972.

Conner, W. Robert. *Thucydides*. Princeton: Princeton University Press, 1984.

Cook, Albert. *Enactment: Greek Tragedy*. Chicago: Swallow Press, 1971.

——. *Oedipus Rex: A Mirror for Greek Drama*. Belmont, Calif.: Wadsworth Publishing Company, 1963.

——. "The Patterning of Effect in Sophocles' *Philoctetes*." *Arethusa* 1 (1968): 82–93.

Cope, Jackson I. "The Rediscovery of Anti-Form in Renaissance Drama." *Comparative Drama* 1.3 (1967): 155–71.

——. *The Theater and the Dream: From Metaphor to Form in Renaissance Drama*. Baltimore: Johns Hopkins University Press, 1973.

Craik, Elizabeth. "The Staging of Sophokles' *Philoktetes* and Aristophanes' *The Birds*." In *Owls to Athens: Essays on Classical Studies Presented to Sir Kenneth Dover*, edited by E. M. Craik, pp. 81–84. Oxford: Oxford University Press, 1990.

Croally, N. T. *Euripidean Polemic: The Trojan Women and the Function of Tragedy*. Cambridge: Cambridge University Press, 1994.

Csapo, Eric, and William J. Slater. *The Context of Ancient Drama*. Ann Arbor: University of Michigan Press, 1995.

Curtius, Ernst Robert. *European Literature and the Latin Middle Ages*. Translated by Willard R. Trask. New York: Pantheon Books, 1953.

Damen, Mark. "Actor and Character in Greek Tragedy." *Theatre Journal* 41 (1989): 316–40.

Davidson, J. F. "Chorus, Theatre, Text and Sophocles." In *Studies in Honour of T. B. L. Webster*, vol. 1, edited by J. H. Betts, J. T. Hooker, and J. R. Green, pp. 69–78. Bristol: Bristol Classical Press, 1986.

———. "Homer and Sophocles' *Electra*." *Bulletin of the Institute of Classical Studies of the University of London* 35 (1988): 45–72.

Davies, M. "Lichas' Lying Tale: Sophocles, *Trachiniae* 260ff." *Classical Quarterly* 34.2 (1984): 480–91.

Des Bouvrie, Synnove. "Aristotle's *Poetics* and the Subject of Tragic Drama: An Anthropological Approach." *Arethusa* 21 (1988): 47–74.

De Wet, B. X. "The Electra of Sophocles: A Study in Social Values." *Acta Classica* 20 (1977): 23–36.

Diller, Hans. "Menschendarstellung und Handlungsführung bei Sophokles." *Antike und Abendland* 6 (1957): 157–69.

Dodds, E. R. "On Misunderstanding the *Oedipus Rex*." In *Greek Tragedy: Modern Essays in Criticism*, edited by Erich Segal, pp. 177–88. New York: Harper & Row, 1983.

Duncan, Thomas Shearer. "Gorgias' Theories of Art." *Classical Journal* 33 (1937–38): 402–15.

Easterling, P. E. "Anachronism in Greek Tragedy." *Journal of Hellenic Studies* 105 (1985): 1–10.

———. "The End of the Trachiniae." *Illinois Classical Studies* 6 (1981): 56–74.

———. "*Philoctetes* and Modern Criticism." *Illinois Classical Studies* 3 (1978): 27–39.

———. "Women in Tragic Space." *Bulletin of the Institute of Classical Studies of the University of London* 34 (1987): 15–26.

Edmunds, Lowell. *Theatrical Space and Historical Place in Sophocles' Oedipus at Colonus*. London: Rowman and Littlefield, 1996.

Egan, Robert G. *Drama within Drama: Shakespeare's Sense of His Art in King Lear, The Winter's Tale, and The Tempest*. New York: Columbia University Press, 1975.

Ehrenberg, Victor. *Sophocles and Pericles*. Oxford: Blackwell, 1954.

Else, Gerald F. *The Origin and Early Form of Greek Tragedy*. New York: Norton Library, 1972.

Epstein, Leslie. "Beyond the Baroque: The Role of the Audience in the Modern Theatre." *Tri-Quarterly* 12 (1968) 213–34.

Errandonea, Ignacio. "Filoctetes. I and II." *Emerita* 23 (1955): 122–64; 24 (1956): 72–107.

Ferguson, John A. *Companion to Greek Tragedy*. Austin: University of Texas Press, 1972.

Fergusson, Francis. *The Idea of a Theater*. Princeton: Princeton University Press, 1949.

Flickinger, Roy C. *The Greek Theatre and Its Drama*. Chicago: University of Chicago Press, 1960.

Foley, Helene. "Tragedy and Democratic Ideology: The Case of Sophocles' *Antigone*." In *History, Tragedy, Theory: Dialogues on Athenian Drama*, edited by Barbara Goff, pp. 131–50. Austin: University of Texas Press, 1995.

Ford, Andrew L. "The Seal of Theognis: The Politics of Authorship in Archaic Greece." In *Theognis of Megara: Poetry and the Polis*, edited by Thomas J. Figueira and Gregory Nagy, pp. 82–95. Baltimore: Johns Hopkins University Press, 1985.

Fraenkel, Eduard. *Beobachtungen zu Aristophanes*. Roma: Edizioni di Storia e Litteratura, 1962.

Freeman, Kathleen. *The Pre-Socratic Philosophers: A Companion to Diels, Fragments der Vorsokratiker*. Cambridge, Mass.: Harvard University Press, 1959.

Friis Johansen, Holger. "Sophocles 1939–1959." *Lustrum* 7 (1962): 94–288.

Fuqua, Charles. "Studies in the Use of Myth in Sophocles' 'Philoctetes' and the 'Orestes' of Euripides." *Traditio* 32 (1976): 29–95.

Furnish, Shearle. "Metatheatre in the First Shepherds' Play." *Essays in Theatre* 7 (1989): 139–48.

Gardiner, Cynthia P. *The Sophoclean Chorus: A Study of Character and Function.* Iowa City: University of Iowa Press, 1987.

———. "The Staging of the Death of Ajax." *Classical Journal* 75 (1979): 10–14.

Garner, Stanton B. *Bodied Spaces: Phenomenology and Performance in Contemporary Drama.* Ithaca: Cornell University Press, 1994.

Gellie, G. H. "The Second Stasimon of the *Oedipus Tyrannus.*" *American Journal of Philology* 85 (1964): 113–23.

———. *Sophocles: A Reading.* Melbourne: Melbourne University Press, 1972.

Gentili, Bruno. *Theatrical Performances in the Ancient World: Hellenistic and Early Roman Theatre.* Amsterdam: J. C. Gieben, 1979.

Goldberg, Sandor M. *The Making of Menander's Comedy.* Berkeley: University of California Press, 1980.

Goldhill, Simon. *Reading Greek Tragedy.* Cambridge: Cambridge University Press, 1986.

———. "Reading Performance Criticism." *Greece and Rome* 36 (1989): 172–82.

Goldman, Michael. *The Actor's Freedom: Towards a Theory of Drama.* New York: Viking Press, 1975.

Goodhart, Sandor. "Ληστὰς Ἔφασκε· Oedipus and Laius' Many Murderers." *Diacritics* 8 (1978): 55–71.

Gould, Thomas. *The Ancient Quarrel between Poetry and Philosophy.* Princeton: Princeton University Press, 1990.

Gredley, Bernard. "Greek Tragedy and the 'Discovery' of the Actor." *Themes in Drama* 6 (1984): 1–14.

Greengard, Carola. *Theatre in Crisis: Sophocles' Reconstruction of Genre and Politics in Philoctetes.* Amsterdam: Adolf M. Hakkert, 1987.

Grene, David. *Reality and the Heroic Pattern: Last Plays of Ibsen, Shakespeare, and Sophocles.* Chicago: University of Chicago Press, 1967.

Grote, Dale Allan. "Electra or Chysothemis?: The Assignment of Sophocles' *Electra* 428–30." *Classical Journal* 86 (1991): 139–43.

———. "Sophocles' 'Electra': A Social Document of Late Fifth Century Athens." Ph.D. dissertation, University of Wisconsin–Madison, 1988.

Guthrie, W. K. C. *The Sophists.* Cambridge: Cambridge University Press, 1971.

Halleran, Michael R. "Lichas' Lies and Sophoclean Innovation." *Greek, Roman and Byzantine Studies* 27 (1986): 239–47.

———. *Stagecraft in Euripides.* Totowa, N.J.: Barnes and Noble, 1985.

Hamilton, Richard. "Neoptolemos' Story in the *Philoctetes.*" *American Journal of Philology* 96 (1975): 131–37.

Haslam, Michael W. "The Authenticity of Euripides' *Phoenissae* 1–2 and Sophocles' *Electra* 1." *Greek, Roman and Byzantine Studies* 16 (1975): 149–74.

Heiden, Bruce. *Tragic Rhetoric: An Interpretation of Sophocles' "Trachiniae."* New York: Peter Lang, 1989.

Heikkilä, Kai. " 'Now I Have a Mind to Dance': The References of the Chorus to Their Own Dancing in Sophocles' Tragedies." *Arctos* 25 (1991): 51–67.

Henrichs, Albert. " 'Why Should I Dance?': Choral Self-Referentiality in Greek Tragedy." *Arion* 3 (1994–95): 56–111.

Herington, John. *Poetry into Drama: Early Tragedy and the Greek Poetic Tradition.* Berkeley: University of California Press, 1985.

Hester, D. A. "Deianeira's 'Deception Speech.'" *Antichthon* 14 (1980): 1–8.

——. "Oedipus and Jonah." *Proceedings of the Cambridge Philological Society* 23 (1977): 32–61.

Hogan, James C. *A Commentary on the Plays of Sophocles.* Carbondale: Southern Illinois University Press, 1991.

Hogan, John T. "The ἀξίωσις of Words at Thucydides 3.82.4." *Greek, Roman and Byzantine Studies* 21 (1980): 139–49.

Holt, Philip. "The End of the *Trachiniai* and the Fate of Herakles." *Journal of Hellenic Studies* 109 (1989): 69–80.

Homan, Sidney. *When the Theatre Turns to Itself: The Aesthetic Metaphor in Shakespeare.* Lewisburg, Pa.: Bucknell University Press, 1981.

Hornby, Richard. *Drama, Metadrama, and Perception.* Lewisburg, Pa.: Bucknell University Press, 1986.

Horsley, G. H. R. "Apollo in Sophokles' Electra." *Antichthon* 14 (1980): 18–29.

Hubbard, Thomas K. *The Mask of Comedy: Aristophanes and the Intertextual Parabasis.* Ithaca: Cornell University Press, 1991.

Hubert, Judd D. *Metatheater: The Example of Shakespeare.* Lincoln: University of Nebraska, 1991.

Huizinga, Johan. *Homo Ludens: A Study of the Play Element in Culture.* Boston: Beacon Press, 1950.

Jameson, M. H. "Politics and the *Philoctetes.*" *Classical Philology* 51 (1956): 217–27.

Johnson, Martha Bancroft. "The Mask in Ancient Greek Tragedy: A Reexamination Based on the Principles and Practices of the Noh Theatre of Japan." Ph.D. dissertation, University of Wisconsin–Madison, 1984.

Johnston, Brian. "The Metamorphoses of Theseus in *Oedipus at Colonus.*" *Comparative Drama* 27 (1993): 271–85.

Jones, John. *On Aristotle and Greek Tragedy.* Stanford: Stanford University Press, 1962.

Kaimio, Maarit. "The Protagonist in Greek Tragedy." *Arctos* 27 (1993): 19–33.

Kamerbeek, J. C. "Comments on the Second Stasimon of the Oedipus Tyrannus." *Wiener Studien* 79 (1966): 80–92.

——. *The Plays of Sophocles.* Vols. 1–7. Leiden: E. J. Brill, 1953–67.

Karavites, Peter. "Tradition, Skepticism, and Sophocles' Political Career." *Klio* 58 (1976): 359–65.

Kells, J. H. "Sophocles' *Electra* Revisited." In *Studies in Honor of T. B. L. Webster,* vol. 1, edited by J. H. Betts, J. T. Hooker, and J. R. Green, pp. 153–60. Bristol: Bristol Classical Press, 1986.

Kennedy, George. *The Art of Persuasion in Greece.* Princeton: Princeton University Press, 1963.

King, W. D. "'Nailed to a Circus of Blood': *Ajax* at the American National Theatre." *Theater* 18.1 (1986): 9–15.

Kirkwood, Gordon M. "From Melos to Colonus: ΤΙΝΑΣ ΧΩΡΟΥΣ ΑΦΙΓΜΕΘ'..." *Transactions and Proceedings of the American Philological Association* 116 (1986): 99–117.

——. *A Study of Sophoclean Drama.* Ithaca: Cornell University Press, 1958.

——. "Two Structural Features of Sophocles' *Electra.*" *Transactions and Proceedings of the American Philological Association* 73 (1942): 86–95.

Kitzinger, Rachel. "Why Mourning Becomes Elektra." *California Studies in Classical Antiquity* 10 (1991): 298–327.

Knox, Bernard M. *Essays Ancient and Modern*. Baltimore: Johns Hopkins University Press, 1989.

——. *The Heroic Temper: Studies in Sophoclean Tragedy*. Berkeley: University of California Press, 1964.

——. *Oedipus at Thebes*. New Haven: Yale University Press, 1957.

——. *Word and Action: Essays on the Ancient Theatre*. Baltimore: Johns Hopkins University Press, 1979.

Kott, Jan. *The Eating of the Gods: An Interpretation of Greek Tragedy*. New York: Random House, 1973.

Lattimore, Richmond. *The Poetry of Greek Tragedy*. Baltimore: Johns Hopkins University Press, 1958.

——. *Story Patterns in Greek Tragedy*. Ann Arbor: University of Michigan, 1964.

Lattimore, Steven. "Oedipus and Teiresias." *California Studies in Classical Antiquity* 8 (1975): 105–11.

Leinieks, Valdis. *The Plays of Sophokles*. Amsterdam: B. R. Gruener Publishing, 1982.

Lesky, Albin. *Greek Tragic Poetry*. Translated by Matthew Dillon. New Haven: Yale University Press, 1983.

Ley, Graham. *A Short Introduction to the Ancient Greek Theater*. Chicago: University of Chicago Press, 1991.

Linforth, Ivan M. "Electra's Day in the Tragedy of Sophocles." *University of California Publications in Classical Philology* 19.2 (1962): 89–126.

——. "Philoctetes: The Play and the Man." *University of California Publications in Classical Philology* 15.3 (1956): 95–156.

Lloyd-Jones, H., and N. G. Wilson. *Sophoclea: Studies on the Text of Sophocles*. Oxford: Clarendon Press, 1990.

McDevitt, A. S. "Shame, Honour and the Hero in Sophocles' *Electra*." *Antichthon* 17 (1983): 1–12.

Mack, Maynard. "The World of *Hamlet*." *Yale Review* 41 (1952): 502–23.

Markantonatos, Gerasimos. "Dramatic Irony in the Electra of Sophocles." *Platon* 28 (1976): 147–50.

Mastronarde, Donald J. "Actors on High: The Skene Roof, the Crane, and the Gods in Attic Drama." *California Studies in Classical Antiquity* 9.2 (1990): 247–94.

Mills, S. P. "The Death of Ajax." *Classical Journal* 76 (1980–81): 129–35.

Moore, John A. *Sophocles and Arete*. Harvard Phi Beta Kappa Prize Essay. Cambridge, Mass.: Harvard University Press, 1938.

Muecke, F. "'I know you by your rags': Costume and Disguise in Fifth Century Drama." *Antichthon* 16 (1982): 17–34.

Müller, Gerhard. "Chor und Handlung bei den griechischen Tragikern." *Sophokles (Wege der Forschung)* 95 (1967): 212–38.

Murray, Gilbert. *The Literature of Ancient Greece*. Chicago: University of Chicago Press, 1956.

——. "Reactions to the Peloponnesian War in Greek Thought and Practice." *Journal of Hellenic Studies* 64 (1944): 1–9.

Musurillo, Herbert. *The Light and the Darkness: Studies in the Dramatic Poetry of Sophocles*. Leiden: E. J. Brill, 1967.

Nelson, Robert J. *Play within a Play: The Dramatist's Conception of His Art: Shakespeare to Anouilh*. New Haven: Yale University Press, 1958.

Newman, Robert J. "Heroic Resolution: A Note on Sophocles, *Philoctetes* 1405–1406." *Classical Journal* 86 (1991): 305–10.

O'Higgins, Dolores. "Narrators and Narrative in the Philoctetes of Sophocles." *Ramus* 20 (1991): 37–52.

———. "The Second Best of the Achaeans." *Hermathena* 147 (1989): 43–56.

Owen, A. S. "The Date of the *Electra* of Sophocles." In *Greek Poetry and Life: Essays Presented to Gilbert Murray on His Seventieth Birthday*, edited by Cyril Bailey, E. A. Barber, C. M. Bowra, J. D. Denniston, and D. L. Page, pp. 145–57. Oxford: Oxford University Press, 1936.

Padel, Ruth. *In and Out of the Mind: Greek Images of the Tragic Self.* Princeton: Princeton University Press, 1992.

———. "Making Space Speak." In *Nothing to Do with Dionysos?: Athenian Drama in Its Social Context*, edited by John J. Winkler and Froma Zeitlin, pp. 336–65. Princeton: Princeton University Press, 1990.

Pavlovskis, Zoja. "The Voice of the Actor in Greek Tragedy." *Classical World* 71 (1977): 113–23.

Pickard-Cambridge, A. W. *The Dramatic Festivals of Athens.* 2nd ed., rev. John Gould and D. M. Lewis. Oxford: Oxford University Press, 1988.

———. *The Theatre of Dionysus at Athens.* Oxford: Oxford University Press, 1967.

Poe, Joe Park. *Genre and Meaning in Sophocles' Ajax.* Frankfurt: Athenaeum, 1986.

Post, L. A. "Sophocles, Strategy, and the Electra." *Classical Weekly* 46 (1953): 150–53.

Rehm, Rush. *Greek Tragic Theatre.* London: Routledge, 1992.

Reinhardt, Karl. *Sophocles.* Translated by Hazel Harvey and David Harvey. New York: Barnes and Noble, 1979.

Righter, Anne. *Shakespeare and the Idea of the Play.* London: Chatto and Windus, 1962.

Ringer, Mark. "Reflections on an Empty Urn." *Drama: Beiträge zum antiken Drama und seiner Rezeption* 4 (1996): 93–100.

Roberts, Deborah H. "Different Stories: Sophoclean Narrative(s) in the *Philoctetes*." *Transactions and Proceedings of the American Philological Association* 119 (1989): 161–76.

———. "Sophoclean Endings: Another Story." *Arethusa* 21.2 (1988): 177–96.

Rorty, Amélie Oksenberg, ed. *Essays on Aristotle's Poetics.* Princeton: Princeton University Press, 1992.

Rose, Peter W. "Historicizing Sophocles' *Ajax*." In *History, Tragedy, Theory: Dialogues on Athenian Drama*, edited by Barbara Goff, pp. 59–90. Austin: University of Texas Press, 1995.

———. "Sophocles' *Philoctetes* and the Teachings of the Sophists." *Harvard Studies in Classical Philology* 80 (1976): 49–105.

Rosenmeyer, Thomas G. "Gorgias, Aeschylus, and *Apate*." *American Journal of Philology* 76.3 (1955): 225–60.

Rosevach, Vincent J. "The Two Worlds of the *Antigone*." *Illinois Classical Studies* 4 (1979): 16–26.

Rutherford, R. B. "Tragic Form and Feeling in the *Iliad*." *Journal of Hellenic Studies* 102 (1982): 145–60.

Schein, S. L. "*Electra*: A Sophoclean Problem Play." *Antike und Abendland* 28 (1982): 69–80.

Schlegel, August Wilhelm. "Lectures on Dramatic Art and Literature," lecture 5. In *Dramatic Theory and Criticism: The Greeks to Grotowski*, edited by Bernard Dukore, pp. 502–5. Fort Worth, Tex.: Harcourt, Brace, Jovanovich, 1974.

Scott, William C. *Musical Design in Sophoclean Theatre.* Hanover, N.H.: University of New England Press, 1996.

Seaford, Richard. "The Destruction of Limits in Sophokles' *Elektra*." *Classical Quarterly* 35 (1985): 315–23.

Seale, David. *Vision and Stagecraft in Sophocles*. Chicago: University of Chicago Press, 1982.

Segal, Charles. *Dionysiac Poetics and Euripides' Bacchae*. Princeton: Princeton University Press, 1982.

——. "The *Electra* of Sophocles." *Transactions and Proceedings of the American Philological Association* 97 (1966): 473–545.

——. *Euripides and the Poetics of Sorrow*. Durham, N.C.: Duke University Press, 1993.

——. "Gorgias and the Psychology of the Logos." *Harvard Studies in Classical Philology* 66 (1962): 99–155.

——. *Interpreting Greek Tragedy: Myth, Poetry, Text*. Ithaca: Cornell University Press, 1986.

——. *Oedipus Tyrannus: Tragic Heroism and the Limits of Knowledge*. New York: Twayne Publishers, 1993.

——. *Sophocles' Tragic World: Divinity, Nature, Society*. Cambridge, Mass.: Harvard University Press, 1995.

——. "Time, Theatre, and Knowledge in the Tragedy of Oedipus." In *Edipo: Il Teatro Greco e la Cultura Europea*, edited by B. Gentile and R. Pretagostini, pp. 459–89. Rome: Edizioni dell' Ateneo, 1986.

——. *Tragedy and Civilization: An Interpretation of Sophocles*. Cambridge, Mass.: Harvard University Press, 1981.

Sheppard, J. T. *Aeschylus and Sophocles: Their Work and Influence*. New York: Cooper Square Publishers, 1963.

——. "*Electra*: A Defense of Sophocles." *Classical Review* 41 (1927): 2–9.

——. "*Electra* Again." *Classical Review* 41 (1927): 163–65.

——. "The Tragedy of Electra according to Sophocles." *Classical Quarterly* 12 (1918): 80–88.

Shucard, Stephen C. "Some Developments in Sophocles' Late Plays of Deception." *Classical Journal* 69 (1974): 133–38.

Skura, Meredith Anne. *Shakespeare the Actor and the Purpose of Playing*. Chicago: University of Chicago Press, 1993.

Slater, Kathleen Field. "Some Suggestions for Staging the Trachiniai." *Arion*, n.s., 3 (1976): 57–68.

Slater, Niall W. "The Idea of the Actor." In *Nothing to Do with Dionysos?: Athenian Drama in Its Social Context*, edited by John J. Winkler and Froma Zeitlin, pp. 385–96. Princeton: Princeton University Press, 1990.

——. *Plautus in Performance: The Theatre of the Mind*. Princeton: Princeton University Press, 1985.

Smith, Craig S. "The Meaning of Καιρός in Sophocles' *Electra*." *Classical Journal* 85 (1990): 341–43.

Stanford, W. B. *Greek Tragedy and the Emotions*. London: Routledge, 1983.

Strasburger, Hermann. "Thukydides und die politische Selbstdarstellung der Athener." *Hermes* 86 (1958): 17–40.

States, Bert O. *Great Reckonings in Little Rooms: On the Phenomenology of Theater*. Berkeley: University of California Press, 1985.

Stroup, Thomas B. *Microcosmos: The Shape of the Elizabethan Play*. Lexington: University of Kentucky Press, 1965.

Styan, J. L. *Drama, Stage and Audience*. Cambridge: Cambridge University Press, 1975.

Swart, Gerhard. "Dramatic Function of the 'Agon' Scene in the *Electra* of Sophocles." *Acta Classica* 27 (1984): 23–29.

"A Symposium: Sophocles' *Electra*." Edited by Eugene H. Falk, Leon Reissman, and Robert W. Corrigan. *Tulane Drama Review* 1 (1955–56): 22–66.

Taaffe, Lauren Kathleen. *Aristophanes and Women*. London: Routledge, 1993.

——. "Gender, Deception, and Metatheatre in Aristophanes' *Ecclesiazusae*." Ph.D. dissertation, Cornell University, 1987.

Taplin, Oliver. "Fifth-Century Tragedy and Comedy: A *Synkrisis*." *Journal of Hellenic Studies* 106 (1986): 163–74.

——. *Greek Tragedy in Action*. London: Methuen, 1978.

——. "The Mapping of Sophocles' Philoctetes." *Bulletin of the Institute of Classical Studies of the University of London* 34 (1987): 69–77.

——. "Sophocles in His Theatre." In *Sophocle*, edited by Bernard Knox and Jacqueline de Romilly, pp. 155–85. Entretiens sur l'antiquité classique 29. Geneva: Vandoevres, 1983.

——. *The Stagecraft of Aeschylus: The Dramatic Use of Exits and Entrances in Greek Tragedy*. Oxford: Oxford University Press, 1977.

Tonelli, Franco. *Sophocles' "Oedipus" and the Tale of the Theater*. Ravenna: Longo Editore, 1983.

Untersteiner, Mario. *The Sophists*. Translated by Kathleen Freeman. New York: Philosophical Library, 1954.

Vellacott, Philip. *The Logic of Tragedy: Morals and Integrity in Aeschylus' Oresteia*. Durham, N.C.: Duke University Press, 1984.

——. *Sophocles and Oedipus*. Ann Arbor: University of Michigan Press, 1971.

Verdenius, W. J. "Gorgias' Doctrine of Deception." *Hermes: Einzelschriften* 44 (1981): 116–28.

Vernant, Jean-Pierre, and Pierre Vidal-Naquet. *Myth and Tragedy in Ancient Greece*. New York: Zone Books, 1988.

Vickers, Brian. *Towards Greek Tragedy: Drama, Myth, Society*. London: Longman, 1973.

Vickers, Michael. "Alcibiades on Stage: *Philoctetes* and *Cyclops*." *Historia* 36 (1987): 171–97.

Waldock, A. J. A. *Sophocles the Dramatist*. Cambridge: Cambridge University Press, 1951.

Walton, J. Michael. *The Greek Sense of Theatre: Tragedy Reviewed*. London: Methuen, 1984.

——. *Greek Theatre Practice*. London: Methuen, 1991.

——. *Living Greek Theatre: A Handbook of Classical Performance and Modern Production*. New York: Greenwood Press, 1987.

Wassermann, Felix M. "Thucydides and the Disintegration of the Polis." *Transactions and Proceedings of the American Philological Association* 85 (1954): 46–54.

Webster, T. B. L. *Greek Theatre Production*. London: Methuen, 1956.

——. *An Introduction to Sophocles*. London: Methuen, 1969.

Weisinger, Herbert. *The Agony and the Triumph: Papers on the Use and Abuse of Myth*. Ann Arbor: Michigan State University Press, 1964.

Whitman, Cedric. *The Heroic Paradox: Essays on Homer, Sophocles and Aristophanes*. Ithaca: Cornell University Press, 1982.

——. *Homer and the Heroic Tradition*. Cambridge, Mass.: Harvard University Press, 1958.

——. *Sophocles: A Study in Heroic Humanism*. Cambridge, Mass.: Harvard University Press, 1951.

Wilamowitz-Moellendorff, Tycho von. *Die dramatische Technik des Sophokles*. Berlin: Weidmann, 1977.

Wiles, David. *The Masks of Menander: Sign and Meaning in Greek and Roman Performance*. Cambridge: Cambridge University Press, 1991.

——. "Reading Greek Performance." *Greece and Rome* 34 (1987): 136–51.

Wilshire, Bruce. *Role Playing and Identity: The Limits of Theatre as Metaphor*. Bloomington: Indiana University Press, 1982.

Wilson, Edmund. *The Wound and the Bow: Seven Studies in Literature*. New York: Oxford University Press, 1941.

Winnington-Ingram, R. P. *Sophocles: An Interpretation*. Cambridge: Cambridge University Press, 1980.

——. "Tragica." *Bulletin for the Institute of Classical Studies of the University of London* 16 (1969): 44–54.

Woodard, Thomas. "The Electra of Sophocles." In *Sophocles: A Collection of Critical Essays*, edited by Thomas Woodard, pp. 125–45. Englewood Cliffs, N.J.: Prentice-Hall, 1966.

Worthen, William B. *The Idea of the Actor: Drama and the Ethics of Performance*. Princeton: Princeton University Press, 1984.

Zeitlin, Froma I. "The Closet of Masks: Role-Playing and Myth-Making in the Orestes of Euripides." *Ramus* 9 (1980): 51–77.

——. "Playing the Other: Theater, Theatricality, and the Feminine in Greek Drama." In *Nothing to Do with Dionysos?: Athenian Drama in Its Social Context*, edited by John J. Winkler and Froma Zeitlin, pp. 63–96. Princeton: Princeton University Press, 1990.

——. "Thebes: Theatre of Self and Society in Athenian Drama." In *Nothing to Do with Dionysos?: Athenian Drama in Its Social Context*, edited by John J. Winkler and Froma Zeitlin, pp. 130–67. Princeton: Princeton University Press, 1990.

Zimmermann, Bernhard. *Greek Tragedy: An Introduction*. Translated by Thomas Marier. Baltimore: Johns Hopkins University Press, 1991.

Index

Abel, Lionel, 11–12; *Metatheatre*, 11

Acropolis, 91

Acting: Sophocles and, 5–6; *Electra* and, 150

Actors: role-playing-within-the-role, ix, 8, 30, 214 (n. 21); three-actor rule in tragedy, ix–x, 10, 92, 93; as celebrities, 1–2; and method acting, 2–3; as supernumeraries, 10; casting configuration in *Oedipus at Colonus*, 10, 92–93; role doubling, 10–11, 93; casting configuration in *Ajax*, 47–48; casting configuration in *Trachiniae*, 52; casting configuration in *Antigone*, 73–74, 131; casting configuration in *Oedipus Tyrannus*, 81–82, 131; casting configuration in *Philoctetes*, 122, 131; casting configuration in *Electra*, 131–32; and tragic masks, 195–96

Aeschines, 69

Aeschylus, 162; influence on Sophocles, 6, 7; *Eumenides*, 34–35, 45, 95, 119, 221 (n. 24); *Prometheus Bound*, 39; *Oresteia*, 39, 95, 129, 177, 203, 217 (n. 25); *Suppliants*, 94; *Seven Against Thebes*, 94, 133; *Choephoroi*, 130, 138–39, 143, 156, 191, 227 (n. 43); *Agamemnon*, 136, 177, 202, 207–8; *Septem*, 225 (n. 13); and *deus ex machina*, 231–32 (n. 88)

Alcibiades, 102

American National Theater, 217 (n. 10)

Apate, 27, 41, 42–43, 86–87, 103

Arete, 39, 42, 61, 69, 105, 122–23, 180

Argos, 133

Aristocratic class, 151

Aristophanes, 106, 182; and *deus ex machina*, 122, 231–32 (n. 88); *Frogs*, 132; *Birds*, 212; *Acharnians*, 219 (n. 6)

Aristotle: on Sophocles, 6, 10, 101; on

conventions of tragedy, 58, 79, 86, 196, 207; *Rhetoric*, 101–2; *Poetics*, 196, 229–30 (n. 61); complaints with *Electra*, 229–30 (n. 61)

Arnott, Peter D.: *Public and Performance in the Greek Theatre*, 15–16, 230 (n. 67)

Athenian Empire, 22, 23, 69, 90

Athens, 26; Peloponnesian War and, 22, 91, 103, 110, 211, 227 (n. 44); *Ajax* and, 46; *Antigone* and, 68, 78; *Oedipus Tyrannus* and, 78; plague of 420s in, 78; as setting for tragedy, 90; *Oedipus at Colonus* and, 90, 91–92, 95, 97, 98, 99; politics of, 101–2, 103; democracy in, 102, 205; *Philoctetes* and, 110; *Electra* and, 167, 205, 211, 227 (n. 44)

Audiences, 14, 86–87, 172

Audience-within-the-play ("internal audience"), 8–9; in *Ajax*, 9, 34, 48–49, 53, 84; in *Trachiniae*, 9, 53, 54, 58, 84; in *Oedipus Tyrannus*, 9, 54, 84

Bain, David, 15

Bassi, Karen Lee: "Euripides and the Poetics of Deception," 214 (n. 36)

Batchelder, Ann G.: *The Seal of Orestes*, 18, 228 (n. 57), 231 (n. 77)

Beckerman, Bernard, 14

Beckett, Samuel, 11; *Endgame*, 89

Bers, Victor, 222 (n. 18)

Bierl, A. F.: *Dionysos und die griechische Tragödie*, 16, 219 (n. 10)

Brecht, Bertolt: *Caucasian Chalk Circle*, 7

Burian, Peter, 96

Cacoyannis, Michael, 233 (n. 107)

Calderwood, James, 12–13

Casting: three-actor rule in tragedy, ix–x, 10, 92, 93; in *Oedipus at Colonus*, 10,

as setting for, 133, 148; and Euripides' *Helen*, 141–42; rhetorical style of Electra in, 146–49, 159–60; Electra and Clytemnestra in, 147–48, 151–52, 155–61, 165, 176–77, 200–202; and "illusion" and "elusion," 150–51; false-messenger speech on death of Orestes, 161–75, 177, 229–30 (n. 61); play-within-the-play in, 162–63, 165, 170, 173–74, 176, 188; and Athens, 167, 205, 211, 227 (n. 44); death of Aegisthus in, 177–78, 208–11; recognition scene of Electra and Orestes, 178, 190–92, 231 (n. 81); and Furies, 184, 211, 231 (n. 75); and *deus ex machina*, 193; and tragic masks, 195–96; death of Clytemnestra in, 199–203; and Aeschylus' *Agamemnon*, 202, 207–8; and *Ajax*, 206, 208; Aristotle's complaints with, 229–30 (n. 61); and Euripides' *Orestes*, 233 (n. 108)

—*Oedipus at Colonus*, 90–99; and appearance versus reality, x, 94, 96–97; casting configuration in, 10, 92–93; moral decay and social background for, 22; date of composition, 68; and Athens, 90, 91–92, 95, 97, 98, 99; and Sophocles as dramatist, 93, 97–98, 99, 102, 127; and *Antigone*, 94, 95; and *Oedipus Tyrannus*, 94, 95; metatheatricality in, 94–95

—*Oedipus Tyrannus*, 78–90; and appearance versus reality, x, 83, 85–86; audience-within-the-play in, 9, 54, 84; moral decay and social background for, 22, 78, 127–28; Chorus in, 43, 77, 87–90, 127–28, 182, 183, 220–21 (n. 20); date of composition, 68, 78; and Athens, 78; and Thebes, 78, 133; and tyranny, 78–79, 80, 81; and *Antigone*, 78–79, 80, 81, 82–83; metatheatricality in, 80, 88–89, 90; playwright-within-the-play in, 81, 85, 87; casting configuration in, 81–82, 131; and theater audience, 83–84, 86–87, 182, 220 (n. 15); and *Ajax*, 87; *Oedipus at Colonus* and, 94, 95; *Electra* and, 128, 182

—*Philoctetes*, 101–25; metatheatricality

in, x, 22, 103, 104; moral decay and social background for, 22; demigod Heracles in, 33, 114, 117, 118, 122–23, 124; Lemnos as setting for, 91, 104, 105; prize won by, 102; and political allegory, 102, 103; *Electra* and, 102, 103, 105, 106, 109, 118–19, 137; and Sophocles as dramatist, 102, 124, 125; role-playing-within-the-role in, 103, 104, 105–6, 111, 114, 119; and *Ajax*, 103, 104, 109; and deception theme, 103, 106, 107–12, 116, 121; and Peloponnesian War, 103, 110; playwright-within-the-play in, 103–4, 107, 122, 132, 222 (n. 12); *deus ex machina* in, 104, 121–22, 123, 124, 224 (n. 39), 231–32 (n. 88); Chorus in, 111–12, 115–16, 119–20, 223 (n. 25); play-within-the-play in, 112–13; casting configuration in, 122, 131; and Shakespeare's *Tempest*, 125; messenger scene, 138; rhetoric of Odysseus in, 149

—*Trachiniae*, 51–66; metatheatricality in, x, 51, 52–53, 66, 81; audience-within-the-play in, 9, 53, 54, 58, 84; Chorus in, 43, 54, 55, 56–57, 62, 77, 182–83; Pound's translation of, 51; and *Ajax*, 51, 52, 55, 58, 61, 66; casting configuration in, 52; "diptych" structure, 52, 73; and *Antigone*, 53; opening speech of Deianeira, 53–54, 145–46, 218 (n. 1); messenger scenes, 55–56, 59, 60, 138; ceremony-within-the-play in, 58; role-playing-within-the-role in, 61; and theater audience, 65–66

Sparta, 98
Stanford, W. B., 37, 216 (n. 4)
Stanislavski, Constantine, 2
Strasberg, Lee, 2
Supernumerary actors, 10
Suppliant dramas, 94, 96

Taafe, Lauren Kathleen: "Gender, Deception, and Metatheatre in Aristophanes' *Ecclesiazusae*," 214 (n. 29)
Talma, François-Joseph, 3
Taplin, Oliver, 27, 187, 220 (n. 18), 222 (n. 16), 232 (n. 90); *Greek Tragedy*